Peirce and the Conduct of

Although Charles Sanders Peirce (1839–1914) is regarded as the founding father of pragmatism and a key figure in the development of American philosophy, his practical philosophy remains under-acknowledged and misinterpreted. In this book, Richard Kenneth Atkins argues that Peirce did in fact have developed and systematic views on ethics, on religion, and on how to live, and that these views are both plausible and relevant. Drawing on a controversial lecture Peirce delivered in 1898 and related works, he examines Peirce's theories of sentiment and instinct, his defense of the rational acceptability of religious belief, his analysis of self-controlled action, and his pragmatic account of practical ethics, showing how he developed his views and how they interact with those of his great contemporary William James. This study is essential for scholars of Peirce and for those interested in American philosophy, pragmatism, philosophy of religion, philosophy of action, and ethics.

RICHARD KENNETH ATKINS is Assistant Professor of Philosophy at Boston College. He is the author of *Puzzled?! An Introduction to Philosophizing* (2015) and numerous essays on the philosophy of Charles Sanders Peirce.

Peirce and the Conduct of Life

Sentiment and Instinct in Ethics and Religion

RICHARD KENNETH ATKINS
Assistant Professor of Philosophy
Boston College

CAMBRIDGE
UNIVERSITY PRESS

University Printing House, Cambridge CB2 8BS, United Kingdom

One Liberty Plaza, 20th Floor, New York, NY 10006, USA

477 Williamstown Road, Port Melbourne, VIC 3207, Australia

314-321, 3rd Floor, Plot 3, Splendor Forum, Jasola District Centre, New Delhi - 110025, India

79 Anson Road, #06-04/06, Singapore 079906

Cambridge University Press is part of the University of Cambridge.

It furthers the University's mission by disseminating knowledge in the pursuit of education, learning and research at the highest international levels of excellence.

www.cambridge.org
Information on this title: www.cambridge.org/9781316613856

© Richard Kenneth Atkins 2016

First published 2016
First paperback edition 2018

A catalogue record for this publication is available from the British Library

Library of Congress Cataloging in Publication data
Atkins, Richard Kenneth, author.
Peirce and the conduct of life : sentiment and instinct in ethics and religion / Richard Kenneth Atkins, Assistant Professor of Philosophy, Boston College.
New York : Cambridge University Press, 2016. | Includes bibliographical references.
LCCN 2016014776 | ISBN 9781107161306
LCSH: Peirce, Charles S. (Charles Sanders), 1839–1914. | Conduct of life.
LCC B945.P44 A853 2016 | DDC 191–dc23
LC record available at https://lccn.loc.gov/2016014776

ISBN 978-1-107-16130-6 Hardback
ISBN 978-1-316-61385-6 Paperback

For Božanka

Contents

Acknowledgments

A number of people have made it possible for me to write this book and see it to publication. Foremost among them is my wife, to whom this book is dedicated and whose love and support through the years have afforded me both the time and peace of mind to think about these philosophical questions. My parents-in-law, Petar and Cvetanka, have provided invaluable help in keeping our household functioning, ensuring our children are attended to, and just generally making our lives more pleasant. The community of Peirce scholars is a constant source of support, encouragement, and insights. There are too many people to mention here, but I am especially grateful to Robert Lane, Cheryl Misak, Cornelis de Waal, and André De Tienne. Boston College and my colleagues in the Philosophy Department have seen to it that I have ample time and a pleasant environment in which to conduct my research, for which I am thankful. Much of the research for this book was conducted in Houghton Library at Harvard, and I thank the staff there for their kind support. I am especially grateful to Hilary Gaskin and Cambridge University Press for bringing this book to print.

Portions of this book have previously appeared in print. Chapter 1 – "Peirce's 'Paradoxical Irradiations' and James's *The Will to Believe*" – is reprinted with permission of Indiana University Press, Journals, and appeared in *Transactions of the Charles S. Peirce Society*, 51:2, 173–200, © 2015. The portion of Chapter 4 on Peirce's esthetics is a modest revision of an article first published as "The Pleasures of Goodness: Peircean Aesthetics in the Light of Kant's *Critique of the Power of Judgment*," *Cognitio*, 9:1, 13–25. The material is reprinted here with the authorization of *Cognitio*'s editors. Finally, the portion of Chapter 5 on psychological hedonism originally appeared as "Peirce's Critique of Psychological Hedonism" in *British Journal for the History of Philosophy*, 23:2, 349–367. I thank each of these publishers for permission to reprint the essays here, and I thank the editors and reviewers for their time and energies spent on these essays.

Introduction

Charles Sanders Peirce is not well known for his practical philosophy. Scholars widely appreciate his groundbreaking work in mathematics, logic, and semiotics, abstruse though it sometimes is. But of the pragmatists, William James is typically regarded as the one who has the most to tell us about the conduct of our lives. Peirce's air is too rarified.

The aim of this book is to correct this misapprehension. Not only did Peirce have a practical philosophy – an account of how we should conduct our lives – it is remarkably different from William James's. In fact, Peirce develops his own views in response to positions that James espouses in *The Will to Believe*. Peirce's theories are both plausible and relevant to contemporary debates in ethics, the philosophy of religion, and the philosophy of action.

Peirce believes that philosophy, including ethics and the philosophy of religion, should be strictly scientific. As such, its inquiries must be conducted rigorously and its present conclusions regarded as provisional. Yet if our best ethical and religious theories are provisional and investigation into them is ongoing, how ought we to conduct our lives in the meantime? In the opinion of William James, we ought not to let our ethical and religious theories "lie hid each under its bushel" but should allow them to directly inform our conduct. By allowing our theories to vie for champions in the public sphere, James believes that we will be able to discern which theory is true. The true theory will be the one that survives by gaining champions.

James first articulates this position in *The Will to Believe*, which he dedicates to his old and good friend Charles Sanders Peirce. Peirce, however, finds James's view appalling. In his lecture "Philosophy and the Conduct of Life," Peirce takes a staunch stance, arguing that given the "infantile condition" of philosophy as compared with other sciences such as physics and chemistry, we ought not to conduct our lives according to our philosophical theories but on the basis of our sentiments and instincts. On his view, we *should* allow our theories to lie hid under their bushels.

1

Peirce's position is remarkably different from what might be assumed. Suppose, for instance, that a man's mother suffers from a debilitating disease, that one can extend her life through medical intervention, but that extending her life will utilize resources that can be utilized in ways that will bring about more happiness and less misery in the world than if they are utilized for her. Now suppose, moreover, that that man endorses act utilitarianism. If James is correct, it follows that the man ought not to extend his mother's life. If Peirce is correct, it follows that the man's philosophical commitments ought not to bear much on his deliberations. He would not be blameworthy for failing to conform his conduct to his philosophical commitments.

That is a thinly veiled example, but it highlights the central difference between the views of James and Peirce. Yet it might also sound like a strange position for a philosopher – the founder of pragmatism, no less – to adopt. In fact, no other piece in Peirce's corpus has produced such divergent opinions among Peirce scholars as "Philosophy and the Conduct of Life" has. On one side, Cheryl Misak has claimed that because Peirce's comments in the lecture are doubtful and because Peirce was ashamed at having to rely on the goodness of William James, "these remarks simply cannot be taken seriously" (2004, 164). Similarly, Christopher Hookway has maintained that some of Peirce's comments in the lecture are out of line with the rest of his writings and are rather a "temporary lapse from philosophical good sense" (2000, 23).

In stark contrast to the assessments of Misak and Hookway, Mark Migotti has asserted that Peirce's lecture is "as carefully crafted and searching a piece of philosophy as any in his corpus. So far from being anomalous, the lecture seems to me to provide strong evidence for the claim that Peirce's *oeuvre* bears throughout the stamp of 'a completely determinate philosophical sensibility'" (2004, 302). Migotti (2005) has shown in particular that one of Peirce's more doubtful claims in the lecture – that belief has no place in science – is much more palatable if we read it in the context of other claims that Peirce makes.

In my judgment, Migotti is correct that Peirce's lecture is as carefully crafted and as searching as any of Peirce's other works. Yet much more must be done to show that the ideas Peirce develops in "Philosophy and the Conduct of Life" continue to inform his later work. Whereas other scholars have focused on Peirce's epistemological commitments in that lecture, this book examines what Peirce has to tell us about the conduct of our lives and connects what Peirce says there to his later philosophical work.

The book is divided into six chapters. In Chapter 1, I argue that "Philosophy and the Conduct of Life" has vexed Peirce scholars because Peirce intentionally wrote the lecture to be paradoxical. He did so because it is an oblique criticism of positions James espouses in *The Will to Believe*. Since James had arranged the lectures for Peirce and was the only person with clout trying to help him, Peirce felt the need to express his criticisms obliquely. Yet he also felt compelled to express the criticisms at all because James had dedicated *The Will to Believe* to him, and so Peirce wanted to distance his own philosophical theories from those of James.

Chapter 2 explores Peirce's claim that instead of trusting to reason and philosophical theories in the conduct of life, we should trust to our sentiments and instincts. In his 1898 lecture "Philosophy and the Conduct of Life" and the drafts for it, Peirce calls this position sentimental conservatism. Yet on the face of it, trusting to our conservative sentiments sounds like a recipe for social stagnation, continued prejudice, and oppression. Peirce, for instance, appears to trust to his conservative sentiments when he objects to female and universal male suffrage. Daniel Campos (2014) shows that Peirce was prejudiced against Hispanics and other ethnic groups and argues that his prejudices are inconsistent with his own philosophical views. Had Peirce allowed his philosophy to inform his conduct, he might have been on the better side of history. Cornelis de Waal (2012) has argued against Peirce's sentimental conservatism on the grounds that our sentiments should sometimes be rejected on the basis of reasoning and that sometimes our sentiments compete, other times we have no sentiments, and yet other times our sentiments are too coarse grained. Even Peirce's friend Lady Welby objects to Peirce's view on the grounds that it will preserve that which "once promoted growth and development and now stunts, backens, withers it" (SS 21). I examine Peirce's arguments for sentimental conservatism and show that in his later work Peirce shifts toward a greater emphasis on instinct and instinct-based sentiments and away from sentiments inculcated by tradition. As a consequence, Peirce's more mature conception of sentimental conservatism can accommodate these worries.

The drafts for "Philosophy and the Conduct of Life" are rife with religious themes. One of those themes, consonant with his view that philosophy should affect the conduct of life with "secular slowness," is that if we should hear the call of our Savior, we ought not to waste time "adjusting a philosophy difficulty" but should respond without hesitation and with full commitment. This, however, seems inconsistent with what Peirce states in a letter to William James, namely, that we ought with haste and vigor to collect evidence about the trustworthiness of a man with whom we go into business. Ought we not similarly to collect evidence about the trustworthiness of a putative call from our Savior? In Chapter 3, I argue that Peirce's essay from 1908, "A Neglected Argument for the Reality of God," addresses this problem. I contend that the essay is best read not as an argument for the reality of God but as an argument for the rational acceptability of a living belief in God. That is, it is rationally acceptable for some people to allow their conduct to be informed – even transformed – by putative calls from their Savior.

At one point in the drafts for "Philosophy and the Conduct of Life," Peirce claims that the "supremest commandment" of sentiment is that we should generalize and become welded into a universal continuum and that in doing so we prepare ourselves for "a joyful Nirvana." These claims, though, are obscure and in need of elucidation. I draw on Kant's *Critique of the Power of Judgment* to elucidate Peirce's views on the aim of theoretical inquiry. I then extend this idea to Peirce's theory of sentiment and religion. God, on Peirce's view, is loving the world into greater and greater loveliness. That God is doing this is not a properly scientific or philosophical doctrine but a faith commitment. Moreover, the task of welding us into the universal continuum is not accomplished primarily through the development of human reason and the discovery of new theories but through the evolutionary development of our sentiments and instincts.

Chapter 5 explores Peirce's account of self-controlled action and his responses to various challenges to moral responsibility. The mechanical hypothesis, God's foreknowledge, and psychological hedonism all pose challenges to moral responsibility. In his letters to James about *The Will to Believe* and in his drafts for "Philosophy and the Conduct of Life," we see Peirce touching on each of these issues. He rejects the mechanical hypothesis: It was a provisional belief taken up into the cart of science but should now be kicked off. He contends that by placing God outside of time, we can preserve God's foreknowledge and human freedom. Most importantly, in 1903, he develops a unique critique of psychological hedonism based on a detailed descriptive analysis of self-controlled action. That analysis also shows how Peirce's account of self-controlled action can preserve moral responsibility.

Chapter 6, the final chapter, extends Peirce's ideas to contemporary debates in practical ethics. I argue that Peirce would reject highly theoretical approaches to practical ethics. The task of practical ethicists should not be to take an antecedent ethical theory – such as deontological or utilitarian ethics – and show how the theory is relevant to some contemporary, particular problem. Rather, Peirce himself endorses casuistic approaches to ethics. I argue that on the Peircean view, the casuistry of Albert Jonsen and Stephen Toulmin and the principlism of Tom Beauchamp and James Childress are complementary with respect to both methodology and moral justification. Moreover, Peirce's views on sentiment and instinct can place each on firmer footing.

Before closing this introduction, I should make one last comment. I believe that we have much to learn from Peirce about the conduct of life from a philosophical perspective. I do not believe, though, that we have much to learn from him by emulation. Peirce was a notorious crank and, as James puts it at one point, a most "peppery personage." He had difficulty controlling his temper. He had fallings out with friends over lies and unkept promises. His financial decisions were, to put it mildly, unwise. This book, though, is not about Peirce's own life. It is about his views on the conduct of life. It is a book about his practical philosophy, which is to be distinguished from his science of ethics as well as theoretical political philosophy. The latter two are to be rigorous sciences proceeding on the basis of arguments and evidence. The former is what he advises us to do while we wait for those sciences to conclude their businesses, conclusions he believes are far off in the future.

1 | *Peirce's "Paradoxical Irradiations" and James's* The Will to Believe

In 1898, Charles Sanders Peirce delivered a series of lectures titled *Reasoning and the Logic of Things*. Peirce desperately needed the $1,000 he would earn from these lectures. As he worked on them in the winter, he could not afford to heat his house above 40 degrees. He lived off a loaf of bread bought every three days. No one would publish his books. He could not even persuade the local newspaper, *Pike County Press*, to publish a few of his philosophical letters. William James came to Peirce's aid. He had long known that Charles Eliot, the president of Harvard, would not extend a teaching position to Peirce. Instead, James solicited money from subscribers and organized a series of lectures at the private home of Sarah Bull, the widow of a famed violinist. James was effectively saving Peirce's life.

Peirce hoped to lecture on logic, but James encouraged him to deliver lectures on more popular topics. Peirce was none too happy with this request, but he complied. The result was a lecture titled "Philosophy and the Conduct of Life," the first of the series. No other piece in Peirce's corpus has produced such divergent opinions among Peirce scholars as that one lecture has.

Some scholars have a decidedly negative assessment of Peirce's lecture. Cornelis de Waal, for example, maintains that Peirce's claims in the lecture are doubtful. He states, "Peirce, however, takes a radical stance, arguing emphatically that science should stay away from 'matters of vital importance,' moral problems being among them, thereby denying the validity of a science of ethics" (2012, 87). He writes, "on Peirce's account, the ethics of inquiry seems to preclude ethical inquiry. The scientific attitude ... appears to break down when we seek to resolve doubt with regard to moral issues" (89). De Waal, then, reads Peirce's 1898 comments as denying that there is, or could be, a science of ethics at all.

Other commentators have maintained that Peirce's claims are an embarrassing anomaly in his otherwise profound corpus of writings.

Christopher Hookway has written that in the lecture Peirce "defended views that fit poorly with the most natural reading of 'The Fixation of Belief.'" He points to two doubtful claims Peirce makes: "First he claimed that belief had no place in science ... And second, he argued that it was wrong to trust theory or scientific reflection in connection with 'vitally important matters'" (2000, 14). Hookway maintains that some of Peirce's comments were just "a temporary lapse from philosophical good sense" (23).

Misak claims that Peirce's 1898 lectures are "not the best place for discerning Peirce's considered view about science and vital matters" (2004, 163). She points to the exchanges between him and James regarding the lectures: "He was extremely irritated at James, who had charitably set up the lectures so that Peirce might quite literally be able to put a bit of food on his plate" (163). Peirce, she notes, was "struggling no doubt with the shame of having to be rescued by James and having been shut out of an academic job by Harvard" (163). As a consequence, she asserts, "these remarks simply cannot be taken seriously" (164).

In contrast with de Waal, Hookway, and Misak, other scholars have defended Peirce's lecture and offer a more charitable interpretation of it. Rosa Maria Mayorga has argued that Peirce's comments in the lecture are best understood against the background of his realism, the view that there are real, general features of the universe. She writes that "as Peirce uses the term here, 'vitally important matters' are those everyday matters having to do with the individual's existence and survival ... Now these matters are certainly important, but it is a nominalist mistake to assume that these concerns are the most 'vital' in the end" (2012, 106). On her view, Peirce is arguing that we ought to turn away from our local and private concerns and instead focus on "pure ethics," which is concerned with the aims and purposes of humanity as a whole (108).

Mark Migotti has also defended Peirce's comments in the first lecture. He contends that Peirce speaks of belief in two ways, first as a possession for all time and second as a holding for true for now. Understood in the first way, belief has no place in science, as Peirce claims in the lecture. But understood in the second way, belief does have a place. He states, "the need to distinguish full, practical belief from provisional scientific belief is rooted in the idea that belief of the former kind very thoroughly and very insidiously impedes and discourages honest, fruitful investigation" (2005, 53). Migotti, more-over, responds to Hookway's reading of Peirce's first lecture in general. He writes,

Hookway's frustration with "Philosophy and Conduct" stems, I think, from his misprising the lecture's priorities. While he allows that Peirce "was certainly determined to dissociate himself from those who anticipated vital benefit from the study of metaphysics and to urge that a true scientific spirit should govern work in that discipline," he appears to regard this theme as relatively inconsequential. I take it to be the main point of the lecture. (2004, 307)

That Peirce scholars should be so at loggerheads over "Philosophy and the Conduct of Life" suggests a paradox. How could all of these astute interpreters of Peirce's work stand so far apart in their appraisal of this one lecture? And they are not alone in being vexed by it. Even William James, who read a draft of the first lecture, complained that it was "full of 'sass' to the audience and paradoxical irradiations in all sorts of directions" (CWJ 8:338). In response to James's letter, Peirce set about rewriting the lecture, which is how we got "Philosophy and the Conduct of Life." After doing so, he wrote to James that he has removed "every trace of personal vexation as well as of condemnation for the present state of the university" (CWJ 8:340). However, he noted, "as for the paradoxes, since the doctrine remains the same, they are really untouched." He hoped, though, that he had diminished the paradoxes by treating them "as the well-known doctrines of famous philosophers" (CWJ 8:340).

And it is here that we get to the heart of the matter and the reason why the lecture has vexed Peirce scholars: It is because Peirce intentionally made it paradoxical. Peirce had written to James, "you know that my style of 'brilliancy' consists in a mixture of irony and seriousness – the same things said ironically & also seriously, I mean" (CWJ 8:334).[1] And though Peirce tries to push the paradox to the background, it is likely that doing so only made the lecture more paradoxical to scholars famil-iar with the entire body of his work.

But why should Peirce compose such a paradoxical lecture in the first place? Peirce wrote this lecture to be paradoxical because it is an oblique criticism of ideas found in James's book *The Will to Believe*. While other scholars have noted that Peirce likely had James's essay

---

[1]   This is in addition to what Short calls Peirce's "baroque archness" (2007, 33). See also Colapietro (2007) for a study of Peirce's rhetoric.

"The Will to Believe" in mind while writing his first lecture, Peirce was responding not merely to that essay but to James's philosophical outlook in general, especially as expressed in the preface and first several essays of the book *The Will to Believe*. Peirce objects to James's self-avowed pluralism, to James's "rational radicalism" in contrast with Peirce's own sentimental conservatism, and to James's view that adopting beliefs on the basis of the sentiments is rational.[2]

Peirce's lecture is not merely an oblique criticism of James's book. Other issues are raised in the lecture that do not directly concern James's views, such as Peirce's classification of the sciences. There are, moreover, important points of overlap between James's and Peirce's views in other respects. Also, Peirce is not merely interested in needling James when they do disagree. As the previous comments on the works of de Waal, Hookway, and others indicate, real, serious, and broad philosophical issues are at stake in the essay. Furthermore, while Peirce's lecture provides an occasion for him to criticize James's *The Will to Believe*, Peirce is not led to the views he espouses simply from reflection on James's book, as Mathias Girel (2011) has argued. Nonetheless, the more vexing and paradoxical features of Peirce's "Philosophy and the Conduct of Life" become less so when read in light of how they differ from and constitute criticisms of James's views as expressed in *The Will to Believe*.

We might initially wonder why Peirce should make these criticisms at all and why he should make them obliquely. On the one hand, they are oblique so that Peirce might avoid offending his most influential ally,

---

[2] One topic I shall not directly address in this book is Peirce's theory/practice distinction. Part of the reason for this is that I believe Peirce has no fewer than seven theory/practice distinctions and all of them make an appearance in some way in the drafts for "Philosophy and the Conduct of Life" and the lecture itself. Those distinctions are between (1) theoretical science and practical science; (2) the theoretical person and the practical person; (3) theoretical beliefs and practical beliefs, where the former guide hypothesis adoption and the later guide action; (4) theoretical beliefs and practical beliefs such that the former are always provisional whereas the latter are sometimes treated as infallible; (5) theoretical and practical infallibility; (6) theoretical concerns (such as discovering the truth and eliminating error) and practical concerns (such as persuading people or making money); and (7) what the scientific man says that he does in theory and what the scientific man in fact does in practice. For these reasons, I have preferred to let what theory/practice distinctions are relevant to the present discussions emerge in those discussions. For more direct examinations of Peirce's theory/practice distinction, its consistency throughout his writings, and its plausibility, see Massecar (2013), Boyd (2012), Bergman (2010), and Colapietro (2006).

William James. As noted earlier, by organizing the lectures, James was effectively saving Peirce's very life. On the other hand, Peirce feels compelled to express the criticisms because James had dedicated *The Will to Believe* "To My Old Friend, Charles Sa[u]³nders Peirce, ... to whose writings in more recent years I owe more incitement and help than I can express or repay" (WWJ 6:3). Peirce wishes to distance himself from the objectionable philosophical outlook found in James's book and to stake out his own views. Let us now turn to what those Jamesian views are and how Peirce distances himself from them. We shall do so by first seeing how each difference is developed in a series of letters from 1897, then in the drafts for 1898's "Philosophy and the Conduct of Life," and lastly in the lecture itself.

Pluralism and Monism

James's Pluralism

In the preface to his book, James announces that he is a pluralist. He contrasts his position with monism, writing,

The difference between monism and pluralism is perhaps the most pregnant of all the differences in philosophy. *Primâ facie* the world is a pluralism; as we find it, its unity seems to be that of any collection; and our higher thinking consists chiefly of an effort to redeem it from that first crude form. Postulating more unity than the first experiences yield, we also discover more. But absolute unity, in spite of brilliant dashes in its direction, still remains undiscovered, still remains a *Grenzbegriff*. (WWJ 6:5–6)

Two claims characterize monism as James conceives of it here. The first is that there is some absolute unity to the universe itself. The second is that our "higher thinking" is an attempt to conceive this absolute unity.

In contrast with this view, the pluralist maintains that "the negative, the alogical, is never wholly banished ... Something is always mere fact and *givenness*; and there may be in the whole universe no one point of view extant from which this would not be found to be the case" (WWJ 6:6). Moreover, the radical empiricist is "he who takes for his hypothesis the notion that it [pluralism] is the permanent form of the world"

---

³ The critical edition corrects the spelling of Peirce's middle name, a correction made in the second printing (see CWJ 8:458). Peirce had received a copy from the first printing. James later sent him a corrected copy.

(WWJ 6:6). In other words, the Jamesian pluralist denies both of the claims that characterize monism: The world is not an absolute unity, and our "higher thinking" cannot make it one because "the negative, the alogical" will always be left out.

Peirce's Monism

The Correspondence: James's pluralism does not come to the fore in the correspondence until Peirce's second letter, dated March 18, 1897. In this letter, Peirce focuses on James's "The Dilemma of Determinism" and comments that he is particularly struck by how James "resolv[es] the matter [of whether we are determined] into a question of plurality, which is another name for my 'variety' of nature" (CWJ 8:247). Although it appears that Peirce is here endorsing James's pluralism, it must be noted that this is not a wholesale endorsement of the two claims that characterize the Jamesian position. Peirce is here only affirming that there is variety – "fortuitous variation" of a Darwinian sort, as he calls it in "Evolutionary Love" (W 8:190, 1892) – in nature. In short, it is Peirce's tychism.

But in his first letter from March 13, 1897, the one thing that Peirce does want to drive home to James is that his tychism "is only a part and corollary of the general principle of Synechism" (CWJ 8:245 and see also CWJ 8:337). In other words, to the extent that Peirce endorses some version of "plurality," it is only as a corollary of the view that "ideas tend to spread continuously" and in doing so they "gain generality and become welded with other ideas" (W 8:136, 1892), as Peirce characterizes synechism in "The Law of Mind." The fact that ideas gain in generality and become welded together entails that *now* there is something omitted from any given point of view. But the *aim* of thought is generality and continuity. On Peirce's view, unity, continuity, is the limiting concept, the *Grenzbegriff*.

The Drafts: We have seen that in the correspondence Peirce does not directly attack James's pluralism. But in the drafts for his first lecture, we find otherwise. It is likely that James's pluralism becomes a salient issue for Peirce because of James's request that he lecture on "separate topics of a vitally important character" (CWJ 8:326) rather than on logic. This frustrates Peirce because it means that he cannot present a unified philosophical outlook or his recent research; he writes, "it is most embarrassing to me to find myself muzzled as regards my studies, which I am burning to recount" (R 436:32). With respect to lecturing on – as Peirce comes to call these "separate topics" – detached ideas, he writes to James that "however little time people may have for connected thought outside their business, yet it is better to make it as connected as possible, not shunning detached ideas but seeking to assimilate them" (CWJ 8:335).

Accordingly, in contrast with the Jamesian position, we find Peirce opting for a monism but of a surprising variety. As already noted, Peirce insists that tychism is a corollary of synechism: While there is chance and variation, ideas tend toward generalization and "welding" with each other. Peirce denies that the universe is an absolute unity but affirms that thinking aims at it. We see in R 435s an echo of his letter to James about detached ideas: "Detached ideas are idle things and until there is some promise of them drawing together into a system are as silly as they are idle. The only use of ideas at all is to bind facts into one great continuum, by a logic at once subjective and objective" (R 435s).

But whereas James conceives of monists as asserting that our higher thinking tries to attain to absolute unity, Peirce takes a different position. It is not higher thinking alone – or even primarily – that attains to absolute unity but our sentiments come to fruition in religion. Reasoning helps us attain it only secondarily:

But reasoning has no monopoly of the process of generalization – Sentiment also generalizes itself; but the continuum which it forms instead of being like that of reason merely cognitive, superficial, or subjective is ["entitative" and "existential" are crossed out] penetrates through the whole being of the soul, and is objective or to use a better word ["existential" is crossed out] is ["exstantial" is crossed out] exstant, and more than that is exsistant. (R 435s)

Thus it is that while reasoning and the science of reasoning strenuously proclaim the subordination of reasoning to sentiment, the very supremest command of sentiment is that man should generalize, should become welded into the universal continuum, which is what true reasoning consists in, as the logic of relatives demonstrates, and that this should come about not merely in his cognitions which are the surface of his being but objectively in the deepest springs of his life. In fulfilling this command man prepares himself for transmutation into a new form of life, the joyful Nirvana in which the discontinuities of his will shall have almost disappeared. (R 436:34 and 27)[4]

---

[4] The pagination here is out of order but only because the original "26" on 34 was crossed out as Peirce rearranged the pages.

The complete generalization, the complete regeneration, of sentiment is religion, which is poetry but poetry completed. (R 435:35/CP 1.676)

Sentiment generalizes and so it, too, is capable of welding the disparate features of the universe into a continuum. How sentiment does so I shall take up in Chapters 2 and 4. Reasoning, "higher thinking," assists in this process but it does not bear the burden alone.

A brief comment on Peirce's conception of religion is in order; I shall have more to say about it in Chapter 3. In a letter to James, Peirce states that "religion *per se*" – that is, religion taken at face value – "seems to me a barbaric superstition" (CWJ 8:245). But in its more perfectly embodied forms, such as we find in Buddhism rather than the "miracle monger" of the gospels, its chief value lies in teaching "the degradation of all arts of propi[ti]ating the higher powers" so that "the clergymen who do any good don't pay much attention to religion. They teach people the conduct of life, and on the whole in a high and noble way" (CWJ 8:245). Peirce's claim that religion generalizes and regenerates is not, then, the claim that Christianity, say, is true. It is rather the claim that religion teaches us how to conduct our lives. It teaches us how to be "welded" to each other: "The supreme commandment of the Buddhisto-christian religion is, to generalize, to complete the whole system even until continuity results and the distinct individuals weld together" (R 435:34/CP 1.673). We become welded with each other when we not only hold the same beliefs but feel and will the same way: "This does not reinstate reasoning for this generalization should come about, not merely in man's cognitions, which are but the superficial film of his being, but objectively, in the deepest emotional springs of his life" (R 435:35/CP 1.673). I shall have more to say about this in Chapter 4.

Admittedly, Peirce's monism sounds mystical, and it may well be informed by a religious experience he had in 1892. He acknowledges its peculiarity but tries to make it more comprehensible:

If this sounds unintelligible, just take for comparison the first good mother of a family that meets your eye, and ask whether she is not a sentimentalist, whether you would wish her to be otherwise, and lastly whether you can find a better formula in which to outline the universal features of her portrait than that I have just given. (R 435:34/CP 1.673)

A good mother does not care to advance her own interests but those of her offspring and family. Likewise, the truly religious person does not seek to advance her own interests but those of the whole "social organism" that is humanity.

The Lecture: Peirce's antipathy toward pluralism is perhaps best captured in a comment made in a letter to Lady Welby dated May 14, 1905: "I have not a very high admiration for the philosophical calibre of pluralists" (SS 57). In 1898's "Philosophy and the Conduct of Life," we find Peirce's endorsement of monism evidenced only obliquely in the final paragraphs of the lecture. After classifying the sciences, Peirce claims that they are "slowly but surely converging" to mathematics (RLT 120). He then writes of the mathematician, "he is not indeed in the habit of publishing any of his sentiments nor even his generalizations" but "the typical Pure Mathematician is a sort of Platonist. Only ... he corrects the Heraclitan error that the Eternal is not Continuous. The Eternal is for him a world, a cosmos, in which the universe of actual existence is nothing but an arbitrary locus" (RLT 121). The sciences, Peirce maintains, find their center in a science (pure mathematics) that seeks to identify the continuities in "the real potential world" (RLT 121). This is in keeping with James's characterization of monists who claim that higher thinking aims at conceiving of reality as an absolute or continuous unity.

While this is well and good for mathematicians, it is not possible to do so "in this workaday world" where we are "mere cells in a social organism itself a poor and little thing enough" (RLT 121). Here we must,

> draw upon all our powers, reason included. And in the doing of it we should chiefly depend not upon that department of the soul which is most superficial and fallible, – I mean our reason, – but upon that department that is deep and sure, – which is instinct. Instinct is capable of development and growth ... And just as reasoning springs from experience, so the development of sentiment arises from the soul's Inward and Outward Experiences. (RLT 121)

That is, reasoning alone does not generalize and weld the features of the universe into a continuum. Sentiment and instinct do so too.

Rational Radicalism and Sentimental Conservatism

James's Rational Radicalism

James, we have just seen, endorses the metaphysical (in some sense of that term) theses of pluralism and radical empiricism: The world is not an absolute unity and higher thought cannot conceive of the universe as one. But James also thinks that his metaphysics should be brought directly to bear on matters central to the conduct of our lives, especially religion and ethics. This is at the heart of what I shall call James's "rational radicalism" in contrast with Peirce's self-avowed sentimental conservatism.

Although I had initially thought "rational radicalism" was my own coinage, I afterward found that Peirce himself distinguishes his own conservatism from rational radicalism. In a letter dated April 22, 1904, Lady Welby advocates for replacing the decimal system with a binary system and states, "I believe that if even one generation were brought up from the first in the assurance that no desirable and really progressive reform was impossible or even unduly difficult to a trained and fully developed social will, the result in utilizing the latent potencies of man would be amazing and seem at first miraculous" (SS 18–19). Peirce responds that her "note developes [sic] this difference between us, that you are a rationalistic radical, while I am a conservative on rationalistic & experiential grounds" (SS 19). As to Welby's suggestion that we endeavor to be rid of the decimal system, Peirce responds,

The only way to get rid of it would be to persuade the human race to set a day when we should all commit suicide & so leave room for the evolution of a new race of rational animals who might adopt some other base of numeration, & might not. There are some evils that, once embraced, had better be adhered to. (SS 20)

James, too, is a rationalistic radical, and his rational radicalism consists of three claims. The first is that we should allow our philosophical theories to directly influence our conduct. The second is that our theories should vie with one another in the public sphere through our conduct. The third is that the true theory will be the one that works in the sense of gaining champions.

In the preface to *The Will to Believe*, James begins by drawing a connection between his pluralism and religious and ethical questions pertaining to the conduct of daily life. He writes,

There is no possible point of view from which the world can appear an absolutely single fact. Real possibilities, real indeterminations, real beginnings, real ends, real evil, real crises, catastrophes, and escapes, a real God, and a real moral life, just as common-sense conceives these things, may remain in empiricism as conceptions which that philosophy gives up the attempt either to "overcome" or to reinterpret in monistic form. (WWJ 6:6–7)

The first sentence in this quotation expresses James's pluralism. We see in this quotation, though, an immediate transition from a philosophical hypothesis to its bearing on belief in "a real God, and a real moral life." These, James asserts, may "remain in empiricism" – and recall for James the radical empiricist embraces pluralism – as commonsense beliefs without being drawn into "monistic form."

But James makes an even stronger claim. Not only are philosophical theories and conduct connected, James suggests we ought to allow our philosophical theories *directly* to inform how we conduct ourselves with respect to ethical and religious matters. He admits that he has "preached the right of the individual to indulge his personal faith at his personal risk" (WWJ 6:8). James imagines a scenario in which we put our faiths to the test so that they can vie with one another in the public sphere. The best ideas, he maintains, will be the ones that survive and find champions:

The truest scientific hypothesis is that which, as we say, "works" best; and it can be no otherwise with religious hypotheses ... The freest competition of the various faiths with one another, and their openest application to life by their several champions, are the most favorable conditions under which the survival of the fittest can proceed. They ought therefore not to lie hid each under its bushel, indulged-in quietly with friends. They ought to live in publicity, vying with each other; and it seems to me that (the régime of tolerance once granted, and a fair field shown) the scientist has nothing to fear for his own interests from the liveliest possible state of fermentation in the religious world of his time. (WWJ 6:8–9)

James extends the same general point of view from religion to morality in "The Moral Philosopher and the Moral Life," writing:

Although a man always risks much when he breaks away from established rules and strives to realize a larger ideal than they permit, yet the philosopher must allow that it is at all times open to anyone to make the experiment, provided he fear not to stake his life and character upon the throw ... These [various radical movements of the time, such as those led by the anarchists, the free-traders, and the anti-vivisectionists] and all the conservative sentiments of society arrayed against them, are simply deciding through actual experiment by what sort of conduct the maximum amount of good can be gained and kept in this world. These experiments are to be judged, not *à priori*, but by actually finding, after the fact of their making, how much more outcry or how much appeasement comes about. (WWJ 6:156–157)

In these two quotations, we see all three claims involved in James's rational radicalism: We ought to allow our religious and moral theories to directly influence our conduct. These theories will thereby be tested in the public sphere. The "fittest" theories will be those that survive by gaining champions.

Peirce's Sentimental Conservatism

The Correspondence: Peirce denies all three of the claims that comprise James's rational radicalism. He begins by conceding that theories do need to be put to the test: "That everything is to be tested by its practical results was the great text of my early papers; so, as far as I get your general aim in so much of the book as I have looked at, I am quite with you in the main" (CWJ 8:243). However, he objects to the Jamesian view that the truth of a theory is to be determined by whether it gains champions and survives. The purpose of such testing is not the "brute exercise of strength" but "generalization, such action as tends toward regularization, and the actualization of the thought which without action remains unthought" (CWJ 8:243). After noting how miserable the past several years have been, he states that a consequence of this misery is that it "has led me to rate higher than ever the individual deed as the only real meaning there is [in] the Concept, and yet at the same time to see more sharply than ever that it is not the mere arbitrary force of the deed but the life it gives to the idea that is valuable" (CWJ 8.244).

For Peirce, the purpose of putting theories to the test is not to see what survives by being perpetuated in the minds of believers but to ascertain which hypotheses are sufficiently general so as to explain the phenomena the best. This point is, I judge, closely related to Peirce's comments on his own miserable condition, which are "not so aside from the subject of your book as it might seem at first blush" (CWJ 8:244). Peirce's failure to find an audience for his philosophical work and, consequently, his failure to get his theories to "survive" by gaining champions does not make them "unfit." It is not mere perpetuation of the theory that is valuable but the generality of the theory, how well it accounts for the phenomena it is intended to explain. By putting the idea to the test, we animate the idea; we show that it does in fact satisfy the conditions for being a good hypothesis. These claims are more in line with Peirce's monism: Our theoretical aim is to generalize such that our theories should explain diverse phenomena.

Peirce also expresses doubts about calling commonsense morality into question. He states that morality "is not a bad thing, taking it in the true evolutionary sense" (CWJ 8:245). But taken in the true evolutionary sense, we individuals cannot have an effect on whether it survives: "There really is no evolution in the proper sense of the word if individuals have any arbitrary influence on the former" (CWJ 8:245). *We* do not select for what survives but what survives is what fits nature best. Peirce writes that if our own choices could arbitrarily affect evolution, "it would fully justify Napoleon's remark to Josephine, 'Madam, the rules of morality were not meant for such men as I'" (CWJ 8:245). What we ought to do is mainly trust to our sentiments and instincts. Philosophers may well doubt traditional morality – Peirce says that the "philosopher is considerably emancipated from morality" – but we should also doubt that we can "be wiser than the experience of the race on a complicated question" we have not studied (CWJ 8:245).

The Drafts: Although Peirce's comments in the correspondence are well tempered, in the drafts he comes out swinging. Peirce states, "it angers [crossed out: disgusts] me to open a book of religious philosophy and to read in the preface that the writer offers his metaphysics as a guide for the soul" (R 436:3 and see also R 435:4/CP 1.654). As we have seen, this is what James does in his preface, where he also states that the "first four essays are largely concerned with defending the legitimacy of religious faith" (WWJ 6:7) and several of the other essays concern religion and morality.

On Peirce's view, we ought not to trust too much to our capacity for reasoning or to our philosophical theories. He calls this conservatism. "Reason," he writes, "upon which we so plume ourselves, though it may answer for little things, yet for great decisions is hardly surer than a toss up" (R 435:1/CP 1.649). As we have already seen, Peirce maintains that we should instead trust to our sentiments, and so he identifies himself – perhaps picking up on James's reference to the "conservative sentiments of society" – as embracing a "conservative sentimentalism," which in the lecture he will call a sentimental conservatism. As already noted, the sentiments are also capable of generalizing, and so Peirce writes:

Embrace, on the other hand, a conservative sentimentalism, modestly rate your own reasoning powers at the mediocre price they would fetch if they were put up at auction, and what do you come to then? Why *then* the very first command that is laid upon you, your quite highest business and duty becomes to recognize a higher business than your business, not merely an avocation after your vocation has done its daily task, that of melting into continuity with the neighboring parts of the universal cosmos. (R 436:34; see also R 435:34/CP 1.673)

Here, then, we see Peirce disagreeing with James's view that our philosophical theories should directly inform our conduct. Our proper business is not to care about our interests and to find champions for our ideas but to join together the "neighboring parts of the universal cosmos." Accordingly, we should instead trust to our sentiments, which while not absolutely infallible are practically so: "Of course, sentiment makes no claim whatever to infallibility, – that is, to *theoretical infallibility*, which is a phrase without meaning at all events. But that which *I* ought to take as my highest and ultimate teacher and authority is *for me practically* infallible; – and such sentiment is" (R 435:33; n.b. this passage is crossed out but the idea reappears in the lecture).

Importantly, Peirce is not denying that there can be a science of ethics or a philosophy of religion. He claims,

Somewhat allied to the philosophy of religion is the science of ethics. It is equally useless. [Here Peirce mentions the value of casuistry and then states that the treatises on ethics] chiefly occupy themselves with reasoning out the basis of morality and other questions secondary to that. Now what's the *use* of prying into the philosophical basis of morality? We all know what morality is: it is behaving as you were brought up to behave, that is, to think you ought to be punished for not behaving. But to believe in thinking as you have been brought up to think defines *conservatism*. It needs no reasoning to perceive that morality is conservatism. But conservatism again means as you will surely agree not trusting to one's reasoning powers. To be a moral man is to obey the traditional maxims of your community without hesitation or discussion. Hence, ethics, which is reasoning out an explanation of morality is I will not say immoral, – that would be going too far. But it is composed of the very substance of immorality. (R 435:30/CP 1.666)

He is not denying that we might have a *philosophy* of religion or a *science* of ethics. To the contrary, he is clear that there could be such sciences but they are useless and should not directly inform our daily conduct: "I have not said one single word in disparagement of useless inquiries" (R 435:31; n.b. this is crossed out in favor of "Far be it from me to decry useless inquiries"). He emphasizes this point:

As long as ethics is recognized as not being a matter of vital importance or in any way touching the student's conscience, it is to a normal and healthy mind, a civilizing and valuable study, – somewhat more so than the theory of whist, much more so than the question of the landing of Columbus, which things are insignificant not at all because they are useless, nor even because they are little in themselves, but simply and solely because they are detached from the great continuum of Ideas. (R 435:31/CP 1.669)

As long as they [the other sciences] are not looked at as practical and so degraded to Pot-boiling Arts, – as our modern writers degrade the Philosophy of Religion, in claiming that it is practical, – for what difference does it make whether the pot to be boiled is Today's or the Hereafter's? – they are all such that it would be far too little to say that they are valuable to us. (R 435: 31–32/CP 1.670)

Here we turn to Peirce's criticism of James's third claim, viz. that the truth of an idea is to be judged by its ability to gain champions. For these comments also imply a rejection of James's evolutionary criterion for the valuation of ideas. Their value is not measured by their survivability in the sense of being perpetuated in the minds of believers. To the contrary, a theory's value is measured by its generality, its ability to "fuse," "weld," or "melt" together the various features of the universe. Peirce maintains,

As soon as a [crossed out: science] proposition becomes vitally important, – then in the first place, it is sunk to the condition of a mere utensil; and in the second place, it ceases altogether to be scientific because concerning matters of vital importance reasoning is at once an impertinence toward its subject matter and a ["sophism" is crossed out] treason against itself. (R 435:32/CP 1.671)

On Peirce's view, when science is properly conducted it aims at settled belief by virtue of ascertaining the truth, not some good for the person conducting the inquiry.

Here it is helpful to appeal to Peirce's distinctions among three kinds of inquirers: the pure scientist, the applied scientist, and the "practical man." The first kind of inquirer investigates to discover the truth for truth's sake. Accordingly, science consists in "diligent inquiry into truth for truth's sake" (CP 1.44, c. 1898[5]). The applied scientist, in contrast,

---

[5] This is from a drafted *History of Science*. The editors of the *Collected Papers* state that this was written c. 1896, but we find James first mentioning Peirce's work on

inquires into the truth but to solve a practical problem and not for the sake of truth itself: "There are numbers of scientists who occupy themselves exclusively with the study of dyestuffs. They discover facts that are useful to scientific chemistry, but they do not rank as genuine scientific men" (CP 1.45, c. 1898). But the final sort of inquirer is the practical man, who "must believe with all the force of his manhood that the object for which he strives is good and that the theory of his plan is correct" (CP 6.3, 1898). This is in contrast with the pure scientific man who "is above all things desirous of learning the truth and, in order to do so, ardently desires to have his present provisional beliefs ... swept away, and will work hard to accomplish that object. This is the reason that a good practical man cannot do the best scientific work" (CP 6.3, 1898).

These distinctions help contextualize Peirce's claim that "inquiry" so that the inquirer may gain some good leads to barbarism:

Do you know what it was that was at the root of the barbarism of the Plantagenet period and arrested the progress of awakening science from the days of Roger Bacon to those of Francis Bacon? ... It was the exaggerated interest that was taken in matters of vital importance.

Do you know what it is in Christianity which when recognized makes that religion an agent of reform and of progress? It is that it marks duty at its proper finite value. Not that it in any degree detracts from its vital importance, but that behind the outline of that huge mountain we descry a silvery peak of many times its height. (R 436:31 and see also R 435:35/CP 1.674–675)

The practical man is convinced that his theory is true and will stop at nothing to ensure it "survives." Such a commitment to one's beliefs is especially dangerous in religious cases where a theory can be made to survive through tortures and inquisitions. The pure scientist, in contrast, cares about the truth and is willing to put her own interests aside for the sake of the truth. Accordingly, the truth of a hypothesis is not to be judged by how well it works in the course of our daily lives, as we put it to work and as it gains champions. That is rather the practical man's standard. To the contrary, a theory is to be judged by whether it stands up to the rigors of scientific inquiry, of inquiry into the truth for the sake of the truth.

History of Science on February 3, 1899 (see CWJ 8.493). Prior to then, Peirce was working on a series of monographs titled *The Principles of Philosophy*, and James merely urged him to work on his magnum opus. So, it is likely Peirce suggested a *History of Science* to James while delivering the lectures of *Reasoning and the Logic of Things*, which would date this manuscript to mid to late 1898.

I should stress that Peirce is not denying that philosophical theories may well have enormous consequences for our lives: "I do not deny that a philosophical or other scientific error may be fraught with disastrous consequences for the whole people. It might conceivably bring about the extirpation of the human race. Importance in that sense it might have in any degree. Nevertheless, in no case is it of *vital* importance" (R 435:28/CP 1.663). He is only affirming that the investigator must put those consequences out of mind when conducting an investigation.

The Lecture: As noted earlier, James expresses his extreme displeasure with the draft he read of Peirce's first lecture and finds it full of "paradoxical irradiations." In response, Peirce writes that he has treated the paradoxes "as the well-known doctrines of famous philosophers, and put their paradoxical character almost entirely into the background" (CWJ 8:340). This is what we find in the first several paragraphs of the lecture. But Peirce also gives a hint that he has in mind not the doctrines of famous philosophers but William James's doctrines. After a long discussion of the relation of philosophy to practice, he writes, "Do you think that the physiologist who cuts up a dog reflects while doing so, that he may be saving a human life? Nonsense. If he did, it would spoil him for a scientific man; and *then* the vivisection would become a crime" (RLT 107). This example is taken directly from James's "Is Life Worth Living?":

Take another case which used to impress me in my medical-student days. Consider a poor dog whom they are vivisecting in a laboratory. He lies strapped on a board and shrieking at his executioners, and to his own dark consciousness is literally in a sort of hell. He cannot see a single redeeming ray in the whole business; and yet all these diabolical-seeming events are often controlled by human intentions with which, if his poor benighted mind could only be made to catch a glimpse of them, all that is heroic in him would religiously acquiesce. Healing truth, relief to future sufferings of beast and man, are to be bought by them. (WWJ 6:52–53)

Peirce's statement also alludes to his comment, in the drafts, about the Plantagenet period's barbarism: Vivisection is a crime and not science if it is conducted with an eye to its practical utilities.

Peirce's discussion of famous philosophers divides them into two camps. The first are the Greeks:

The Greeks expected philosophy to affect life, – not by any slow process of percolation of forms, as *we* may expect that researches into differential equations, stellar photometry, the taxonomy of echinoderms, and the like will ultimately [affect] the conduct of life, – but forthwith in the person and soul of the philosopher himself rendering him different from ordinary men in his views of right conduct. (RLT 106).

The Greeks, we see, endorse the first claim of James's rational radicalism: that our philosophical theories ought to directly inform our conduct.

In contrast to the Greeks are – let us say – the Macedonians. Peirce writes that Aristotle, who "was not much of a Greek," held that "theoretical science was for him one thing" whereas "Morals, and all that relates to the conduct of life" forms a different department of intellectual activity (RLT 106–107). Importantly, the Macedonians admit that philosophy might influence conduct by a "slow process of percolation." He states,

I have not one word to say against the Philosophy of Religion or of Ethics in general or in particular. I only say that for the present it is all far too dubious to warrant risking any human life upon it. I do not say that Philosophical science should not *ultimately* influence Religion and Morality; I only say that it should be allowed to do so only with secular slowness and the most conservative caution. (RLT 108, emphasis added)

The problem is not with metaphysics or philosophy of religion or a science of ethics but allowing those sciences directly to inform our conduct.

Peirce declares that he is an Aristotelian, a Macedonian, "condemning with the whole strength of conviction the Hellenic tendency to mingle Philosophy and Practice" (RLT 107). In saying this, he is objecting not to a science of ethics or to the philosophy of religion but to directly applying a philosophical theory to one's conduct as James recommends. On this point, Vincent Colapietro (1998, 248) notes that Peirce had two senses of the practical: that which concerns immediate satisfaction and that which is apt to affect conduct. Mats Bergman maintains, "Philosophy and Theory should be severed from practical concerns in the first sense, but theory (with a small "t") cannot be wholly isolated from conduct in the second pragmatistic meaning" (2010, 30). Both of these claims are correct, and another important distinction as concerns Peirce's and

James's views is the directness of the manner in which theory is apt to affect conduct.

As already noted in our discussion of the drafts, Peirce thinks we should instead trust to our sentiments and be conservative about our reasoning abilities:

Sentimentalism implies Conservatism; and it is of the essence of conservatism to refuse to push any practical principle to its extreme limits, – including the principle of conservatism itself. We do not say that sentiment is *never* to be influenced by reason, nor that under no circumstances would we advocate radical reforms. We only say that the man who would allow his religious life to be wounded by any *sudden* acceptance of a philosophy of religion or who would *precipitately* change his code of morals, at the dictate of a philosophy of ethics, – who would, let us say, hastily practice incest, – is a man whom we should consider *unwise*. (RLT 111, some emphases added)

He makes the same claim a little later on: "as for the man who should in truth allow his moral conduct to be vitally changed by an ethical theory, or his religious life by a philosophy of religion, I should need a strong word to express my view of his unwisdom" (RLT 114).

Peirce's reason for distrusting the science of ethics and the philosophy of religion is straightforward: He thinks philosophy is in an "infantile condition" because it has "chiefly been pursued by men who have not been nurtured in dissecting-rooms and other laboratories" (RLT 107). Our sentiments and instincts, in contrast, are the outcome of human evolution. He writes that the "regnant system of sexual rules is an instinctive or Sentimental induction summarizing the experience of all our race" (RLT 111). As he had in the drafts, Peirce admits that our sentiments are not absolutely infallible but are "practically infallible for the individual" (RLT 111).

If we ought not to allow philosophical theories to directly affect our conduct, it follows that we cannot put them to the test in the Jamesian sense, that is, allow them to vie with one another in the public sphere and see which one gains champions. It also follows that the true belief must not be the one that "works" in the sense of gaining champions, as James claims. Instead, Peirce maintains that if we want to know whether a theory is true, "practical utilities, whether low or high, should be **put out of sight** by the investigator" (RLT 113). As in the drafts, he is not denying that scientific results might have practical implications. He is claiming that when investigating whether a theory is true, we ought not to be concerned with its practical implications and we certainly ought not to be concerned with gaining champions for it, as the practical man might do. Being concerned with gaining champions rather than with the truth is liable to lead us into error by weighing evidence unfairly or ignoring evidence that might be inconsistent with our views, as Migotti (2005) argues. As Peirce states, "the two masters, *theory* and *practice*, you cannot serve" (RLT 113).

Our philosophical theories ought not to directly influence our conduct, but that is not to deny religion and ethics can be investigated scientifically:

It is far better to let philosophy follow perfectly untrammeled a scientific method, *predetermined* in advance of knowing to what it will lead. If that course be honestly and scrupulously carried out, the results reached . . . cannot but be highly serviceable for the ultimate discovery of truth. Meantime, sentiment can say "Oh well, philosophical science has not by any means said its last word yet; and meantime I will continue to believe *so and so.*" (RLT 114)

Our ethical and religious theories ought not to be tested in the public sphere, in our individual deeds, and their claims to truth ought not to be assessed by their ability to be perpetuated in the minds of believers. To the contrary, their claims to truth should be assessed according to the results of a rigorously followed scientific method, as the pure scientist would conduct such inquiries. Our daily conduct, in contrast, should primarily be guided by our sentiments and instincts.

Sentimental Rationality and Scientific Rationality

James's Theory of Sentimental Rationality

Whereas James embraces rational radicalism about how we conduct our lives, he endorses a variety of sentimentalism about rationality. James's view begins with his conception of belief in "The Will to Believe." He regards a hypothesis as "anything that may be proposed to our belief" (WWJ 6:14). Some of these hypotheses are live whereas others are dead. A live hypothesis is one that "appeals as a real possibility to him to whom it is proposed" (WWJ 6:14). Some hypotheses appeal to us as highly probable and not merely as real possibilities. James writes, "The maximum of liveliness in an hypothesis means willingness to act *irrevocably*. Practically, that means belief" (WWJ 6:14, emphasis added). Beliefs, then, are hypotheses that seem so highly probable to us that we are willing to act on them irrevocably. It should be stressed that, on James's view, it must be the *willingness to act* that is irrevocable and not the act itself, for an *act* once done obviously cannot be undone though we may break our commitments to continue to act in some way.

James's thesis in "The Will to Believe" is that sometimes we can adopt beliefs – that is, treat a hypothesis as highly probable, so highly probable we are willing to act irrevocably on it – merely on sentimental grounds: "*Our passional nature not only lawfully may, but must, decide an option between propositions, whenever it is a genuine option that cannot by its nature be decided on intellectual grounds*" (WWJ 6:20). We confront a genuine option when we have two hypotheses proposed to our belief, a decision between them is forced such that not to decide is ipso facto to decide, and what we decide is momentous for our lives. James believes not only that it is lawful but rational to make a decision based on our passional nature when we confront a genuine option: "*where faith in a fact can help create the fact*, that would be an insane logic which should say that faith running ahead of scientific evidence is the 'lowest kind of immorality'" (WWJ 6:29) and "*a rule of thinking which would absolutely prevent me from acknowledging certain kinds of truth if those kinds of truth were really there, would be an irrational rule*" (WWJ 6:31–32).

James indicates that these considerations apply to moral and religious decisions as well as to scientific beliefs. He says, "moral questions immediately present themselves as questions whose solution cannot wait for sensible proof" (WWJ 6:27). "Science," moreover, "consults her heart when she lays it down that the infinite ascertainment of fact and correction of false belief are the supreme goods for man. Challenge the statement and science can only repeat it oracularly, or else prove it by showing that such ascertainment and correction bring man all sorts of other goods which man's heart in turn declares" (WWJ 6:27). And, of course, James also thinks that religious beliefs may be adopted on the basis of our passional natures (see WWJ 6:29–31).

In "The Sentiment of Rationality," James makes another claim regarding the relation between our sentiments and rationality. On James's view, "rationality mean[s] only unimpeded mental function" (WWJ 6:65), and a mark of that lack of impediment is the fluency, the ease, with which our reasoning proceeds. He states, "custom must be one of [rationality's] factors" and that "inasmuch then as custom acquaints us with all the relations of a thing, it teaches us to pass fluently from that thing to others, and *pro tanto* tinges it with the rational character" (WWJ 6:67). Thus, the feeling of fluency or ease in our reasonings is an indicator that they are rational.

James's theory of sentimental rationality, then, involves two claims. The first is the one he makes in "The Will to Believe": On some occasions, we may adopt beliefs – that is, be willing to act irrevocably – on the basis of our passions and in the absence of evidence, and doing so is rational. The second is the one he makes in "The Sentiment of Rationality": The feeling of ease when we draw a conclusion *pro tanto* tinges that reasoning with a rational character. Peirce, we shall see, attacks both of those claims.

Peirce's Scientific Rationality

The Correspondence: Peirce attacks James's conception of belief in his first letter. He writes, "'faith' in the sense that one will adhere consistently to a given line of conduct, is highly necessary in affairs. But if it means you are not going to be alert for indications that the moment has come to change your tactics, I think it ruinous in practice" (CWJ 8:244). Peirce then gives the example of entering into business with a man. One must proceed on the basis of trust in the man, but "that won't prevent my collecting further evidence with haste and energy, because it may show me it is time to change my plan" (CWJ 8:244). Here, Peirce is criticizing James's conception of belief on sentimental grounds as willingness to act irrevocably. Sometimes, one's willingness to act must be revoked, as when future evidence comes in indicating it is time to change one's tactics.

Furthermore, Peirce claims that making the grounds for the adoption of hypotheses to require some degree of probability is a mistake, especially in the sciences. Scientists will draw up plans of research, and probability "will be a prominent factor in a well considered plan of research" (CWJ 8:244). Nevertheless, "the hypothesis to be taken up is not necessarily a probable one. The cuneiform inscriptions could never have been deciphered if very unlikely hypotheses had not been tried" (CWJ 8:244).

Peirce, then, rejects the first claim in James's theory of sentimental rationality: It is not rational to be willing to act irrevocably on some hypothesis (i.e., believe it) on sentimental grounds alone. But this is not to deny it is rational to adopt – or, as Peirce says later, *try* – some hypothesis on sentimental grounds alone. In fact, Peirce's sentimental-ism implies that it is sometimes rational. This may seem like unchari-table quibbling over James's use of "irrevocably," and there is some suggestion that even Peirce thinks it is for he is generally approving of "The Will to Believe." Indeed, he starts his letter by noting that "I have read the first essay ['The Will to Believe'] which is of great value, and I dont [sic] see that it is so very 'elementary' as you say, unless you mean that it is very easy to read and comprehend, and it is a masterpiece in that respect" (CWJ 8:243).

The Drafts: In the drafts, Peirce assumes the Jamesian conception of belief as willingness to act irrevocably, but his target shifts from being willing to *act* irrevocably in practical affairs to being willing to *adopt* irrevocably a hypothesis in science. Accordingly, in the context of a long excursus on the mechanical hypothesis in physics – Boyle's "doctrine that 'the phaenomena of the world are physically produced by the mechanical affections of the parts of matter, and that they operate on one another according to mechanical laws'" (R 435:19) – and showing that scientists are beginning to reject it, he writes,

Science has nothing to do with belief.[6] A scientific conclusion ought not to be believed, but only supposed or provisionally adopted [crossed out: admitted or assumed or provisionally adopted], taken up on the tail of the cart until we find reason to kick it off. [crossed out: But the rank and file of] But the democracy of science do not *see* this. [crossed out: They are not logicians.] They *practice* it about their ordinary conclusions. But not being logicians, knowing no more of the theory of their practice than does the billiardist when it comes to a proposition like the mechanical hypothesis, which lies outside their specialty, they *believe* in it, in the same sense in which they believe that

---

[6] Peirce's claim that science has nothing to do with belief has been especially vexing to Peirce scholars (see especially Hookway 2000, ch. 1, and Migotti 2005). But as far as I have seen, no one has noted the context in which this claim is originally stated: The mechanical hypothesis is not to be believed as a scientific conclusion – it is not an "established truth" that really does threaten freedom of the will and our commonsense moral beliefs – but only provisionally adopted. I shall say more about this in Chapter 5.

incest is wicked, – and with just about as much idea of the reasons for it. (R 435:24–25)

There is an important difference between how scientists treat hypotheses and what scientists say about how they treat them. Whereas scientists are in the habit of saying that some hypothesis is established and that they believe it, they do not believe it in the Jamesian sense of being willing to adopt it irrevocably. They believe it only in the sense that they are unwilling to reject it for now. They have a conviction that it is true, just as they are convinced incest is wicked. But when we look at what scientists – pure scientists – actually do, they only adopt hypotheses provisionally. There is no belief they are unwilling to kick off the cart and so no belief that they are willing to adopt irrevocably. Presumably, that would even include the belief that, as James says, the infinite ascertainment of fact and the correction of false belief are the supreme goods for man.

Peirce's vitriol in the drafts, though, is primarily aimed at James's second claim that the feeling of fluency in reasoning is an indicator that it is rational. Peirce claims that "powers of reasoning in any but the most rudimentary way are a somewhat uncommon gift, about as uncommon as a talent for music" (R 435:5/CP 1.657) and that "comparatively few persons are originally possessed of any but the feeblest modicum of this talent" (R 435:7/CP 1.657). Consequently, if we feel as though we are being rational, we probably are not. Peirce states, "the metaphysician who adopts a reasoning because he is impressed that it is sound, might just as well adopt his conclusions direct without any reasoning because his impression is that they are true" (R 435:12).

He drives this point home with an example of a boy studying Euclid's geometry. Peirce comments that if such a boy meets with a difficulty, "two to one the reason is that there is a logical flaw" (R 435:5/CP 1.657). However, a teacher may well urge the boy on. Peirce writes,

The teacher probably never really saw the true logic of the passage. But he thinks he does because owing to long familiarity he has lost that sense of coming up against an invisible barrier that the boy feels. ... Having worn out the sense of difficulty by familiarity, he simply cannot understand why the boy should feel any difficulty. (R 435:5–6/CP 1.657)

The failure of the teacher to recognize the logical flaw of the passage comes from the fact that he is accustomed to it. He no longer senses the problem the student does just because he is familiar with the passage. Whereas James would say the teacher's ease of reasoning *pro tanto* tinges his reasoning with a rational character, on Peirce's view there is no tinge of rational character here at all, *pro tanto* or otherwise. There is only a failure of the teacher to make himself useful to the student.

The Lecture: In the lecture, we find the same criticisms as are found in the drafts repeated but more obliquely. Peirce disingenuously makes reference to Paul Carus's conception of a belief as a possession for all time, but when it comes to characterizing belief he reveals he is really working with a Jamesian conception of belief as willingness to act: "*Full belief* is willingness to act upon the proposition in vital crises, *opinion* is willingness to act upon it in relatively insignificant affairs" (RLT 112). Peirce, though, claims that "pure science has nothing at all to do with *action*" (RLT 112), and so this Jamesian conception of belief is inapplicable to science, that is, "what is properly and usually called *belief* . . . has no place in science at all" (RLT 112).

As Migotti has noted and as I mentioned earlier, there is another sense of belief – an improper or unusual one – that does have a place in science. In science, "the propositions it accepts, it merely writes in the list of premises it proposes to use . . . The whole list is provisional" (RLT 112). As in the drafts, Peirce concedes that the scientist is in the habit of claiming that there are established truths, but such propositions are merely those "to which no competent man today demurs" (RLT 112). Peirce, then, is objecting to James's first claim. Whereas a scientist may adopt some hypothesis on sentimental or instinctual grounds – as Peirce states, "we are driven oftentimes to try the suggestions of instinct" (RLT 112) – the scientist is not willing to adopt them irrevocably, as (to use Carus's phrase) a possession for all time. The scientist holds the beliefs only provisionally.

Peirce also criticizes James's second claim that the fluency of thought confers *pro tanto* rationality on a line of reasoning. As he had in the drafts, he states, "unless the metaphysician is a most thorough master of formal logic . . . he will inevitably fall into the practice of deciding upon the validity of reasonings . . . by the impressions those reasonings make upon his mind" (RLT 109). The sentiment of rationality, on Peirce's view, is no indicator that a line of reasoning really is rational.

Peirce continues to stress this view. He states that he "would not allow sentiment or instinct any weight whatsoever in theoretical matters, not the slightest" (RLT 111). Note that Peirce is not claiming sentiment and instinct play no role whatsoever in theoretical matters. We have already seen Peirce admit that we will sometimes try the suggestions of instinct. Moreover, note that Peirce is not denying that sentiment and instinct have no weight in our everyday conduct. Once again, as previously discussed in relation to Peirce's sentimental conservatism, they clearly do. Rather, Peirce's claim is that we should give no weight whatsoever to sentiment and instinct in pure scientific matters. The sentiment of rationality – the fluency or ease with which we think – is no indicator of the rationality of our thinking. Though we may try the suggestions of instinct, "we only *try* them ... we hold ourselves ready to throw them overboard at a moment's notice from experience" (RLT 112). That is, they hold no weight.

One final point bears mentioning here. Peirce endorses the view that the validity of the laws of logic rests on logical sentiments. He had defended this claim as early as 1869's "Grounds for the Validity of the Laws of Logic" (see W 2:270–72). He continues to endorse it in 1878's "The Doctrine of Chances":

> It may seem strange that I should put forward three sentiments, namely, interest in an indefinite community, recognition of the possibility of this interest being made supreme, and hope in the unlimited continuance of intellectual activity, as indispensible requirements of logic. Yet, when we consider that logic depends on a mere struggle to escape doubt ... and that, furthermore, the only cause of our planting ourselves on reason is that other methods of escaping doubt fail on account of the social impulse, why should we wonder to find social sentiment presupposed in reasoning? (W 3:285)

On Peirce's view, these sentiments are presupposed and ground the validity of logic's laws because mental processes that have the form of a valid inference – and the early Peirce thinks that all mental processes have the form of a valid inference[7] – will eventually hit upon the truth

---

[7] "We must, as far as we can, without any other supposition than that the mind reasons, reduce all mental action to the formula of a valid inference" (W 2:214, 1868). Peirce proceeds to argue that "every sort of modification of consciousness – Attention, Sensation, and Understanding – is an inference" (W 2:223, 1868) and addresses objections to the effect that inference is general and so experiences of singulars cannot be reduced to valid inference and invalid inferential processes

and root out all error. Hence, as Peirce states in 1878, truth is the "opinion which is fated to be ultimately agreed to by all who investigate" (W 3:273) – provided, that is, the presuppositions set forth in the sentiments are met. What is important in the present context, though, is that Peirce claims that the validity of the laws of logic is grounded in or presupposes certain sentiments. This, though, is a far cry from the Jamesian view that Peirce is criticizing: that our sentiments are indicators of the rationality of some particular line of thought and that it is rational to adopt some beliefs on passional grounds alone.[8]

Conclusion

I have been arguing that Peirce's 1898 lecture "Philosophy and the Conduct of Life" is best read as an oblique criticism of James's philosophical views as found in *The Will to Believe* because by reading the lecture in this way some of the more paradoxical features of Peirce's essay become less so. We find, for example, that while Peirce thinks there is a place for a science of ethics and a philosophy of religion, we ought not make our everyday decisions on the basis of what we conclude in those sciences. This is in contrast with the Jamesian position

cannot be reduced to valid inference. My own view is that Peirce rejects aspects of this position in 1902 and thereafter, but a full defense and examination of these claims lies outside the purview of the present book (though see Atkins, forthcoming).

[8] There is an important question here, though one secondary to the concern of this chapter since it does not arise specifically in "Philosophy and the Conduct of Life." It is the question of what licenses these sentiments and presuppositions on Peirce's view. William Gavin has argued that they are licensed by something like James's will to believe: "in the last analysis, Peirce's 'cheerful hope' involves a Jamesian 'will to believe' in a *situation* that is forced, living, and momentous" (1980, 346). Misak, in contrast, argues that Peirce scorned James's view and instead glosses the cheerful hope as a regulative assumption of inquiry not reasoned to but accepted by a leap (2011, 264–65). Most recently, Andrew Howat (2014) has argued that Peirce is a quietist about what grounds the laws of logic. The debate as to whether Peirce's view is Jamesian hinges on two issues: Whether choosing in favor of or against the regulative assumptions really meets the standards of being a genuine option that cannot be decided on intellectual grounds and if it does, whether it is our "passional nature" that lawfully may and must make the decision. This is a matter I shall not attempt to settle here, but I would be remiss not to point out that Peirce himself claims any reasoning about these sentiments is a "trifling impertinence" (W 2:272, 1869). At least with respect to the sentiments (if not the rules of inference), Howat is correct to describe Peirce as a quietist.

that we ought to allow our philosophical theories directly to inform our conduct and to vie for champions in the public sphere. While Peirce denies that there is in science a place for belief understood in the Jamesian way as a willingness to act irrevocably, he concedes that there is a place for provisional belief in science. Whereas James maintains that fluency of thought is an indicator of the rationality of that line of thought, Peirce denies that such sentiments should have any weight in theoretical matters at all. And Peirce is a unique sort of monist rather than a Jamesian pluralist. Consistent with his realism, the truth of a theory consists in its generality, its ability to explain diverse phenomena. But on Peirce's view, it is not rationality alone that generalizes; sentiment does, too. In short, far from refusing to take "Philosophy and the Conduct of Life" seriously because Peirce was irritated with James, we should do just the opposite. For it is in this lecture we find obliquely expressed what sets Peirce's own philosophical views apart from those of James.

2 | A Defense of Peirce's Sentimental Conservatism

For those of us with more progressive moral and social inclinations, Peirce's sentimental conservatism seems doubtful. Peirce's own moral and social views should certainly give us pause. He opposed female and universal male suffrage. In 1908, Peirce writes, "as to us Americans, who had, at first, so much political sense, we always showed a disposition to support such aristocracy as we had; and we constantly experienced, and felt but too keenly, the ruinous effects of universal suffrage and weakly exercized [sic] government" (SS 78).[1] Daniel Campos (2014) has shown that Peirce was prejudiced against Hispanics and other ethnic minorities.[2] Even Peirce's examples to illustrate logic belie prejudice. Consider, for instance, this argument he uses in 1866 to illustrate a valid syllogism:

> No one overthrown &c. is pleasing to God
> Some Jews were overthrown &c.
> Some Jews were not pleasing to God.
> (W1:377)

And then this one to illustrate an invalid syllogism:

> All men are equal in their political rights
> Negroes are men;
> ∴ Negroes are equal in political rights to whites.
> (W 1:444)

Peirce's condescending comment after that last example does not help: "Far be it from me to say anything which could hinder justice from being done to that people whose guardianship the people of the North have assumed. By altering their social condition we have made

---

[1] See Westbrook (2005, ch. 1) for a discussion of Peirce's political views. Westbrook describes James, not Peirce, as "our kinsman." See Talisse (2007) for a Peircean defense of democracy and see also Misak (2000).

[2] See also Brent (1998, esp. 34 and 61–62) for more on the Peirce family's political views.

ourselves responsible for their welfare, to some extent" (W 1:444). Peirce then advises those who wish to understand the Declaration of Independence to "read Locke's Essay on Government" (W 1:444). Notably, Locke defends both natural equality and slavery as a prolongation of the state of war. One wonders whether Peirce believed the North ought not to have "altered their social condition"; even late in his life, he states that he did not find the cases for or against slavery particularly persuasive (see Brent, 1998, 61).

Peirce's sentimental conservatism looks like an ugly thing indeed. We are inclined to make the same objection to it that Lady Welby had. When Peirce states that they differ in that he is a conservative whereas she is a "rationalistic radical," Welby responds bitingly, "conservative of what? Of the antiquated, the obsolete, the effete? Of the once fitting, now misfitting? Of the once congruous, now incongruous? Of the once workable, now unworkable? Of that which once promoted growth and development and now stunts, backens, withers it" (SS 21, 1904)? Those prejudices that Peirce had inculcated from his aristocratic Cambridge upbringing are precisely those sentiments that are antiquated, now misfitting, now incongruous, now unworkable. Many of us are no doubt blinded by similar prejudices, perhaps against persons of different religious groups, of different gender identities, of different sexual preferences, or of different ethnicities. And yet these are the very sentiments on which Peirce apparently encourages us to rely in the conduct of our lives.

Furthermore, Cornelis de Waal has expressed serious doubts about Peirce's sentimental conservatism. What de Waal finds objectionable is that Peirce seems to leave no room – or at least very little – for critical reflection in our moral decision making. But this is a problem, he notes, for two reasons. First, some ancient and trenchant moral sentiments, such as xenophobia, ought to be rejected and are rejected on the basis of critical reflection (2012, 92). Second, there are other times when we have competing moral sentiments (e.g., with respect to the moral permissibility of abortion), when we have no sentiments (e.g., with newly emerging issues such as genetic research), or when our sentiments are not sufficiently finely grained (e.g., with respect to digital privacy) (see 2012, 93). Presumably, we will need to appeal to reason to determine what we ought to do in such cases. And, it should be noted, these sorts of moral questions are the ones most salient and challenging to us.

Yet if we start to untangle the skein of ideas and pronouncements in "Philosophy and the Conduct of Life" and read them in light of some of Peirce's other writings, then his sentimental conservatism is not as questionable as it may, at first glance, appear. Ultimately, Peirce defends a restricted sort of sentimental conservatism – what I would call instinctual sentimental conservatism – and what should be emphasized in his theory are not our sentiments primarily but our instincts and those sentiments that are based on them.

Peirce's own views on those of other ethnicities, on suffrage, and on slavery are clearly indefensible. Moreover, an examination of the complex ethical issues surrounding such issues as genetic engineering and digital privacy, for example, would be far too immense to undertake here. As ethical issues that have arisen only recently, Peirce has nothing to say about them directly. Furthermore, whether Peirce's *theoretical* philosophy can be used as a model to advocate for social change I shall not discuss here.[3] As I argued in the previous chapter, Peirce's sentimental conservatism is not an ethical theory – much less is it a political theory – but a bit of advice about how we should conduct our lives while we wait for our philosophical investigations to reach their conclusions in a properly scientific manner. Nonetheless, Peirce's practical philosophy – more specifically, his sentimental conservatism – can accommodate the worries just canvased.

Peirce's Sentimental Conservatism

In 1898, Peirce declares himself for sentimental conservatism. James had dedicated *The Will to Believe* to Peirce, and although Peirce thought James's dedication was "a truly sweet thing" (CWJ 8:246), he also expresses serious reservations about James's views. As explained in the previous chapter, one of the theories that Peirce rejects is James's rational radicalism in contrast with Peirce's sentimental conservatism. James maintains that we ought to allow our philosophical theories directly to inform how we conduct our lives, that these theories will then vie for champions in the public sphere through our conduct, and that the true theory will be the one that works in the sense of gaining champions or being perpetuated in the minds of believers.

---

[3] Trout (2010) and Campos (2014) argue that it can be.

In contrast, in the drafts for "Philosophy and the Conduct of Life," Peirce embraces "conservative sentimentalism" or "sentimental conservatism" (R 435:27/CP 1.661; R 435:28/CP 1.662; R 435:34/CP 1.673; and R 436:34). In R 435, he distinguishes between true conservatism and false conservatism. False conservatism consists in doing what is necessary to gain favors or, as Peirce says, "looks to see on which side bread is buttered" (R 435:27/CP 1.661). In contrast, true conservatism – which Peirce maintains is sentimental conservatism – "means not trusting to [crossed out: one's] reasonings about questions of vital importance but rather to hereditary instincts and traditional sentiments" (R 435:27/CP 1.661). We shall see that later in his life, Peirce would drop the "traditional" in favor of "instinct-based." True and false conservatism are alike in that their adherents do not trust much to their own reasonings when it comes to how they conduct their lives. They differ in that the adherent to false conservatism trusts instead to political or religious authorities and does so with the hope of gaining favors from them. The adherent to true conservatism mainly trusts to instinct and sentiment.

In 1892, Peirce states that sentimentalism is "the doctrine that great respect should be paid to the natural judgments of the sensible heart" (W 8:180). It is not clear in what sense hearts can make judgments. What he surely means is that in making judgments about events or considered courses of action, when those judgments are accompanied by pleasing feelings of approval or unpleasing feelings of disapproval and when those feelings are those of a "sensible heart," we ought to pay them great heed. Note, for what follows, that paying them great respect is not the same as always following their dictates.

As there is a true and a false conservatism, Peirce thinks there are ridiculous and non-ridiculous varieties of sentimentalism. He notes that sentimentalism is not widely endorsed at the time he is writing. This is excused because sentimentalism was made "a little ridiculous" "when it was the fashionable amusement to spend one's evenings in a flood of tears over a woeful performance on a candle-litten stage" (W 8:180, 1892). When sentimentalism is not ridiculous, it is the sentiments of the fully developed person that are trustworthy, not those of your average tear-soaked audience member. As he would assert much later, "esthetic good and evil are closely akin to pleasure and pain. They are what would be pleasure or pain to the fully developed superman" (EP 2:379, 1906). The fully developed superman will feel pleasure when considering those actions that are in fact good and pain on considering those that are in fact bad. Those feelings of pleasure and pain that accompany our perception or contemplation of actions, as we shall see later in this chapter, are the sentiments.

As explained in the previous chapter, in R 436, Peirce makes an oblique reference to James's preface to *The Will to Believe* when he writes, "it angers [crossed out: disgusts] me to open a book of religious philosophy and to read in the preface that the writer offers his metaphysics as a guide for the soul" (R 436:3). On Peirce's view, what should guide the soul are not our ethical or metaphysical theories but our sentiments and instincts. He maintains that if we embrace sentimental conservatism, then we will "modestly rate" our own reasoning powers and instead come "to recognize a higher business than your business, not merely an avocation after your vocation has done its daily task, that of melting into continuity with the neighboring parts of the universal cosmos" (R 436:34). It is not entirely clear what this means, though as noted in the previous chapter, it seems likely that the comment is related to Peirce's mystical experience in St. Thomas Episcopal Church in 1892, since he also makes the "supreme commandment of the Buddhisto-christian religion... to complete the whole system even until continuity results and the distinct individuals weld together" (R 435:34/CP 1.673). We shall try to shed some light on these claims in Chapter 4.

Earlier I stated that adherents to sentimental conservatism *mainly* trust to instinct and sentiment. This is because "it is of the essence of conservatism to refuse to push any practical principle to its extreme limits, – including the principle of conservatism itself" (RLT 111). There may well be times when we should not trust our sentiments: "we do not say that sentiment is *never* to be influenced by reason" (RLT 111). Indeed, Peirce writes, "I do not say that Philosophical science should not ultimately influence Religion and Morality; I only say that it should be allowed to do so only with secular slowness and the most conservative caution" (RLT 108). Peirce even admits that there may be some circumstances under which a sentimental conservative would "advocate radical reforms" (RLT 111).

In a letter dated May 7, 1904, Peirce provides two considerations when deliberating about whether to endorse a radical reform. First, he writes, "I insist, before favoring any extensive change, upon evaluating, as well as I can, the cost of it, on the one hand, and the *present value* (as we speak of the present value of an annuity) of all the good it would do, on the other" (SS 19). Suppose, for example, an interest rate of 4 percent. Assume, moreover, that one were to receive $10,000 paid in $1,000 dollar increments over 10 years. That $10,000 over 10 years would be equivalent to receiving $8,110.90 now invested at the same rate. So, less money now (say $9,000) will yield a greater return than $10,000 paid out in $1,000 increments over 10 years. And this is Peirce's point: Having a less than perfect policy at present might yield greater returns in the long run than embracing a radical reform that might take years to institute.

A second consideration Peirce introduces when considering radical reforms is that "the past cannot be reformed; and consequently, its memory and records subsisting still, no prevalent mode of expression can be annihilated. The most you can do is to introduce an *additional* way of expressing the same meaning" (SS 20). He continues, "there are some evils that, once embraced, had better be adhered to" (SS 20). Whatever reform might be introduced, the institutions being reformed cannot be utterly forgotten. Accordingly, sometimes it is best to stick with what one has, not because it promises to yield greater dividends (as in the case of the present value of an annuity) but because it promises to avoid greater harms.

In sum, in embracing conservatism, Peirce is objecting to allowing the adoption of a moral or political philosophy, a religious theory, or our own reasonings about morality and religion suddenly or precipitately to affect our conduct. As he states in the lecture, a man who allows the acceptance of a philosophical theory to directly influence his conduct, "who would, let us say, hastily practice incest, – is a man whom we should consider *unwise*" (RLT 111). He provides a similar example in a draft:

Place before the conservative arguments to which he can find no adequate reply and which go, let us say, to demonstrate that wisdom and virtue call upon him to offer to marry his own sister, and though he be unable to answer the arguments, he will not act upon their conclusion, because he believes that tradition and the feelings that tradition and custom has [sic] developed in him are safer guides than his own feeble ratiocination. Thus, true conservatism is sentimentalism. (R 435:27/CP 1.661)

Peirce's position, then, is contrary to James's. We should allow our moral and religious philosophies and our reasonings about them to lie hid under their bushels. Then, while we work out the truth of our moral and religious philosophies scientifically, in a way in which the conclusion is not predetermined, "sentiment can say 'Oh well, philosophical science has not by any means said its last word yet; and meantime I will continue to believe *so and so*'" (RLT 114).

It ought also to be clear from the preceding that Peirce is not proposing sentimental conservatism as an ethical theory established by the philosophical sciences. Philosophy – including the science of ethics – is in an infantile condition, in Peirce's judgment. Rather, his sentimental conservatism is a piece of advice on how we individually should live our lives while we wait for our ethical inquiries to reach their conclusions. Instead of conducting our lives according to whatever spurious ethical theory we should happen to endorse at the moment, we should mainly trust to our sentiments and instincts. This is an important point because if our scientific researches into ethics and religion should reach their conclusion, then we should allow their results to inform the conduct of our lives. Until then, Peirce advises us mainly to follow our instincts and our sentiments.

Peirce's Argument for Conservatism

Sentimental conservatism consists of two claims. One is the conservative claim: We ought not to trust too much to our own reasonings or to our moral and religious philosophies in the conduct of our lives. The other is the sentimental claim: In the conduct of life, we ought mainly to trust to our sentiments and instincts. But does Peirce have any good arguments for these theses?

He does have an argument for conservatism, and it is clearly stated in "Philosophy and the Conduct of Life." First, Peirce maintains that the talent for reasoning is actually quite rare. He claims that "powers of reasoning in any but the most rudimentary way are a somewhat uncommon gift, about as uncommon as a talent for music" (R 435:5/CP 1.657) and that "comparatively few persons are originally possessed of any but the feeblest modicum of this talent" (R 435:7/CP 1.657). Rather, what tends to be the case is that people think they are shaping their conduct to reason when really they are shaping their reason to what they would like to do: "a great many people think they shape their lives according to reason, when it is really just the other way" (RLT 114). If a talent for reasoning really is so uncommon and if we are sometimes deluded into thinking we are acting rationally when we are not, then we probably ought not to trust to our own reasonings too much. This, though, is not to say we ought never to trust them. We have already seen Peirce claim that there will be times when reason may inform our conduct.

Furthermore, Peirce maintains that we ought not trust to our philosophical theories because philosophy is in an "infantile condition" (RLT 107). He believes this is because philosophy has not, in the main, been pursued by investigators "animated by the true scientific Eros" but by seminarians "inflamed with a desire to amend the lives of themselves and others" (RLT 107). Hence, "for the present it is all far too dubious to warrant risking any human life upon it" (RLT 108). One hallmark of science is that investigators using sound methods of inquiry who begin their inquiries at different points nevertheless reach the same conclusions. This, I am confident a survey of the literature in philosophical ethics and the philosophy of religion shows, has yet to occur.

Taken together, these two claims show that we ought not to trust much to our own reasonings or philosophical theories, which is the very doctrine of conservatism. They also explain why Peirce states that he is a conservative "on rationalistic & experiential grounds" (SS 19, 1904). Science, when rightly conducted, is rigorous and thorough. It cannot be quickly accomplished. As Peirce writes to James of his own philosophical work, "it is a serious research to which there is no royal road" (CWJ 8:330, 1897). Philosophical investigations into ethics and religion are still ongoing.

While these considerations support conservatism, they do not support sentimentalism. Take, for example, the first argument. If a talent for reasoning really is uncommon, perhaps we should instead trust to those who do possess this uncommon talent rather than to our own sentiments and instincts. In that case, we will not trust to our own reasonings too much but we will trust to theirs. A similar consideration applies to the second argument: perhaps we should instead look to those philosophers of ethics who are animated by the true scientific Eros for advice on how to conduct our lives. Or perhaps we ought not trust to anything at all. A flip of the coin might be used to decide which course of action to take. Why, then, should we also be sentimentalists?

Two Arguments for Sentimentalism Considered

Reason as the Fly on the Wheel

Aside from supporting conservatism in the way just mentioned, Peirce also claims, "Sentimentalism implies Conservatism" (RLT 111). He then proceeds to argue for sentimentalism. Peirce's strategy is to argue that reason, in "vital crises," must appeal to instinct, which in turn appeals to our sentiments. But if that is so, then we should mainly trust to sentiments rather than to reason or, perhaps better, in trusting to reason we are actually just trusting to sentiment.

The "instinct" Peirce refers to in his argument is the abductive instinct. Abduction is that mode of reasoning that generates hypotheses. Yet abduction only renders tentative suggestions. In 1903, he writes,

> The form of [abductive] inference therefore is this:
> The surprising fact, C, is observed;
> But if A were true, C would be a matter of course.
> Hence, there is reason to suspect that A is true.
>
> (EP 2:231)

I shall have more to say about this particular passage in Chapter 3, but for now the statement of the conclusion is important: The hypothesis is but a suspicion.

Moreover, although abduction can be represented as having an argument form, Peirce contends that abductive reasoning is ultimately instinctual in nature.[4] He writes, "An Insight, I call it, because it is to be referred to the same general class of operations to which Perceptive Judgments belong. This Faculty is at the same time of the general nature of Instinct" (EP 2:217, 1903). Abduction as such is an ability to guess rightly in a way that is not overwhelmingly wrong: "abduction is, after all, nothing but guessing" (EP 2:107, 1901), and this power is "not strong enough to be oftener right than wrong, but strong enough not be overwhelmingly more often wrong than right" (EP 2:217, 1903).

Peirce maintains that in vital crises reason must appeal to the abductive instinct because the other two modes of reasoning – deduction and induction – have nothing to say. First, consider deduction. Deduction, as Peirce states, "only professes to give us information concerning the

---

[4] See Paavola (2005) for various stances on this matter and his own.

matter of our own hypotheses, and distinctly declares that if we want to know anything else, we must go elsewhere" (RLT 111). Hence, it cannot advise us as to what we should do in vital crises. It can only tell us what necessary consequences follow from the options at hand.

Second, consider induction. Induction, Peirce tells us, is of value "where we have ... an endless multitude of insignificant risks" (RLT 111). However, because vital crises are rare – as Peirce states, "in the conduct of life, we have to distinguish everyday affairs and great crises" (RLT 109) – we do not have an endless multitude of them. Also, because vital crises are significant – they are our *"greatest* concerns" and not "minor practical affairs" (RLT 112) – for the course of one's life, they do not involve insignificant risks.

If reason must appeal to abduction in vital crises and if abduction is instinctual, then in vital crises reason must appeal to instinct. The sort of "reason" it will appeal to is not scientific reasoning, however, but "egotistical" reasoning (RLT 111) or as Peirce states in R 435, "unconsciously unfair" reasoning (R 435:6/CP 1.657). He writes, "in many matters [reason] acts the fly on the wheel" (RLT 111). As a fly on a moving chariot's axle thinks it is kicking up a lot of dust by flapping its wings, reason thinks it is doing a lot of work in these cases when in fact "the reasons [men] attribute to themselves are nothing but excuses which unconscious instinct invents to satisfy the teasing 'whys' of the *ego*" (RLT 111). When we confront vital crises, we must appeal to our abductive instinct. But in appealing to our abductive instinct, we will actually invent some sham reasoning (see CP 1.57) to accord with what we desire: "The extent of this self delusion is such as to render philosophical rationalism a farce" (RLT 111). Peirce makes a similar claim in an unpublished essay titled "Analysis of Propositions," likely written a few years before he delivered "Philosophy and the Conduct of Life." He writes,

Men seem to themselves to be guided by reason. There is little doubt that this is largely illusory: they are much less guided by reason, much more guided by instinct, than they seem to themselves to be; because their reasonings are prominent in their consciousness, and are attended to, while their instincts they are hardly aware of, except later when they come to review their conduct. Even then, they are so immersed in instinct that they are hardly able to perceive it. (R 410:1–2, c. 1894)

Even when we think we are being guided by reason, and even when we reflect on the soundness of reasonings, most of us tend to be under the influence of instinct rather than strict ratiocination. This is Peirce's defense of sentimentalism: In vital crises, our reasonings can be but abductions. Our abductions are instinctive, but these abductive "reasonings" in vital crises are but sham reasonings invented to justify satisfying our desires in accordance with our sentiments. So, in vital crises, our reasonings are, at bottom, but appeals to sentiment: "Reason, then, appeals to sentiment in the last resort" (RLT 111).

Peirce is surely correct that in vital crises we will have to appeal to our abductive instinct, but this argument as a whole supports neither sentimentalism nor sentimental conservatism. There are three problems with it. First, it shows nothing about the utility of reason in the conduct of life generally, only in vital crises. But as a practical principle, Peirce's sentimental conservatism is not supposed to be limited to vital crises but to the conduct of life even for everyday affairs.

Second, it succeeds only by failing to distinguish among instinct, sentiment, and desire. But we have already seen in R 435 that Peirce makes mention of "hereditary instincts and traditional sentiments," suggesting that he does recognize some distinction between them, namely that instincts are inherited whereas sentiments (at least some) are inculcated by tradition. Also, we might indulge in some sham reasoning so that we can satisfy our desires even though we feel some repugnance (a sentiment) in doing so. Imagine, for example, a rebellious Hindu teenager who feels disapproval when considering eating beef but, when presented with a delectable sausage pizza and under peer pressure, reasons that cows are, after all, only animals. Or consider a Muslim who, though he feels disapproval when considering drinking alcohol, nevertheless reasons that it is good to "disinfect" his digestive system. In these cases, it is not sentiment to which the abductive instinct appeals but desire. I shall have more to say about Peirce's theory of desire in Chapter 5.

Third, even if we sometimes do engage in such sham reasoning, Peirce could hardly maintain that we always do. Sometimes our reasonings are contrary to our sentiments and desires and rightly so. Take, again, Peirce's opposition to female suffrage. Anyone with his wits about him would realize that there are no rational grounds for opposing female suffrage and good ones for supporting it. Peirce's attitude was surely informed by his own aristocratic upbringing in Cambridge and the "traditional sentiments" inculcated there.

Peirce's Irony and Another Argument for Sentimentalism

But perhaps – in fact, quite likely – Peirce was only being ironic in making that last argument in "Philosophy and the Conduct of Life." Perhaps what he meant to claim is that what you, that is, his audience of Harvard students and professors, call "reasoning" is nothing more than an appeal to your own sentiments and desires. But nevertheless, reason really does recommend sentimentalism. This would be consonant with Peirce's rejection of the Jamesian theory of sentimental rationality, explained in the previous chapter. Furthermore, there can be little doubt that Peirce was quite intent on insulting his audience when he delivered "Philosophy and the Conduct of Life." Insulting their conception of reasoning in this way would be oblique enough to avoid offending them but no doubt satisfying for Peirce. In fact, the drafts are dripping with sarcasm. For instance, in R 435, he writes,

One may well be struck with pity for the masses of population concentrated in New York and living under such unnatural conditions that they are forced to think mathematically. However, it is not as if they had the tender nurture of a cultured modern Harvard, that great eleemosynary institution that Massachusetts has established to the end that the *élite* of her youths may be aided to earning comfortable incomes and living softly cultured lives. The brains of those New York plebeians are coarse, strong, laboring brains, who don't know what it is to be free from mathematics. Their conceptions are crude and vulgar enough, but their vigor of reasoning would surprise you. (R 435:2/CP 1.650)

Perhaps, then, Peirce's argument given earlier for sentimental conservatism was supposed to be serious in one respect but ironic in another.

In "The Fixation of Belief," Peirce had suggested that in circumstances when we are unable to employ scientific reasoning – and a vital crisis would surely be such a circumstance – we should instead "let the action of natural preferences be unimpeded, then, and under their influence let men, conversing together and regarding matters in different lights, gradually develop beliefs in harmony with natural causes" (W 3:252, 1877). That is, we should follow what Peirce calls the a priori method and adopt beliefs that seem agreeable to reason. He maintains that "this method is far more intellectual and respectable from the point of view of reason" (W 3:253) than are the methods of fixing belief by appealing to authorities or by tenaciously retaining one's belief in the face of doubt. And in a late manuscript in which he set about revising that essay, he adds a note connecting this method explicitly to instinct: "Indeed, as long as no better method can be applied, it ought to be followed, since it is then the expression of instinct which must be the ultimate cause of belief in all cases" (EP 1:377n22, c. 1909).

Furthermore and as mentioned at the end of Chapter 1, in 1878's "The Doctrine of Chances," Peirce argues that logic itself rests on the sentiments of "interest in an indefinite community, recognition of the possibility of this interest being made supreme, and hope in the unlimited continuance of intellectual activity" (W 3:285). In "The Doctrine of Chances," Peirce argues that logic depends on the sentiments mentioned in the quotation because the probability of a form of inference is determined by the number of times the premises A and the conclusion B are true divided by the number of times A is true (see W 3:281). But, he contends, "death makes the number of our risks, of our inferences, finite, and so makes their mean result uncertain" (W 3:283–4). Consequently, "logicality inexorably requires that our interests shall *not* be limited. They must not stop at our own fate, but must embrace the whole community" (W 3:284).[5] Peirce's sentimental basis for logic is essentially a hope that the valid processes of mental action never cease, that they embrace all rational life forms, and that the exercise of reason is not limited to local or trivial concerns, for then the truth about any matter of fact should be discovered and error should be eliminated.

Richard L. Trammell has argued that a consequence of making reason or logicality depend on social sentiment is that matters of personal concern cannot be treated logically. He states, "according to Peirce's view of reason, a merely private concern can not be treated logically at all. The truth of any belief (or hypothesis) can be ascertained only by extended testing of its implied consequences so that sooner or later any error will be detected and corrected" (1972, 9–10). The truth is what will be believed after a sufficiently long and rigorous course of inquiry. It is the "predestinate opinion" (W 3:273, 1878). The conduct of our everyday lives, though, is concerned with the present, with what we must do now.

Here, then, we find many claims akin to those made in "Philosophy and the Conduct of Life": In vital crises, reason must appeal to instinct.

---

[5] In fact, Peirce had argued that logicality rests on the sentiments as early as 1869's "Grounds of Validity of the Laws of Logic" (see W 2:271–72, which "The Doctrine of Chances" echoes).

Reasoning – but in this case scientific reasoning – rests on the sentiments. And we ought not to trust too much to our own reasonings, for the "mean result" is "uncertain."

But as with Peirce's argument in "Philosophy and the Conduct of Life," this argument from the *Illustrations of the Logic of Science* series does not support the claim Peirce wishes to endorse: that even in the conduct of our everyday lives we ought mainly to trust to sentiment and instinct rather than to our reasonings and philosophical theories. First, Trammell's claim is doubtful. Certainly, the beliefs I act on may not be true and may not have been subjected to sufficient scientific scrutiny. But this does not mean my beliefs cannot be treated logically in the sense of being taken up into a process of inquiry. Neither does it follow that the belief is not true. At best, it only follows that I cannot assert that my own beliefs have been demonstrated or otherwise proven to be true in some strong sense of the terms "demonstrate" and "proven." For Peirce's view leaves open the possibility that my beliefs have some measure of scientific support.

Second, this line of argument only shows that the validity of probable reasoning depends on sentiments when those probable reasonings are put to use in scientific endeavors. But in 1904 in the context of discussing his conservatism with Lady Welby, Peirce acknowledges, "in my logic there is a great gulf between the methods proper to practical and to theoretical question[s]" (SS 19). Peirce's sentimental conservatism is on the practical side of that gulf; his resting the validity of the laws of logic on the sentiments is on the theoretical side. As Christopher Hookway has remarked regarding Peirce's early theory, the best reading of Peirce's comments in these early papers is that "in science – where, alone, rational self-control is possible – our practice of reasoning depends upon our membership in a community of inquirers bound together by these fundamental altruistic 'logical sentiments'" (2000, 230). In short, this argument supports a sentimental basis for our theoretical endeavors and not for the conduct of our everyday lives.

A Better Argument for Sentimental Conservatism

We have just seen that in his *Illustrations of the Logic of Science* series, Peirce contends that reason rests on sentiments. But as Peirce set about editing those lectures late in his life (c. 1909), he reveals an interesting shift: a focus away from the sentiments and toward instincts. In fact, he objects to sentimentalism and instead emphasizes instinct and the importance of pain and anxiety:

It is an obvious corollary from this principle [Malthus's principle of "struggle for existence" adopted by Darwin] that if pain, anxiety, and fear are the greatest stimuli to exertion, far from regarding them as evils, we should think of them as the main safeguards of our race, and persons infected with anything like hedonism and its offspring, sentimentalism, as disseminators of the seeds of racial extinction. (R 334:B2)

And he notes that our ability to engage in just reasoning is an instinct that has been developed in us over the past several thousand years:

Yet unless we are prepared to accuse all of the ancient civilized people either of laziness [for not performing an experiment] or of stupidity [for not making an obvious inference], the numerous cases in which easy experiments would have refuted their opinions ought to incline us toward the supposition that the Instinct of Just Reasoning had not in those days attained as full a development in the human genus as it has in ours. (R 334:F2)

Peirce continues to claim that this position receives "some colour of support" from the fact that the Greeks in the *Iliad* are "absolutely devoid of that Moral Instinct upon which the plots of Sophocles are pivoted" (R 334:F2). On Peirce's late view there are three instincts that have been undergoing development in human evolution: "Each of three human Instincts of Beauty, of Morality, and of Just Reasoning has undergone strange fluctuations in the course of history; and yet, if we are really descended from anything like apes, there has certainly been an upward growth of each on the whole" (R 334:F3).

But that Peirce means by sentimentalism as an offspring of hedonism the same thing he means by sentimentalism in 1898 is not clear. Sentimentalism as an offspring of hedonism might be of that ridiculous variety rather than the non-ridiculous variety. To clarify these issues, we need to take a look at Peirce's distinction between sentiment and instinct and his theory of instinct more generally. This will lead us to an evolutionary account of the origins of our sentiments and instincts. That, in turn, will lead us to another way of defending sentimental conservatism, an argument supporting a more instinct-focused version of it.

Sentiment and Instinct

In his discussion of Peirce's sentimentalism, Cornelis de Waal characterizes moral sentiments as "acquired or inherited moral habits of which we have ourselves only a partial cognitive understanding, or even awareness" (2012, 90). De Waal also characterizes sentiments as instincts (93). Similarly, Rosa Maria Mayorga identifies sentiment and instinct when she writes that Peirce's "notion of 'sentiment' or 'instinct' is that of an inherited characteristic, the result of evolution, which has as its aim the preservation of the community over the individual" (2012, 107).

Yet we have already seen that a statement from Peirce in R 435 suggests sentiment and instinct are distinct. Sentiments are traditional whereas instincts are inherited. But in "Philosophy and the Conduct of Life," Peirce sometimes conflates them, as when he writes, "it is the instincts, the sentiments, that make the substance of the soul" (RLT 110), "the regnant system of sexual rules is an instinctive or Sentimental induction" (RLT 111), and "matters of vital importance must be left to sentiment, that is, to instinct" (RLT 112).

In his later work, he quite clearly distinguishes between sentiments and instincts. On the one hand, it ought to be obvious that not all of our instincts are sentiments. For example, an infant's rooting and sucking reflexes can hardly be called sentiments though they are instinctual. When an infant's cheek or chin is touched, she will turn toward the stimulus and begin to make sucking motions as if to breastfeed. That is the rooting reflex. And the sucking reflex is such that when anything touches the roof of an infant's mouth, she will suck. These are instincts but not sentiments.

Are all of our sentiments instinct-based? That is less clear. Some anthropological studies suggest that they are not. For example, Catherine A. Lutz, in her book *Unnatural Emotions: Everyday Sentiments on a Micronesian Atoll and Their Challenge to Western Theory*, examines the sentiments of the Ifaluk people and argues for the cultural construction of emotions. While sentiments are not identical to emotions, all sentiments do involve the emotions, for sentiments, as David Savan writes, are "enduring and ordered systems of emotions, attached either to a person, an institution, or, in Peirce's case, a method" (1981, 331). Hence, if emotions are not instinctual, we may be led to conclude that some sentiments are not either.

As one example Lutz explores, the Ifaluk people have an emotion called *fago*. This emotion defies direct translation, and so Lutz characterizes it as compassion/love/sadness. But she notes,

> From the perspective of the implicit notions entailed in the American-English terms ... that together best translate *fago*, the concept involves some basic internal contradictions ... The ethnotheoretical notions surrounding the emotions with which I had come to Ifaluk created the structure of bafflement that I felt at seeing the diverse contexts within which the term *fago* ... was used. (1988, 119–120)

For instance, a man might feel *fago* for a stranger who is both disabled and homeless as well as for his father just before leaving for a long trip. If, as Lutz argues, emotions are culturally constructed and socially defined, it strongly suggests that not all sentiments are instinctual, assuming instincts are shared across the human race. Lutz's claim is doubtful, though. Perhaps the Ifaluk language is too coarse grained compared to American English to express the complexities of emotional life, just as, arguably, some languages have a more coarse-grained color vocabulary than does American English (see Lucy 1997). Or perhaps *fago* is tracking some feature that is common to both experiences just mentioned, such as heaviness in one's heart, as we say in English. Let us, then, look more closely at what Peirce says about sentiment and instinct.

Peirce characterizes the sentiments as "whatever the dictates of the human heart may approve" (EP 2:59, 1901) – or, presumably, disapprove. This is in line with the views of the British moralists, especially Hutcheson and Hume, with whose views Peirce was familiar. Hume's moral theory makes moral praise and blame depend on the sentiments. Hutcheson maintains that we have a moral sense by which we perceive the rightness or wrongness of actions, and he understands a sense to consist not merely in the reception of ideas (in the case of the moral sense, moral ideas) but also in accompanying pleasures and pains: "Every Determination of our Minds to receive Ideas independently on our Will, and to have Perceptions of Pleasure and Pain, [I call] A SENSE" (1756, 4). A moral sentiment, then, is a pleasing feeling of approval or an unpleasing feeling of disapproval regarding some proposed or actual course of action. For example, we have pleasing feelings of approval on consideration of a person acting benevolently. We have unpleasing feelings of disapproval on consideration of a person committing incest. In contrast to his account of sentiments, Peirce understands an instinct to be an "inherited habit" (CP 2.170, 1902) or

a way of voluntary acting prevalent almost universally among otherwise normal individuals of at least one sex or other unmistakable natural part of a race (at some stage, or during recurring periods of their lives), which action conduces to the probable perpetuation of that race, and which, in the present stage of science, is not at once satisfactorily and fully explicable as a result of any more general way of mental action. (EP 2:464–65, 1913)

Sentiments are feelings; instincts are inherited habits.

A habit, according to Peirce, is "some general principle working in a man's nature to determine how he will act" (CP 2.170, 1902). It might be preferable to state that a habit is a principle that determines how a person will respond under certain conditions, for as Joshua Black (2013, 8) has noted, Peirce sometimes writes of habits of feeling (see EP 2:377–378) and habits of imagination (CP 2.148). Nevertheless, habits of action are paradigmatically habits for Peirce. Peirce regards habits as "general law[s] of action," such that a person who has inculcated the habit of biting her nails whenever she is under stress will be "more or less apt" to bite her nails when she is in fact under stress (CP 2.148, 1902). The habit is the readiness to act in a certain way under certain conditions. Accordingly, habits are both general and conditional, as Shapiro (1973, 26) notes. They are not identical to the actions themselves but rules or tendencies of action. Moreover, they issue actions when certain conditions are met. Also, Shapiro writes, habits are "of a purposive, rather than a mechanical type" (29) in that the purpose of a habit is to bring about a certain result. We may or may not be conscious of the habits that we possess. Peirce maintains that some habits are inherited (instincts), whereas others are acquired. Nonetheless, he acknowledges that we may have difficulty discerning which habits are inherited and which are acquired at a young age (CP 2.170, 1902). For reasons that shall become evident later, the distinction between inherited habits and those acquired at a young age is vague. Presumably, it is for this reason that in 1913 he adds the qualification that an instinct is such that "in the present stage of science, [it] is not at once satisfactorily and fully explicable as a result of any more general way of mental action."

Peirce also draws – but does not always respect – a technical distinction between habits and dispositions (see EP 2:413, 1907). On Peirce's view, dispositions, properly speaking, are not alterable. A glass vase has the dispositional property of breaking if one drops it on a tile floor. In contrast, we can form or alter habits by action or by imagination. For instance, I can form the habit of taking a vitamin every morning simply by repeatedly taking a vitamin first thing every morning. The more I do it, the less I will think about the activity. It will become, as we say, second nature. This is the development of a habit by action. As one striking example of gaining a habit through imaginative exercises, Peirce tells the story of his brother Herbert putting out a fire on their mother's dress. Herbert acted quickly, without deliberation, and Charles was amazed. When he asked Herbert how he acted so quickly, Herbert stated that he had heard the story of how Fannie Longfellow's dress had caught on fire and she died. Herbert had considered what he would do were his own mother's dress to catch fire and through these imaginative exercises formed a habit of action (see CP 5.487n1 and CP 5.538). On Peirce's view, our ability to form or alter our habits is at the heart of self-controlled action and thought and is essential to moral responsibility, a topic I shall take up in Chapter 5. For now, it is important to note that our instincts or inherited habits are under a degree of control. However, the amount of control we can exercise over them is sometimes quite limited. For instance, we can train ourselves to hold our breath for a long time, but it is impossible to commit suicide merely by holding one's breath. Moreover, some of our instincts may fade in the natural course of human development, as do the rooting and sucking reflexes.

As noted earlier, these instincts are sometimes accompanied by sentiments, but not always. Moreover, in later comments from 1905, Peirce is quite clear that some sentiments have a basis in instinct, but not all of them do. This is evident in his discussion of incest and suicide. Of our belief in the criminality of incest, Peirce notes the "intensity of our sentiment" of disapproval about it. He goes on to claim that when we consider "the thrill of horror which the idea excites in us, we find reason in that to consider it [the incest taboo] to be an instinct" (EP 2:349–50). In contrast, although we have a strong sentiment of disapproval about suicide, Peirce denies that the sentiment has an instinctual basis (EP 2:350). This is for two reasons. First, the sentiment is not common to all cultures. Second, the sentiment is given little consideration when we confront a situation in which suicide is a reasonable option (e.g., committing suicide so as to save another's life).

Clearly, then, Peirce thinks that some moral sentiments (feelings of approval or disapproval with respect to some course of action) do have their basis in instinct (inherited habits), whereas others do not. Recent studies on infant morality suggest that children do in fact have moral sentiments but lack acquired habits. One conclusion we may reasonably draw from this is that they have an instinct for morality. Recent work at the Yale Infant Cognition Center lends credence to this view. Paul Bloom has argued that babies have a sense of right and wrong, however coarse grained and primitive it may be. He gives an example:

Not long ago, a team of researchers watched a 1-year-old boy take justice into his own hands. The boy had just seen a puppet show in which one puppet played with a ball while interacting with two other puppets. The center puppet would slide the ball to the puppet on the right, who would pass it back. And the center puppet would slide the ball to the puppet on the left ... who would run away with it. Then the two puppets on the ends were brought down from the stage and set before the toddler. Each was placed next to a pile of treats. At this point, the toddler was asked to take a treat away from one puppet. Like most children in this situation, the boy took it from the pile of the "naughty" one. But this punishment wasn't enough – he then leaned over and smacked the puppet in the head. (2010)

Presumably a one-year-old child has not yet acquired moral habits, but here we see a child acting on a sentiment of disapproval toward the naughty doll. The child, Peirce would claim, has an instinct for morality.

With respect to de Waal's characterization of moral sentiments as "acquired or inherited moral habits," this raises a question: Do sentiments that do not have a basis in instinct nevertheless have a basis in acquired habits? One route to answering the question of whether there might be some moral sentiments that do not have a basis in habits is to consider instances when adults confront novel situations that elicit moral sentiments, but, since they are novel, the person cannot have acquired habits pertaining to those situations. Consider de Waal's example of digital privacy. Since digital privacy is a recent phenomenon, we cannot have instincts pertaining to it. Neither can we have acquired moral habits pertaining to novel sorts of intrusions into digital privacy since they are novel. However, it may be that such sentiments do in fact have some basis – perhaps analogically or because the novel situation is a species of some more generic situation – in inherited or acquired habits. For example, one might have unpleasing feelings of disapproval regarding invasions of digital privacy, but that may be rooted in an acquired habit pertaining to privacy in general.

It is difficult to discern whether all sentiments *in fact* have some basis in habits. However, we can be content with a weaker claim: that on Peirce's view, it must be *in principle possible* for us to have moral sentiments without corresponding moral habits. Why is this so? For Peirce, sentiments are feelings and feelings are Firsts, the "mode in which anything would be for itself, irrespective of anything else, so that it would not make any difference though nothing else existed, or ever had existed" (RLT 147). In other words, a universe consisting only of the sentiment of disapproval is conceivable (see CP 1.305), which means it need not be based on a habit.[6]

To sum up, our moral sentiments are feelings of approval or disapproval about certain proposed or accomplished courses of action. Instincts are inherited habits, though the line of demarcation between inherited habits and those resulting from infantile conditioning is vague and so the latter may also be regarded as instincts. Some of our moral sentiments have a basis in instincts, but not all of them do. It is not clear whether all of our sentiments have a basis in some habit, whether inherited or acquired. Nonetheless, on Peirce's view it must at least be possible in principle to have a moral sentiment without it being based on a corresponding habit. Furthermore, it should be clear now that characterizing sentiments as habits is not quite accurate. Whereas it *may* be the case that all of our sentiments in fact have some basis in acquired or inherited moral habits, sentiments themselves are not habits but pleasing or unpleasing feelings of approval or disapproval, respectively, regarding some course of action. We must distinguish between habits and instincts, on the one hand, and sentiments, on the other.

Although I have been focusing on the distinction between sentiments and instincts, they are obviously related. The parental instinct to care for one's young is clearly accompanied with feelings of love, of compassion, of pride, and so on. Similarly, the so-called fight or flight response involves the sentiments, namely, feelings of courage and fear. Sentiments and

---

[6] Someone might object that the moral sentiment is clearly an emotional interpretant of the considered course of action, but that only shows the moral sense depends on interpretation, not that the sentiment does. At any rate, Peirce is quite clear that even if the feeling is a logical ingredient of the moral sense, it may still be considered in itself by ignoring the other ingredients (see EP 2:364–65).

instincts are to be distinguished, but our instincts are felt or made conscious to us way by of our sentiments. Indeed, that feeling is part of what makes our instincts effective guides to action. The habit to flee in the presence of seeing a fox is the rabbit's instinct. The instinct effectively causes the rabbit to flee when it sees a moving patch of red fur. The sentiment is the conscious effectuation of the instinct. This thought sheds light on why Peirce rejects sentimentalism as an offspring of hedonism in his late comments on "The Fixation of Belief." Sentimentalism regarded as an offspring of hedonism is the view that what we ought to do is to seek out the pleasurable feelings of sentiment and avoid painful ones. But true sentimentalism, the sort of sentimentalism that Peirce endorses, finds value not merely in the positive, pleasurable sentiments but the painful ones as well. As Peirce writes, they are "safeguards of our race."

Peirce on the Instincts

At this juncture, we will do well to turn to Peirce's classification of the instincts, which he undertakes in 1902. His motivation for classifying the instincts is an attempt to develop a classification of the practical, as opposed to theoretical, sciences. As the practical sciences arise because we have some purpose or goal we hope to successfully accomplish and because our purposes are ultimately rooted in desires and our desires in our instincts, Peirce believes that a classification of our instincts will provide the key for classifying the practical sciences.[7]

Such is Peirce's motivation, but it is harder to ascertain who inspires his theory and classification of the instincts. Charles Darwin's chapter on instinct in *The Origin of Species* and his views in *The Descent of Man* are likely one significant influence on Peirce's theory, as Maryann Ayim has noted (1982, 69–73). First, we know that as Peirce worked on his classification of the sciences in 1902, he returned to the work of zoologists in classification. His classification of the theoretical sciences draws on Louis Agassiz's *Essay on Classification* (see CP 1.229ff. and

---

[7] This poses a problem in that it would seem to make the theoretical sciences practical sciences, for we have the purpose of acquiring knowledge and that is based on what Peirce calls our gnostic instinct. He replies, questionably, to this worry: "It is quite true that the Gnostic Instinct is the cause of all purely theoretical inquiry, and that every discovery of science is a gratification of curiosity. But it is not true that pure science is or can be successfully pursued *for the sake* of gratifying this instinct" (R 1343:75–76/CP 7.58), and "curiosity is their motive; but the gratification of curiosity is not their aim" (R 1343:77/CP 7.58).

Atkins 2006), which he also remarks "appeared at a most inauspicious epoch" (CP 1.205n1). Accordingly, it would not be surprising if Peirce turned to another zoologist, the one who made that epoch inauspicious for the appearance Agassiz's book, to work out his classification of the practical sciences.

Second, the examples Peirce uses to illustrate the instincts are similar to Darwin's. Darwin singles out three examples of instinct for extended discussion: the instinct of cuckoo birds to lay their eggs in the nests of other birds; the slave-making instinct of ants; and the making of hives by bees. With respect to the first, he notes,

> Every one understands what is meant, when it is said that instinct impels the cuckoo to migrate and to lay her eggs in other birds' nests. An action, which we ourselves should require experience to enable us to perform, when performed by an animal, more especially by a very young one, without any experience, and when performed by many individuals in the same way, without their knowing for what purpose it is performed, is usually said to be instinctive. (1870, 185)

Peirce makes a similar point but with respect to wasps: "wasps having no experience of the destiny of an egg will lay its eggs so that the young will find a kind of food that would not be food at all to the mother, even if she knew that any young were to come forth" (NEM 3:203, 1911). Peirce's preference for the wasp example may well be inspired by controversy at the time surrounding how common it was for cuckoos to lay eggs in the nests of other birds, and Darwin himself indicates bees and wasps provide a better example:

> Many bees are parasitic, and always lay their eggs in the nests of bees of other kinds. This case is more remarkable than that of the cuckoo; for these bees have not only their instincts but their structure modified in accordance with their parasitic habits; for they do not possess the pollen-collecting apparatus which would be necessary if they had to store food for their own young. Some species, likewise, of Sphegidae (wasp-like insects) are parasitic on other species; and M. Fabre has lately shown good reason for believing that although the Tachytes nigra [a species of wasp] generally makes its own burrow and stores it with paralysed prey for its own larvae to feed on, yet that when this insect finds a burrow already made and stored by another sphex, it takes advantage of the prize, and becomes for the occasion parasitic. (1870, 194–195)

Peirce also regularly makes reference to the instincts of birds, bees, wasps, and ants (see, e.g., RLT 111, CP 6.476, and EP 2:464 and

467). Nonetheless, it must also be admitted that these examples were in wide use.

Third and most significantly, like Peirce, Darwin regards instincts as inherited habits. Darwin writes,

Frederick Cuvier and several of the older metaphysicians have compared instinct with habit. This comparison gives, I think, a remarkably accurate notion of the frame of mind under which an instinctive action is performed, but not of its origin. How unconsciously many habitual actions are performed, indeed not rarely in direct opposition to our conscious will! yet they may be modified by the will or reason. Habits easily become associated with other habits, and with certain periods of time and states of the body. When once acquired, they often remain constant throughout life. Several other points of resemblance between instincts and habits could be pointed out ...

If we suppose any habitual action to become inherited – and I think it can be shown that this does sometimes happen – then the resemblance between what originally was a habit and an instinct becomes so close as not to be distinguished. (186)

Here we see many of the ideas we find in Peirce: Instincts are inherited habits. Habits are not always conscious. However, they can be modified by effort. Instincts are typically acquired by natural selection (hence Darwin's qualification "not of its origin") but might also be acquired by habitual action.

It may be surprising to see Darwin here treating habitual action as capable of driving evolutionary changes – that "it can be shown" that "habitual action [may] become inherited" – and resulting in inherited characteristics. To our ears, such a notion sounds positively Lamarckian, whereas Darwin thinks that the driving force of evolution is natural selection. But as Robert J. Richards has pointed out,

In the early editions of the *Origin*, he [Darwin] did attempt to explain most adaptations by use of natural selection, but he certainly admitted the significance of other factors. For example, he allowed that "habit, use, and disuse have, in some cases, played a considerable part of the modification of the constitution, and of the structure of various organs." And in explaining the instincts of domestic animals, he forthrightly acknowledged the role of inherited habit. (1987, 193–194).

Moreover, Richards notes, Darwin's late *The Expression of Emotions in Man and Animals* relies on the principle of the inheritance of acquired characteristics (see p. 203). There was, moreover, an important question as to whether natural selection could account for the mental and moral characteristics of humans, especially given the shortness of geological time, even if it could fully account for the physiological characteristics of humans. Even if natural selection is the primary force driving evolution, Darwin does not commit himself to the claim that it is the sole force.

As a Lamarckian, Herbert Spencer (unlike Darwin) regarded acquired habits becoming inherited habits as the primary driving force of evolution. But in one passage that sounds positively Darwinian, he writes, "it is clear that by the ceaseless exercise of the faculties needed to contend with [the dangers of existence], and by the death of all men who fail to contend with them successfully, there is ensured a constant progress towards a higher degree of skill, intelligence, and self-regulation – a better co-ordination of actions – a more complete life" (1852, 267). Peirce, as we shall see in Chapter 4, also regarded evolutionary processes as tending toward an ideal state. Unlike Spencer, though, Peirce thought of this religiously and quasi-mystically, as a state in which the discontinuities of wills disappear and individuals are "welded" together. Moreover, as we shall see in Chapter 5, Peirce was fiercely critical of Spencer for regarding evolution as a mechanical process and, consequently, as reversible. Peirce understood that some processes are nonconservative and regarded evolution as one such process.

Nevertheless, that passage from Spencer's work does suggest something like the Baldwin Effect: An organism's ability to learn new behaviors will affect its reproductive success. And, indeed, the work of James Mark Baldwin may also have influenced Peirce's theory of instinct. Peirce wrote several of the entries for Baldwin's *Dictionary of Philosophy and Psychology* and would have been familiar with the main ideas of his work. He also reviewed of some of Baldwin's books for *The Nation*. Not unlike Darwin, Baldwin defines instincts as "original tendencies of consciousness to express itself in motor terms in response to definite but generally complex stimulations of sense; i.e. they are inherited motor intuitions" (1894, 311). As tendencies, they are habits, and so like Peirce, Baldwin regards instincts as inherited habits. Moreover, Baldwin urges that his theory of organic selection accommodates an account of how intelligence and imitation can influence evolution within a Darwinian framework. In 1902's *Development and Evolution*, he writes,

We reach a point of view which gives to organic evolution a sort of intelligent direction after all; for of all the variations tending in the direction of an instinct, but inadequate to its complete performance, *only those will be supplemented and kept alive which the intelligence ratifies and uses for the animal's individual accommodations.* The principle of selection applies strictly to the others or to some of them. So natural selection eliminates the others; and the *future development of instinct must at each state of a species' evolution be in the directions thus ratified by intelligence.* (1902, 69)

If a culture, for instance, regards youthful acts of courage as a sign of future greatness and if some offspring have neural anatomy that makes them more prone to act courageously in their youth than others or that aids them in catching on to how to act courageously from a young age, then those offspring with that neural anatomy will be selected for over successive generations. Darwin himself suggested that the inherited structure of the brain causes instincts (see Richards, 1987, 94). From this, his theory of natural selection, and his recognition that conspecifics exert some of the most significant selection pressures, it is only a short step to claim that within communities, certain neural anatomies might be selected for over others and, in this way, new instincts might emerge. (Of course, those communities themselves must also be selected for if those neural anatomies are to survive, as Darwin realized.) For reasons such as this, Baldwin was sometimes accused of saying nothing that was not already to be found in Darwin. Moreover, it is because of accounts such as these that Peirce would regard the line of demarcation between inherited habits and those acquired in infancy as vague.

I make these points to forestall a certain objection against Peirce's theory of instinct, namely, that Peirce apparently endorses Larmarckian evolution in his "Evolutionary Love" of 1892. I have no interest here in defending that essay; there can be little doubt it was written in the thralls of a religious fervor. Nonetheless, some points in defense of Peirce are in order. First, Peirce quite clearly limits his discussion of evolution in the third part of that essay to the development of mind and not to anatomical structures. Second, Peirce nowhere proposes a mechanism for how an acquired habit could become inheritable. Third, as already argued, Peirce's views would not have been regarded as peculiar for his time, as Darwin at times leans in a Lamarckian direction and Spencer at times leans in a Darwinian one. Fourth, by 1902 when he develops his theory and classification of instincts, Peirce would have been familiar with

Baldwin's ideas and so would have had available to him a Darwinian framework to accommodate his more Larmarckian inclinations. In fact, in "Evolutionary Love" he had already asserted, "the line of demarcation between the three modes of evolution [viz. Darwinian, Lamarckian, and evolution by necessity, such as we find in Hegel's thought] is not perfectly sharp" (W 8:195, 1892). And finally, late in his life, Peirce resolves the worry that there had not been sufficient geological time for the instincts to evolve by way of natural selection when he notes that evolutionary changes can accrue geometrically rather than arithmetically (R 334.F2x–F7x, c. 1909). In short and in sum, Peirce does regard instincts as inherited habits, but he is not obviously committed to a Lamarckian account of how acquired habits might become inherited. Indeed, Peirce is not committed to any particular view on how an acquired habit might become inheritable.

However influential Darwin and Baldwin may have been on Peirce's theory of the instincts – and however less influential Lamarck and Spencer may have been – neither Darwin nor Baldwin provides a classification of instincts. In 1898, Peirce reviewed Henry Rutgers Marshall's *Instinct and Reason* for *The Nation*, and Marshall does provide a classification of the instincts. However, it bears no obvious relation to Peirce's classification. Nonetheless, Marshall does make a clear distinction between instinct-based sentiments and instincts proper, referring to the latter as instinct feelings and the former as instinct actions. This distinction may have played a role in Peirce more clearly distinguishing between sentiments and instincts after 1898, as explained earlier.

We do find a rather haphazard list of the instincts in James's *The Principles of Psychology* (WWJ 9:1004–1057), and it is likely that Peirce's first of two attempts to classify the instincts draws on James's list. The instincts listed in Peirce's first classification are the instincts for food, health, clothes, house, collecting, play, imitation, conversation, war, morals, progeny, and magic (by which Peirce means having emotions to the service of society) (R 1300). This list of the instincts lines up nicely with James's, who lists instincts for sucking, biting, clasping an object, and carrying to the mouth an object (food); turning the head aside as a gesture of rejection, holding the head erect, sitting up, standing, locomotion, and cleanliness (health); modesty and shame, as when we hide parts of our bodies in clothing; constructiveness as when we build "like the bee or beaver" (house); appropriation or acquisitiveness (collecting); play; imitation; pointing, crying, voca-lization, sociability, and shyness (conversation); emulation or rivalry and hunting and fighting (war); love, paternal love, and sex (progeny); and various emotions, such as pugnacity, sympathy, jealousy, and fear (magic). The only instinct on Peirce's list that does not obviously correlate with those on James's is the instinct for morals, but this instinct has a place alongside many of the others on James's lists, such as the various emotions, sociability, and love. However, Peirce thought that his own first list was incomplete and overlapped in some respects. For instance, health and play are closely related in that we play to maintain our health. Accordingly, Peirce undertook a better classification.

Peirce begins his second classification by noting that there are two general instincts:

The instincts of every animal appear to have for their quasi-purpose the preservation of the race of which that animal is a member, and this in one or other of two ways,

1st by preserving that individual alive,
2nd by causing him to reproduce his kind, and rear his offspring.
(R 1343:18)

Peirce calls instincts that fall under the first sort *suicultural* because they aim at the preservation and flourishing of the self. He calls instincts that fall under the second sort *civicultural* because they aim at the preserva-tion and flourishing of the stock. Peirce's use of the prefix "quasi-" in "quasi-purpose" stems from the fact that natural selection does not act with a purpose as humans have purposes: "Should there be no human purpose, there may, nevertheless, be an evolutionary agency that acts like a purpose, or there may [be] a principle similar to such agency except that it is related, not to a temporal, but to a logical sequence of results" (R 1343:12).

Humans, though, have another sort of instinct in addition to these two. He writes, "such instincts as that for Art and Scientific Curiosity do not deal with persons so much as with ideas; nor do we find among Artists and Scientific Men that power of handling men that we find among those in whom civic instincts, say those for Politics, Education, and War, are strong" (R 1343:34–35). Whereas the first two sorts of instincts concern our dealings with other people, the last kind concerns our dealings with ideas. These are the *specicultural* instincts.[8] Accordingly, Peirce writes,

> Let us ask our own hearts what if anything, makes the human race worthy of preservation. The answer would seem to be, its promise of ultimately developing ideas and of rendering the arrangements of its sphere of influence reasonable. Are not the words 'worthy' and 'reasonable', in the perfect sense of each, synonymous? If so, the third group of instincts will be those that concern ideas; so that the division of Instincts will be into the Suicultural, the Civicultural, and the Specicultural. (R 1343:36–37)

   Peirce proceeds to identify the more specific instincts that fall under each of these classes (R 1343:37–42). The suicultural instincts are these four: (1) the Gambol instinct, which is an instinct for exercise of body and mind; (2) the Gust instinct, which is an instinct to take pleasure in sensations, especially those related to food; (3) the Getting instinct, which is an instinct to amass treasures, whether money or books or other things; and (4) the Gentleman instinct, which is for the enjoyment of one's own grandeur, for example, in having a great house. The civicultural instincts are (5) the Govern instinct, which is an instinct for ordering one's neighbors; (6) the Ghost instinct, which is an instinct for having emotions that serve society, as, for example, magicians and shamans who stir up emotions for the service of a tribe; (7) the Gore instinct, an instinct for combat and ruthless destruction; and (8) the Gamic instinct, which is an instinct for the production, rearing, and training of children. Finally, these are the four specicultural instincts: (9) the Grouping instinct, an instinct for asso-ciation and associational suggestion; (10) the Garb instinct, which causes sensuous and unintentional expression and blossoming of the soul, manifest in clothing, especially; (11) the Graphic instinct, which is a disposition to work energetically with ideas and to "wake them up" by expressing them in action or in imagination; and (12) the Gnostic instinct, which is an instinct to look beyond ideas to their upshot and purpose, which is the truth. Peirce's mnemonic device of naming all of

---

[8] In her treatment of Peirce's theory of instinct, Maryann Ayim neglects R 1343, excepting the excerpts published in CP. As a consequence, she asserts that there are only two distinct kinds of instinct, selfish and social (1982, 21) and her classification of 37 instincts does not follow Peirce's own. Like Robert Beeson (2008) and William Davis (1972), Ayim is primarily concerned with instinct and sentiment as they relate to scientific inquiry. Beeson does an admirable job of situating Peirce's theory of emotion in its historical context.

the instincts with a word beginning with the letter "G" is certainly strange, but we should not conclude from this that his classification is ill-considered. As noted earlier, his classification is likely a development of James's attempt to provide a list of the instincts. Peirce believes that the second list is complete, but he provides no argument for this claim.[9]

Furthermore, Peirce believes that all twelve of these instincts are somehow inherited, passed down from parent to progeny, though the means of their being passed down may not be known. He writes that "an animal instinct is a natural disposition, or inborn determination of the individual's Nature (his 'nature' being that within him which causes his behavior to be such as it is), manifested by a certain unity of quasi-purpose in his behavior" (R 1343:21) and "the three essential characters of instinctive conduct are that it is conscious, is determined to a quasi-purpose, and that in definite respects [it] escapes all control" (R 1343:23). Peirce's claim that instincts escape all control is too strong. As he would state c. 1909, these instincts can be refined through training (see the earlier quotation from R 334:A4). Even in the manuscript itself, he notes that only parts of the instinct are beyond control. Other parts can be "partially controlled by the deliberate exercise of imagination and reflexion" (R 1343:21).

What is noteworthy about Peirce's comment here is that these instincts are conscious, even if minimally so. They are accompanied with feelings, with emotions or sensations. Although Peirce does not provide an account of what these feelings may be, he does provide some hints. The Gentleman and Ghost instincts involve enjoyment and emotions at the service of society, respectively. The Graphic instinct is energetic. The Garb instinct will be accompanied with feelings of what looks good, what is stylish, what is visually pleasing. In the manuscript, he notes that the Gore instinct is associated with irascibility. And obviously the Gamic instinct will be accompanied with feelings of love and care for one's offspring. These, then, are the instincts according to Peirce. Many of them are effectuated in various sentiments.

---

[9] Though he does not say so, it is possible Peirce thought the general, tripartite division of instincts into the suicultural, civicultural, and speciculurary is complete because of his view that Firstness, Secondness, and Thirdness exhaust the list of categories. This, though, could hardly support his claim that the list of 12 instincts is complete. He might also think the list is complete because it includes all of the instincts James lists and more.

Animals, Instinct, and Sentiment

One of the more peculiar features of Peirce's 1898 lecture and its drafts is his frequent reference to animals and how they conduct their lives. He begins his draft thusly:

Among the advantages which our humble cousins whom it pleases us to refer to as "the lower animals" enjoy over some of our own family is that they *never* reason about vitally important topics, and never have to lecture nor to listen to lectures about them. Docilely allowing themselves to be guided by their instincts into almost every detail of life, they live exactly as their Maker intended them to live. The result is, that they very rarely fall into error of any kind, and *never* into a vital one. What a contrast to our lives! (R 435:1/CP 1.649)

And in the lecture, he makes a similar point:

Those whom we are so fond of referring to as the "lower animals" reason very little. Now I beg you to observe that those beings very rarely commit a *mistake*, while we – – – ! We employ twelve good men and true to decide a question, we lay the facts before them with the greatest care, the "perfection of human reason" presides over the presentment ... and it is generally admitted that the parties to the suit might almost as well have tossed up a penny to decide! Such is man's glory! (RLT 110)

He also notes:

Do not doubt that the bee thinks it has a good reason for making the end of its cell as it does. But I should be very much surprised to learn that its reason had solved the problem of isoperimetry that its instinct has solved. (RLT 111)

And again:

The instincts of those animals whose instincts are remarkable present the character of being chiefly, if not altogether, directed to the preservation of the stock and of benefitting the individual, very little, if at all, except so far as he may happen as a possible procreator to be a potential public functionary. Such, therefore, is the description of instinct that we ought to expect to find in man, in regard to vital matters. (RLT 113)

Peirce's references to nonhuman animals are telling and indicative of how he thinks of human animals. It is implausible – and certainly Peirce would think it false – to claim that animals reason in any sense like humans are capable of reasoning. Although animal instincts are, on

Peirce's account, conscious, animals themselves are not reflective. They are incapable of formulating premises, of drawing conclusions from them, of evaluating the soundness of their reasonings, and of following out a predetermined method of investigation into a question.

Nevertheless, nonhuman animals do very well for themselves. They are able to learn from one another. They avoid danger. They find food and shelter. They manage to eek out an existence in harsh environments or during catastrophic meteorological events. As Peirce writes in "Analysis of Propositions,"

> If we compare the results of the two methods of determining conduct, it certainly seems that instinct works far better than reasoning. The small number of mistakes which the lower animals make is most surprising. Most men fail in life. A great percentage of men make utter failures; a very few make complete successes; and the majority of these few are men of tremendous instincts and little power of ratiocination. (R 410:2, c. 1894)

But how do animals do it? How can they be so successful when they are guided not by reasoning or a "scientific Eros" but by their sentiments and instincts?

Animals are surely capable of some rudimentary sorts of "reasonings." When, for example, a rabbit sees a fox and then feels fear, there is some sense in which it recognizes *this* fox as an instance of a thing *to be feared*. But on Peirce's view, the success of animals is to be explained by the natural selection of their sentiments and instincts. The rabbit has suicultural instincts aimed at survival. Those instincts give rise to feelings, such as the feeling of fear on seeing a fox. The feeling of fear is itself a generalization that guides the conduct of the rabbit. As Peirce states, "reasoning has no monopoly of the process of generalization – Sentiment also generalizes itself" (R 435s). In being a generalization, the sentiment reduces a manifold of threatening appearances to a principle. This, though, is a principle of action: to flee when one sees a fox. The instincts and feelings they give rise to work in tandem to ensure the survival of the rabbit. Moreover, the instincts and sentiments are subject to natural selection. The rabbit that should fail to fear things that really are fearful – such as a fox – is sure to be gobbled up if it should come across a fox. But note also that the rabbit that is overly fearful is likely to be selected against since every motion in the grasses is liable to send it scampering back into its rabbit hole.

Peirce is not as clear about this in "Philosophy and the Conduct of Life" as we might like. In a later lecture from the same series, he states that he has "not succeeded in persuading my contemporaries to believe that Nature also makes inductions and retroductions ... I point out that Evolution *wherever* it takes place is one vast succession of generalizations" (RLT 161, emphasis added) and then connects this view to his cosmology. We have also seen him claim that the system of sexual rules is a "Sentimental induction" and that sentiment "penetrates through the whole being of the soul" unlike cognitive generalizations. Sentiments are generalizations that are primarily aimed at preserving an organism's or a species' existence. Our sentiments do not *understand* phenomena in the sense of grouping them under concepts, as cognitive generalizations do. Nonetheless, our sentiments help us *comprehend* the world by identifying those things that are fearful, as in the case of the rabbit fearing a fox. These sentiments and their corresponding instincts are selected for in the process of evolution and the "best" sentiments are those that survive. Importantly, sometimes these sentiments will dictate the sacrifice of the organism for the survival of the species. Such sentiments would be based on civicultural instincts. This is Peirce's point in the previous quotation (see RLT 113): Our instincts – and the sentiments that they may give rise to – are not directed at the preservation of the individual organism alone but also at the preservation of the stock. Good mothers, for example, will subordinate their own interests to the interests of their child.

What, though, is Peirce arguing for here? He is not arguing that our instincts and instinct-based sentiments should be used as a guide for life just because they are a consequence of evolutionary processes. That would be to commit the naturalistic fallacy: Just because we *have* evolved to have these sentiments and instincts, it does not follow that we *should* act on them. Moreover, if this were Peirce's argument, Welby's criticism cited at the start of this chapter – "conservative of what? ... Of that which once promoted growth and development and now stunts, backens, withers it" (SS 21)? – would have real bite.[10] It may well be that our instincts and sentiments have evolved, but it would be outrageous to suggest that we should not act in a manner contrary to our evolved instincts and sentiments when acting on them

---

[10] I suspect the force of this criticism is what leads Peirce to shift toward an emphasis on our instincts and instinct-based sentiments rather than our sentiments in general, but my only evidence for this claim is that Peirce makes that shift after this exchange with Welby.

no longer promises one's well-being, let alone the well-being of one's stock. Indeed, this is presumably the great advantage of being a rational creature. Nonrational animals are nearly fated to act on their instincts and sentiments even to their demise. Rational creatures, in contrast, can foresee circumstances when their habits will be disadvantageous and exercise a degree of self-control to avoid them. The great glory of reason is that we do not have to rely on our instincts and sentiments. And though *not* relying on our instincts and sentiments may well bring about the demise of humanity, relying on them when conditions change may well do the same.

Peirce fails to notice this in 1898, as is evident from his lecture. He writes that sentiment might guide us in two conceivable ways in "terrible crises." The first is that, while our instincts are not as "detailed and featured" as those of animals, sentiment can guide us without the aid of reason (RLT 112). The second is that "sentiment might act to bring the vital crises under the domain of reason by rising under such circumstances to such a height of self abnegation as to render the situation insignificant" (RLT 113). In these cases, we treat our own lives as "small matters" (RLT 113) and are willing to sacrifice our lives for the well-being of the whole. But Peirce overlooks the fact that sentiment might yet bring a vital crisis under the domain of reason, and reason might realize that acting on that sentiment would bring about the demise of one's own life or the stock as a whole. This, I take it, is part and parcel of de Waal's criticisms.

Peirce's point about animals and their instincts and sentiments being honed by evolution is not designed to support sentimentalism but to support his claim that our instincts and sentiments are trustworthy – not perfect – guides for conduct. By and large, our instincts and instinct-based sentiments get things right. But not every time. And not forever. Peirce writes of the system of sexual rules that are a consequence of "Sentimental induction" that "it is abstractly and absolutely infallible we do not pretend" (RLT 111). Nevertheless, since evolutionary processes have honed our sentiments and instincts, they are good enough. They are "*practically* infallible" (R 435:33 and RLT 111).

Peirce's Argument for Sentimental Conservatism

From here, it is a short step to Peirce's sentimental conservatism. We have already seen how Peirce establishes conservatism on "rationalistic &

experiential grounds" (SS 19). This, though, left open the question of on what we should rely if not our own theories and reasonings. Peirce's argument is that we ought to rely on our instincts and sentiment-based instincts because these are the most trustworthy things we *individually* have at our disposal.

This, though, comes with a significant challenge. The challenge is that it can be difficult to discern which sentiments are instinctual and which are merely prejudices inculcated from our society. Peirce makes this problem quite clear in a letter from late in his life. I quote the passage at length:

> The reason for accepting the Retroductive conclusion, is that man must trust to his power of getting at the truth simply because it is all he has to guide him; and moreover when we look at the instincts of various animals, we are struck with wonder at how they lead those creatures toward rational behaviour ... Now man has equally powerful instincts though we do not recognize them any more than the wasp does hers, and for the same reason, because in following our instincts we, like her, seem to ourselves to be acting according to manifest good sense. So it is to us, though it would not be so but for our instincts. The reason we go right in the following of our instincts, is the same as the reason that the wasp does so. Namely, it is because these instincts have been formed under the influence of those very laws of nature that they lead us to conform to ... At the same time, there is a danger in following what appear to be our natural instincts too closely; and partly because we cannot distinguish between true instincts and mere prejudices. (NEM 3:203–204, 1911)

This passage reveals that Peirce's appeal to the evolution of instincts and sentiments is designed to explain why the sentimental conservative is less liable to be led astray than one who trusts to reason and theories. Evolutionary processes have honed our sentiments and instincts.

Moreover, Peirce maintains that we have no other good option but to rely on our sentiments and instincts in the conduct of our lives. We have already seen, in the first argument for conservatism discussed earlier, that our philosophical theories are provisional and our talent for reasoning doubtful. Now suppose that we turn instead to those who do have a talent for reasoning for advice on the conduct of life. First, for each individual to do so in everyday matters is clearly impracticable and, moreover, for them to do so in vital matters is impossible since such crises are rare and time is of the essence. Second, should we decide to do so, we are relying on our abductive instinct, on our suspicion that

that person has the correct answer. Yet our abductive instinct suggests that this is highly doubtful. After all, philosophers are themselves deeply divided about which theory is true. Our philosophical researches have not reached their conclusions. So, why think that any given philosopher is a better guide than our instincts and sentiments, which have been honed by evolutionary processes just as those of the philosopher have? Indeed, what we observe in animals speaks in favor of trusting to our instincts insofar as they reliably guide those animals. To be sure and as Peirce indicates (see RLT 113), there are wise people who might be good guides to the conduct of our lives. But these people are not trustworthy guides because they have an elaborated moral theory but because they have had their instincts honed by long experience, by study and reflection. As we shall see in Chapter 6 when we extend Peirce's ideas to *corporate* decision making, we will need to rely on the discernment of the wise person in these cases. The key point here is that Peirce's sentimental conservatism is a piece of advice about how individuals should conduct their lives with respect to everyday matters and "terrible crises."

Nevertheless, we must be cautious about relying on our sentiments and instincts. Some of our sentiments are not based on instincts but are mere prejudices inculcated from our society. It is our instinct-based sentiments that should guide our conduct, not the prejudices borne of our peculiar social circumstances. As such, there will be times when we ought not to act on our sentiments. We will have to discern which sentiments are instinct based and which are mere prejudices.

To continue unpacking this idea, consider Peirce's distinction between everyday conduct and vital crises. He writes,

In the conduct of life, we have to distinguish everyday affairs and great crises. In the great decisions, I do not believe it is safe to trust to individual reason. In everyday business, reasoning is tolerably successful; but I am inclined to think that it is done as well without the aid of a theory as with it. A *Logica Utens*, like the analytic mechanics resident in the billiard player's nerves, best fulfills familiar uses. (RLT 109)

Peirce is here setting up two tasks: first, to argue for adopting the principle of sentimental conservatism with respect the great decisions or crises; second, to argue for adopting the principle of sentimental conservatism with respect to everyday affairs.

We have already seen Peirce's argument for the view that we should be sentimental conservatives with respect to the great decisions or crises of life. As discussed earlier, Peirce argues that these abductive reasonings will themselves ultimately rest on sentimental grounds. I have already argued that this move in his argument is spurious and rather an ironic condemnation of his audience's own conception of reasoning. Moreover – and in this respect I think de Waal's objection hits the nail on the head – sometimes we will have no instinct-based sentiments to guide us with respect to these great crises. In fact, Peirce had made much the same claim in "Analysis of Propositions": A man's "instincts are feeble and dim; and he is perpetually thrown into novel situations in which instinct would not, at best, work to advantage" (R 410:3, c. 1894). What is correct about Peirce's claim, though, is that in vital crises we will have to rely on our abductive instinct, even if it does not ultimately rest on our sentiments.

Yet when we do have sentiments to guide our action in great crises, we will need to decide which sentiments are instinct based and which are mere prejudices. This is especially pertinent when our sentiments conflict. But how are we to discern which sentiments are instinct based and which are mere prejudices? We might choose to consult Peirce's classification of instincts, but this will not do for the conduct of our everyday lives let alone our decision making in great crises. Not everyone has access to Peirce's manuscripts, and we certainly do not have time to consult the contemporary research on instincts.

As an aid to answering this question of how we can distinguish our sentiments and prejudices, let us consider what Peirce has to tell us about the conduct of our lives with respect to everyday affairs. In our everyday affairs, Peirce notes, reason is "tolerably successful." However, we need only a *logica utens*. Peirce distinguishes between *logica utens* and *logica docens*. In 1901, he writes, "every man who reasons ... has necessarily a rudimentary science of logic, good or bad. The slang of the medieval universities called this his *logica utens*, – his 'logic in possession', – in contradistinction to *logica docens*, or the legitimate doctrine that is to be learned by study" (HP 2:891–892). In a basic or "rudimentary" way, we all engage in reasoning in the conduct of our lives, and we do so without reflection on what we are doing while we reason.

Consider, for example, an everyday matter such as going to the grocery store. I go weekly, about 52 times a year. Which store I choose to go to has little significance. Moreover, if I am willing to be hungry, I don't even have to go. But I can still reason about which store to go to. To illustrate, I may want a particular ingredient that is only sold at store

X, but I may also know that its produce is generally not as good as the produce at store Y. I begin to reason about whether I can find a substitute for the ingredient I want at store Y or whether I should risk inferior produce at store X or whether I should go to both stores. I consider that it is summertime and that the produce I desire is in season. Moreover, I realize that my time is limited. So, I opt to go to store X only. Note, though, that reasoning is quite useful in this case. Deductions and inductions based on the time of the year, the limitations on my time, and prior experiences at both stores help render a decision. But I can engage in this sort of reasoning without reflecting on *how* I am reasoning or whether my reasonings are any good. It would be utterly implausible to claim that only those who have studied logic reason about how to conduct their daily lives and only slightly less implausible to claim that only those who have studied logic reason *well* about how to conduct their daily lives. And this is Peirce's point about the "analytic mechanics resident" in the billiard player's nerves. The billiard player does not reflect on what she is doing as she strikes the billiard ball. She is not reflecting on the computations she is subconsciously making as she decides which balls to strike, which pockets to aim for, and which angles will ensure success. But she nevertheless "reasons" – in some very latitudinous sense of that term – about which shot to take and how to take it. And she does this without reflecting on what she is doing as she "reasons" about which shot to take. That is her *logica utens*.

Interestingly, Peirce makes an appeal to billiards at another place in the drafts when he writes,

Science has nothing to do with belief. A scientific conclusion ought not to be believed, but only supposed or provisionally adopted [crossed out: admitted or assumed or provisionally adopted], taken up on the tail of the cart until we find reason to kick it off. [crossed out: But the rank and file of] But the democracy of science do not *see* this. [crossed out: They are not logicians.] They *practice* it about their ordinary conclusions. But not being logicians, knowing no more of the theory of their practice than does the billiardist when it comes to a proposition like the mechanical hypothesis, which lies outside their specialty, they *believe* in it, in the same sense in which they believe that incest is wicked, – and with just about as much idea of the reasons for it. (R 435:24–25)

What I wish to focus on from this quotation is Peirce's claim about the belief that incest is wicked rather than his claim about belief having no place in science.[11] Peirce's somewhat confused analogy is this: The scientist's belief that a conclusion should be adopted only provisionally is like the belief that a billiard player has about mechanical hypotheses, both of which are like the belief that one has that incest is wicked. These are beliefs we have adopted (in some sense) and on which we act. But they are also beliefs that, to the extent we are even aware of them and are aware we are acting on them, are only vaguely formulated and only dimly recognized as principles guiding our conduct. In the case of the scientist, her practice is to adopt conclusions only tentatively, but her beliefs about how she conducts the practice are actually mistaken. She says some theory is an established truth when in practice she has only provisionally adopted it. In the case of the billiard player, her practice is to select and take those shots and angles most likely to ensure success, but she only has a dim grasp of the principles of analytic mechanics, if she has any explicit grasp of them at all. And for those of us who abstain from incest and judge it to be wicked, we likely cannot give an account of why it is wicked or, perhaps, why we have abstained from it. But it is nevertheless a principle guiding our conduct.

Yet how is it that belief in the wickedness of incest informs our conduct? In most cases, it is probably not by reflection on philosophical ethics or some argument to the effect that incest is wicked. Consider, even, the argument that incest is wicked because it heightens the chance that one's children will have birth defects. That argument must be admitted to be a bad argument. At most it only shows that persons who commit incest should use birth control. In most cases, I submit, belief in the wickedness of incest affects our conduct less by the conscious apprehension that incest is wicked and more by the intense feeling of disgust we have in contemplating acts of incest.

Here we get to the quick of how reasoning informs our conduct when it comes to moral questions (and not just which grocery store to shop at). We oftentimes do not have explicitly formulated beliefs about how we should conduct our lives. Nevertheless, the feeling of repugnance at the thought of incest – which, recall, Peirce maintains has a basis in our instincts – combined with our recognition that, for example, *this* person is one's brother, leads one to abstain from engaging in sexual relations with him. To the extent that there is reasoning involved here

---

[11] On this point about belief in science, see Hookway (2000, ch. 1) and Migotti (2005).

at all, it is of the most rudimentary kind, and no doctrine of reasoning or learned theory of logic is required at all. It is very much like the sort of "reasoning" a rabbit engages in when it sees a fox and flees, as well as the sort of "reasoning" about mechanics that a billiard player engages in when selecting shots.

In the conduct of our workaday lives, we do not need a theory of how to balance our instincts, desires, sentiments, and reasonings. Moreover, we certainly do not have the time to learn a theory of scientific reasoning and to apply it while reflecting on the nature of goodness, morality, and the like. We might consult those who have reflected on these topics, but to the extent that philosophy is not in an "infantile condition," we do not always have time to consult philosophers. Moreover, philosophers themselves disagree intensely about many of these matters. So, we will have to get by. And more importantly, we do get by. We do as we need to do, balancing our sentiments, desires, instincts, and reasons. Miracle of miracles – or by the steady pace of natural selection – we manage to make it work pretty well. But our doing of this is itself guided by instinct and sentiment.

On this score, de Waal has suggested distinguishing between our *ethica utens* and our *ethica docens*, the former of which is the ethics of which we are in possession and the latter of which is an elaborated theory of ethics. What I am calling our ability to "get by" by weighing our instincts, sentiments, and reasonings might as well be called our *ethica utens* insofar as it is concerned with actions. Yet insofar as it is concerned with weighing different reasons for action and the various pushes and pulls of our human nature, it is part of our *logica utens*. Recall also that on Peirce's view, our *ethica docens*, as de Waal calls it, ought not to precipitately or suddenly affect the conduct of our lives. That is the heart of his conservatism. Similarly, Peirce does not think our *logica docens* ought to always be employed in our reasoning processes. He writes,

The writer's rule is to consider whether a question is one for exact reasoning and is quite beyond the jurisdiction of good sense; or whether accuracy of thought ought to give way to sound instinct and wholesome feeling; or whether, finally, it ought first to be carefully reasoned out, the reasoning then being submitted to the review of common sense. (R 617:18, c. 1908)

We have a primitive, instinctual power of navigating the complexities of our animal nature. It is on this power to navigate the various pushes and pulls of instinct, sentiment, desire, and reason that we must rely in our day-to-day decision making as well as in vital crises.

This account of the matter is supported by comments in a letter from Peirce to Lady Welby dated May 7, 1904. Peirce writes,

> It is necessary to take into consideration the fact that we never can foresee all of the consequences of a great change, and that some of its consequences are sure to be corrupting ... Reason blunders so very frequently that in practical matters we must rely on instinct & subconscious operations of the mind, as much as possible, in order to succeed. (SS 19)

Furthermore, this account accords with Peirce's comments in R 334. There, he notes that our ability to distinguish among necessary reasonings, probable reasonings, and those reasonings "worth consideration" is instinctive:

> [It is a] true "instinct" in the sense in which we speak of the wonderful instincts of pidgons [sic] wasps, and salmon, – meaning a faculty which guides them right in the main, but which cannot reasonably be explained as consisting or due to reasoning. That is to say, though our reasonings may be supported by other reasonings, yet their ultimate support is not to be so explained, and is therefore to be called an *Instinct*. We know that the Instincts of dogs, canaries, goldfish, etc. are capable of wonderful modification by wisely conducted exercise and training; and consequently the fact that human reasoning is susceptible of improvement (and it is sufficient to read Aristotle's Organon, to say nothing of his Metaphysics and Physics, to be convinced that it is so) is no objection to the opinion that it ultimately rests upon an Instinct analogous to those of the so-called "brutes" and insects. (R 334:A3–A4)

We have an instinctive capacity to reason and to recognize the strength of reasonings. While that instinct can be modified and shaped by a rigorous course of philosophy or logic, the power itself is ultimately an "Instinct of Just Reasoning" that is refined through study.

Finally, this helps us get traction on the question we asked earlier: How is it that we discern which sentiments are the "true" sentiments based on instinct and which sentiments are merely culturally inculcated prejudices? One way in which we can differentiate instinct-based sentiments and mere prejudices is the way Peirce indicated previously: the strength of a sentiment relative to the breadth of circumstances. The strength of our sentiment of disapproval regarding incest in any circumstance whatsoever is a good indicator that it is instinct based, whereas the variability of our sentiments, both in strength and with respect to circumstance, regarding suicide – if, for instance, one must sacrifice one's life to preserve one's society – suggests that our sentiments against suicide are not instinct based.

A second way in which we can discern those sentiments that are instinctual and those that are prejudicial is by reflection on cultural differences. In some cases, we will find that a way of acting is prevalent among the vast majority of cultures. For example, the vast majority of cultures have an incest taboo and prohibitions on cannibalism. This is a good indication that the intense feelings of disgust we have at the thought of incest and cannibalism are instinct-based sentiments and not mere prejudices.[12] In contrast, in "The Fixation of Belief," Peirce uses polygamy as an example of a philosophical issue that cannot be decided using the a priori method. That prohibitions against polygamy are not shared across cultures is a good indicator that the sentiment we have against (or for) it may be a mere prejudice.

Yet at other times, we may not be able to discern whether a sentiment is instinct based or a mere prejudice. In these cases, we simply will have to rely on our abductive instinct, our instinct for guessing in a way that is not "overwhelmingly wrong." Xenophobia is a good example of such a prejudice. On the one hand, a fear of foreign tribes is nearly universal across primitive societies. Also, it is fairly easy to understand why this sentiment might be selected for in a process of evolution. Strangers may well pose threats to the well-being of a tribe. They may be spies from another tribe bent on warfare. They may carry diseases. They may be usurpers or charlatans looking to take advantage of tribe members. On the other hand, it seems as though the dangers that strangers pose to one's society might well be addressed by an exercise of due caution rather than by xenophobic sentiments. Accordingly, we might be led to the conclusion that xenophobia is a mere prejudice or we might be led to the conclusion that though xenophobia has been selected for by an evolutionary process, that is purely accidental and the same evolutionary end might have been achieved by the selection of different sentiments and instincts. This leads us back to de Waal's objections mentioned at the start of this chapter. Let us return to them now.

---

[12] It might be objected that incestuous and cannibalistic practices previously prevailed among primitive tribes, but even if that were true, the fact that they no longer are practiced suggests that the practices have been selected against.

De Waal's Objections

I should be clear from the outset that my aim in what follows is not to settle the questions of practical ethics that de Waal raises. In fact, to claim that I shall would be contrary to the spirit of Peirce's sentimental conservatism. For the whole point of Peirce's theory is that how *I* should act in any given situation will have to be determined by weighing the various pushes and pulls of instinct, sentiment, desire, and reasoning in the given circumstance. Moreover, it should not be decided by some antecedent ethical or political theory. Peirce's senti-mental conservatism is not a piece of political theory or an ethical theory but a piece of advice about how I should conduct *my* life. All that can be done here is to show that Peirce's theory can accommodate the worries that de Waal has about Peirce's sentimental conservatism.

The First Objection

De Waal's first objection, recall, is that we have some sentiments that should be rejected and are rejected on the basis of critical reflection. His example is xenophobia. As we have just seen, there is an open question as to whether or not xenophobia is an instinct-based sentiment. If not, then we may maintain that it is a mere prejudice and so give it little or no weight as a guide to our conduct.

Let us, though, suppose for the sake of argument that xenophobia is an instinct-based sentiment. It might, after all, have a basis in the Govern instinct, insofar as strangers may be a threat to the ordering of one's neighbors. How might Peirce then address de Waal's objection? Peirce's view, as we have already seen, is not that our sentiments are infallible guides to conduct but that they are inductive generalizations that help guide our action well enough to avoid disaster. They are practically infallible in the sense that they are the best we have. Accordingly, it is perfectly open to Peirce to maintain that xenophobia is a sentiment that will lead us wrong and even that such a sentiment may change. But Peirce would also maintain that where xenophobia has come to prevail as a deeply ingrained, instinct-based sentiment, it does generalize suffi-ciently well to guide our conduct. But why should that be so?

Here we must turn to Peirce's evolutionary account. Imagine a primi-tive humanity with no international laws. Rather, life is essentially tribal and nomadic. Over time, these tribes are sure to come into contact with each other and – more importantly for the present story – come into conflict. In these cases, a sentiment such as xenophobia will help ensure the preservation of the tribe by shunning foreigners who might be a threat. As noted, strangers may well pose threats to the well-being of a tribe, and so evolutionary processes may select for xenophobic sentiments.

Consider a specific example, this one from the Bible. Isaiah 39 tells the story of King Hezekiah, who had recovered from an illness. The son of the king of Babylon sent envoys. Hezekiah had a decision to make: to welcome the envoys or refuse them. He chose the former, showing the envoys all of his riches and his armory. This was, of course, a very bad decision. Isaiah truly prophecies (what would have been obvious to anyone who gave it a second thought) that everything the envoys have seen will be carried off to Babylon, a powerful and emerging empire. With respect to this vitally important matter, a little xenophobia might have gone a long way.

Now it might be objected – quite rightly – that other attitudes would have done just as well in this case. Why not a bit of caution rather than a sentiment such as xenophobia? But recall that sentiments are not absolutely infallible. Also, we have no control over which sentiments may be selected for in any given environment. As Peirce states in a letter to James in 1897, "there really is no evolution in the proper sense of the word if individuals can have any arbitrary influence" on what evolves (CWJ 8:245). So, while cautious sentiments may well be preferable in some contexts, the xenophobic sentiment is sufficient to attain the same end and consequently the instincts that give rise to it might be selected for.

Sentiments, I have been noting, are not absolutely infallible. Moreover, we have already seen Peirce claim that we cannot even push the principle of sentimental conservatism to its extreme. A second example shows that sometimes we will have to act in a manner contrary to our sentiments even when they are instinct based (again, we are assuming for the sake of argument that xenophobia is an instinct-based sentiment). Suppose that a wounded soldier whose fellow soldiers have retreated must either suffer an agonizing death or entrust himself to the enemies, risking torture but also, perhaps, saving his own life. Rather than acting on his xenophobic sentiments, he pleads for mercy from the opposing soldiers, his life is saved, and he is not tortured. In this case, he ought not to trust to his sentiments, and it is because of cases like this that I have been stressing that we ought *mainly* (not entirely) to trust to our sentiments.

Peirce may make one final comment here. It is that as a consequence of changing environmental conditions, xenophobia while once selected for may come to be selected against. In an increasingly globalized and interconnected world where one's success comes to depend on working with others outside of one's own small corner of the world, xenophobic sentiments will be a hindrance to procreation and self-preservation. It is here that Lady Welby's point – "conservative of what? ... Of that which once promoted growth and development and now stunts, backens, withers it?" (SS 21) – comes into play. Even if a sentiment is instinct based, changing conditions may well make it such that acting on that instinct-based sentiment will lead to one's demise. We should not assume that evolution has had its final say.

The Second Objection

Let us now turn to de Waal's second point: that there are times when our sentiments conflict, fall short, or are too coarse grained. I think Peirce would readily concede de Waal's worries. Where de Waal errs is in thinking that this is a problem for Peirce's position. Much to the contrary, Peirce thinks that if one of these instances occurs, we cannot – or, at least, cannot simply – rely on sentiment but must rely on our abductive instinct.

Consider, first, an instance when our sentiments conflict. De Waal's example is abortion, where presumably the conflicting sentiments concern the preservation of the rights of the mother to promote her own well-being and the protection of a putative child-to-be. It is easy to understand how both of these sentiments would evolve in the course of human affairs. On the one hand, we have an instinct for self-preservation. On the other hand, the protection of children – and children-to-be – ensures the preservation of a tribe. This is a case when our suicultural and our civicultural instincts come into conflict.

What, then, shall we do when we confront these competing sentiments? The first point to keep in mind with respect to Peirce's sentimental conservatism is that it is not an ethical or political theory. It is a piece of advice on how any individual should conduct her life. When it comes to how any person should act, Peirce would first encourage us to ask whether or not these sentiments have a basis in instinct and to accord more weight to those sentiments that have an instinctual basis. In the case of abortion, it seems quite clear that both instincts are deeply ingrained. If the woman has no reason for giving more weight to one of the competing sentiments rather than another, then she may be compelled to rely on her abductive instinct and conduct her life according to the best guesses she can muster. That is, what she should do will depend on the given circumstance, and it is up to her to make the decision that she deems best and then to hope for the best.

Let us turn to the second case, when our sentiments fall short. Here, de Waal's example is genetic engineering. I am not sure that we have no sentiments with respect to questions of genetic engineering. It seems clear that when genetic engineering may put our own well-being at risk, we have sentiments of aversion to it. Such is the case when we consider programs to engineer especially virulent infectious agents. But there are other cases when our sentiments are divided. Such would seem to be the case with respect to genetically engineering crops. Doing so may improve yield and help relieve hunger. On the other hand, it may also have unforeseen consequences for health and well-being. In such cases, we will have to make decisions as to what to do and, assuming we have no experimental data and it is unfeasible to obtain it, we will have to rely on our abductive instinct. Our best guesses may well be wrong, though of course we will hope they are correct. But, again, it is important to recall that Peirce's sentimental conservatism is not a political or ethical theory. It is a piece of advice about how individuals should conduct their lives; Peirce is not aiming to answer the question of which policies should be set in place.

Finally, we turn de Waal's third case: when our sentiments are too coarse grained. I have already indicated that, even when our sentiments are coarse grained with respect to issues of digital privacy (de Waal's example), they may nevertheless apply as genera to species or by analogy. Digital privacy is a species of privacy more generally, and some of us have strong sentimental aversions to incursions into our privacy in general. There can be little doubt that we may have to work out what sorts of privacy incursions are permissible and which are not. In these cases, we will once again have to appeal to our abductive instinct. Here our instinct can work in tandem with our sentiments. The strong sentiment of disapproval with respect to making known our own sexual predilections is a good indicator that we should not permit incursions into digital privacy that might reveal them. Yet our indifference to whether others know what country we live in is a good indicator that such data need not be protected. That is, we should adjust our privacy settings and make personal information about ourselves available according to our sentimental, instinctive inclinations. Again, sentimental conservatism was not intended to be a theory of how we should corporately set policies but a piece of advice as to how individuals should conduct their lives.

In "Analysis of Propositions," Peirce himself countenances some of these difficulties. He writes,

> But reaching a conclusion, without knowing why you reach it, cannot be called a thoroughly rational proceeding. As instinct fails in novel situations; so such quasi-reasonings cannot be trusted as reasonings, though they may be so much like other conclusions which have turned out well, that there may be that secondary reason for believing them trustworthy. (R 410:4, c. 1894)

When we must rely on our abductive instinct because we are in a novel situation wherein our sentiments fall short, we have at best a tentative, quasi-reason for acting as we plan to act. It will fail often but not always. We cannot trust it as a good reasoning, one that is thoroughly rational. But we must trust it because we have no other good option. In other cases, though, we might recognize our novel situation as related to some other situation, as with respect to issues of digital privacy. Here, we might appeal to analogical cases to provide a secondary reason for trusting our instincts about the novel situation. Again, it will not be thoroughly rational, but it will be the best we can do.

Peirce's sentimental conservatism, as I stated earlier, is a piece of advice about how individuals should conduct their lives rather than an ethical or political theory. This, I believe, sums up what Peirce's advice is:

(1) Our decision regarding how to conduct our individual lives will be about either an everyday matter or a vital crisis.

(2) In the case of everyday matters, our reasoning, sentiments, desires, and instincts get along just fine in helping us decide what to do. We can generally trust them, but not universally. Sometimes we will have to act in a manner contrary to our sentiments and instincts. But whatever the case may be, we are generally able to navigate the various pushes and pulls of reason, sentiment, desire, and instinct without a *logica docens* and without an ethical theory. Our ability to navigate these diverse facets of human nature so as to render decisions is itself instinctual in nature.

(3) In vital crises, our deductive and inductive reasonings will fail us because such instances are rare and momentous. Here, we have only abductions and sentiments to which we may make an appeal.

(4) Our choice in vital crises may be made either (a) on the basis of sentiments alone, (b) on the basis of our abductive guesses alone, or (c) on the basis of sentiments in conjunction with our abductive guesses.

(5) If (4a), those sentiments will be either instinct based or not. If a sentiment is an instinct-based sentiment, "while human instincts are not so detailed and featured as those of dumb animals yet they might be sufficient to guide us in the *greatest* concerns without any aid from reason" (RLT 112). Guidance with respect to incest would be such an example. If our sentiments are not instinct based, then they may be mere prejudices. In that case, we may wish to make an appeal to reason, in accordance with the principle of conservatism and the fact that we should not push it to extremes, in which case see (7). Moreover, the pronouncements of our sentiments may be inconsistent with one another. If so, we may need to appeal to abduction to render a decision, in which case see (7).

(6) If (4b), because our sentiments make no pronouncements, then we must rely on our abductive guesses alone and hope to avoid the most disastrous consequences. If, for instance, we are lost in the woods, we likely have no sentiments regarding which way to go and so we will have to rely on a guess.

(7) If (4c), either (i) all of our sentiments will be consistent with our abductive guesses and with one another, or (ii) some of our sentiments will be inconsistent with our abductive guesses but all of our sentiments will be consistent with one another, or (iii) some of our sentiments will be inconsistent with our abductive guesses and some of our sentiments will be inconsistent with one another. If (i), there is no problem: We should act accordingly. If (ii) or (iii), what we do should depend, in part, on whether any of the sentiments are instinct based. If they are instinct based, we should *generally but not always* act on the basis of the instinct-based sentiment, even if our abductive guesses are inconsistent with them. Hezekiah would have done well to follow this principle, assuming again that xenophobia is instinctual, but the xenophobic soldier exemplifies why such a qualification "generally but not always" is important. This qualification is also supported by the

possibility that changing environmental conditions may select against such sentiments. If our sentiments are not instinct based, then we must rely on our abductive guesses to arbitrate the inconsistency and issue an action.

Conclusion

At first glance, Peirce's sentimental conservatism might look like an ugly thing. But Peirce does have an argument for the theory: Given that the results of our present philosophical inquiries are but provisional from a theoretical point of view, we ought not to trust to our theories and reasonings until those inquiries reach their conclusions in a properly scientific manner. The best, in the sense of most trustworthy, thing we have to rely on are our instincts and our instinct-based sentiments since these have been honed by evolutionary processes.

Moreover, we have now seen that his view is not inconsistent with progressive agendas or radical reforms. Peirce is willing to embrace reform either when it promises greater returns – as in the present value of an annuity – or when failing to embrace reforms promises greater harms. He distinguishes between instincts and instinct-based sentiments, on the one hand, and mere prejudices, on the other. It is the former alone on which we are to rely in the conduct of our lives. He admits, though, that it can sometimes be difficult to discern which is which. Accordingly, we will sometimes need to rely on our abductive instinct to decide whether or which sentiments to act on, especially when it comes to vital crises. Furthermore, as he comes to realize after Lady Welby's biting remark, our instincts sometimes become antiquated, misfitting, incongruous, or unworkable. When they do, we may need to act in a manner contrary to our instincts and sentiment-based instincts.

3 | *Heeding the Call of One's Savior*

The drafts for Peirce's "Philosophy and the Conduct of Life" reveal a concern for religious action, for living the religious life. In one particularly striking passage, Peirce writes,

> If walking in a garden on a dark night you were to hear the voice of your sister, crying to you to rescue her from a villain, would you stop to reason out the metaphysical question of whether it were possible for one mind to cause material waves of sound and for another mind to perceive them? If you did, the problem might probably occupy the remainder of your days. In the same way, if a man has any religious experience and hears the call of his Saviour, for him to halt till he has adjusted a philosophical difficulty, is worse than silly. It is disgusting. On the other hand, if a man has had no religious experience, any religion that is not pretense is as yet impossible for him; and the only honest course is to wait until such experience comes. No amount of speculation can take the place of experience. (R 436:3–4)

Those who have had religious experiences, who have heard the call of their Savior, ought not to deliberate about how it is possible for an immaterial, perfect being – if God be that – to communicate with a material, woefully imperfect human. They are, rather, called to act, to respond to the voice of their Savior and orient their lives and conduct to the Lord's beckoning.

To be certain, the Savior might call different people to different courses of action. Whereas Mother Teresa was called to serve the poorest of the poor, the neediest of the needy, Georg Cantor believed he had been called by his Savior to present the theory of transfinite numbers. In a draft for a later article titled "A Neglected Argument for the Reality of God," Peirce goes so far as to claim "probably every human being that reaches maturity, at some time feels something like an intimation, as from a higher power, calling upon him for a gathering of his powers for some endeavor, whether active or passive" (R 843:[2]6–7[1]).

---

[1] R 843 consists of at least three attempts to compose "A Neglected Argument." Peirce uses a circle with one dot in the center (1), a circle with two dots in the

Peirce had heard the call of his Savior. In 1892, Peirce reports that he had a mystical experience in Saint Thomas Episcopal Church in Manhattan. In a letter draft, he writes,

No sooner had I got into the church than I seemed to receive the direct permission of the Master to come. Still, I said to myself, I must not go to the communion without further reflection! . . . But, when the instant came, I found myself carried up to the altar rail, almost without my own volition . . . I have never before been mystical; but now I am. (R L482)

He continues, "that which seemed to call me today seemed to promise me that I should bear a cross like death for the Master's sake, and he would give me strength to bear it. I am sure that it will happen. My part is to wait" (R L482). It is likely that Peirce thought his cross to bear was to work out a philosophical system on the basis of logic. It is also likely that Peirce realized this meant he would live a life of penury, which in fact he did. He probably did not realize then how destitute he would be; the economic depression of 1893–94 devastated the Peirce's finances. Nonetheless, Peirce did heed the call of his Savior and did not halt till he had "adjusted a philosophical difficulty."

Even if we should heed the call of our Savior when we hear it, we may also wonder whether future evidence might reveal the need to change our tactics. Peirce criticizes William James for defining belief as willingness to act irrevocably because, in entering into business with a man, one proceeds on the basis of trust, but "that won't prevent my collecting further evidence with haste and energy, because it may show me it is time to change my plan" (CWJ 8:244). Similarly, when conforming our wills – or, perhaps better, having our wills conformed – to the call of our Savior, we might nevertheless collect further evidence with haste and energy. In doing so, we may well find the evidence weighs against heeding our putative Savior's call.

Moreover, to continue with the analogy of working with a businessman, there will be times we will not go into business with someone precisely because we already have reasons to doubt that person's honesty. Similarly, if a person already believes that religious experiences are delusional, then if she has one presumably it

center (2), and a circle with one dot in the center and the word "new" (1 New) to keep track of these drafts. The parenthetical numbers before the page number refer to those different drafts.

would be unreasonable for her to act on the basis of her experience. She should instead doubt it and seek out reasons for why she has succumbed to this delusion. In the course of doing so, she may find that she has no good reasons to doubt her religious experience, but it does not follow from that that she should have heeded the call of her Savior in the first place. If we are going to get anywhere in defending Peirce's claim that we should heed the call of our Savior when we hear it, then we will need a better account of under what conditions it is rationally acceptable do so. Peirce's 1908 article "A Neglected Argument for the Reality of God" does precisely that. The article does not argue, as if often supposed, for the reality of God. Rather, it argues for the rational acceptability of a living belief in God. That is, there are conditions under which it is rationally acceptable to conduct our lives in accordance with some putative experience of God.

I should make two brief comments before proceeding. The first is that heeding the call of one's Savior is, for Peirce, a religious matter and not a theological one. As Douglas Anderson has rightly argued (2004 and 1995, 135–138), Peirce objects to theology insofar as it aims to separate the damned from the saved or to uphold the classic creeds of the church. But for Peirce, Anderson states, "religion involves a feeling for the highest ideals of human life," and Peirce has a "reverence for religion born of human instinct" (1995, 136).

Second, Peirce's conception of God is not the traditional conception of the monotheistic religions, an omniscient, omnipotent, omnipresent, omnibenevolent deity. Peirce regards the idea of God to be vague. In 1909, he would write, "we must not predicate any Attribute of God otherwise than vaguely and figuratively, since God, though in a sense essentially intelligible, is nevertheless essentially incomprehensible" (R 641:22). To the extent that he tries to make that idea more determinate, Peirce states that God is love and as love loves the world into greater loveliness (see W 8:184–186, 1892). And in a draft for "A Neglected Argument," he writes that he means by God "not some god, but that God in whom religious people of all creeds believe in proportion as they are truly religious" (R 842:8). In "A Neglected Argument," Peirce merely states that "God" is a proper name signifying the *Ens necessarium* (EP 2:434). But these claims, of course, are quite vague themselves.

Reconsidering C. S. Peirce's "Neglected Argument"

Peirce is not widely known for his work in the philosophy of religion. Yet those more familiar with his writings know that he published a complex and probing essay toward the end of this life titled "A Neglected Argument for the Reality of God." In the estimation of his critics, Peirce's argument for the reality of God fails miserably. Many of Peirce's critics have understood him to be arguing for the truth of the belief that God is real. I do not believe they are blameworthy for understanding the article in this way, but I also think there is a much more charitable reading of Peirce's article wherein the target is not the truth of the belief that God is real but the rational acceptability of belief in God's reality. On my reading, what we find in "A Neglected Argument" – or, perhaps I should say, what we find that is of real philosophical value – are (1) a *description* of a line of thought that leads some people to belief in God's reality and (2) a defense of the claim that that line of thought and other similar lines of thought are rationally acceptable. Drawing out and defending these claims are the tasks of the present chapter.

Could We Be So Confused?

A consequence of my view is that Peirce's essay is woefully mistitled insofar as it suggests he is presenting an argument for the reality of God. A more *a propos* title might be the clunkier "A Defense of the Rational Acceptability of Certain Lines of Thought That Lead to Belief in the Reality of God." But this will no doubt lead to skepticism as to my thesis: Could Peirce really have been confused about what he was arguing for in his essay so as to mistitle it?

My own view is that Peirce was well aware of what he was arguing for in the essay. Unfortunately, he did a lamentably poor job of stating it in the published article. In the drafts, though, he is much clearer about his aim. In R 842, he states that many people are led to belief in God:

Yet this argument has seldom been much insisted upon by theologians for the reason that, persuasive as it is, it has not seemed to them to be logical. This I conceive has been due to a false theory of logic; and consequently the main substance of the present paper must be a brief abstract of a defense of a theory of logic according to which the theological argument in question is as logically sound as it certainly is persuasive. (R 842:10)

He continues to note that he will give two arguments for belief in God's reality, but these arguments are really more like premises. The first – the minor premise – is what Peirce calls the "humble argument." It is a description of a line of thought that leads to belief in God. The major premise is a theory of logic. Peirce then states, "whoever acknowledges its premisses need have no scruple in accepting its conclusion" (R 842:11). Peirce's point, then, is that one need have no scruples about accepting the belief that God is real on the basis of this line of thought and then conducting one's life in accordance with it. He is not proving that God is real but that it is rationally acceptable to believe it.

Similarly, in R 843, Peirce writes that his aim is not to prove that God is real but to prove that a line of thought leading to belief in God's reality is reasonable. He states, "my main concern is to show that that line of reflexion which I call the Neglected Argument is an argument, and a particularly strong one, of the kind with which every positive scientific inquisition must begin" (R 843:[1]6). The last clause about the kind of argument is there to indicate the sort of argument he takes the Neglected Argument to be, viz. an abductive or hypothetical argument. What I wish to stress here is that Peirce's aim is to show that the Neglected Argument is an *argument*; that is, it is not just a line of thought that produces a belief but also a line of thought that *reasonably* produces a belief. I shall have more to say about this distinction later in this chapter.

But is it possible for many – not all – interpreters of Peirce to have mistaken his aim? I think so. First, the article is poorly titled and, as already noted, Peirce himself was not as clear about his aims in the final version of the article as one would wish him to be. In fact, even the editor of the journal in which the article was published could not discern in Peirce's essay an argument for God's reality. He wrote to Peirce asking for a clarification of the article "in order to forestall careless cavillers who might say, 'what, then, precisely, is your neglected argument?'" (quoted at EP 2:551n14). Peirce wrote two "additaments" to the essay, neither of which he wanted published and leaving it to the editor to select one. Of course, the editor's failure to find an argument for God's reality would be readily explained if there is in fact no argument for God's reality in the article but instead an argument for the rational acceptability of a line of thought that leads to belief in God's reality.

Second, it has not been uncommon for thinkers to confuse *de jure* questions about the rationality of religious belief with *de facto* questions concerning the truth of religious belief. Consider, for example, that only in the past few decades has it become commonplace to distinguish logical versions from probabilistic versions of the problem of evil. The former target the truth of religious beliefs (it is impossible for evil to exist and for God to exist), whereas the latter typically target the rationality of religious belief (given the amount of evil that exists, it is unlikely that God exists and so it is unreasonable to believe that God exists).

Third, some commentators on Peirce have characterized his argument as a defense of religious belief. But we must bear in mind that a defense of religious belief is different from a defense of *a* religious belief (e.g., belief in the reality of God). For example, John E. Smith has maintained that Peirce is "providing a model in which both direct experience and argument are related in an intelligible and convincing way" (1983, 491). But this claim that Peirce is providing a model for defending religious belief on the basis of direct experience and argument is far different from the claim that Peirce is defending an argument for some particular religious belief, such as that God is real. As a second example, Kathleen Hull has stated, "the N.A. is not only an *apologia* for religious belief, but serves as a test case for Peirce's non-mechanistic 'theory about the nature of thinking'" (2005, 494). Her thesis is, I believe, correct, and what I want to emphasize is her characterization of the essay as a defense of religious belief and not of the particular belief in the reality of God. And as a third example, Douglas Anderson writes, "[Peirce] does not intend to give a final proof of God's reality but to provide an opening for a belief in God that is reasonable" (1995, 154). I certainly endorse the final clause but would clarify the first by noting that Peirce is not offering a proof for God's reality *final or otherwise*.

If I am correct that Peirce's "A Neglected Argument" is not aimed at presenting an argument for God's reality, then we are also in a position to sidestep a series of objections that have often been used to dismiss Peirce's essay. To do so, we first need to grasp how Peirce's essay is commonly understood. After that, we will review a series of attempts to dismiss his argument.

The Common Understanding

To put these objections in context, we must first grasp how Peirce's essay is commonly understood. I should state at the outset that although I think that this common understanding of Peirce's essay is mistaken, it is entirely excusable. Peirce's comments in conjunction with the title of essay might easily lead one to believe that Peirce is in fact arguing for the reality of God. The blame for the misunderstanding of what Peirce is actually arguing for lies with Peirce himself.

On the common understanding, Peirce is arguing for the reality of God. His argument has three steps. First, he maintains that if one "muses" about the universe around us and our experiences of it, one will inevitably hit on the hypothesis that there is a God. Second, he argues that the more one considers the hypothesis that God is real, the more one will be ravished by the idea of God and begin to conform one's conduct to that idea. That is, the person will come to *believe* that God is real, since beliefs – or *living* beliefs –are just habits of action on Peirce's view. Third, this is true not merely for oneself but for all normal people. That is, this is not just a case when intellectual processes malfunction. Belief in God's reality is a consequence of normal mental activity. And so we have here an abductive – that is, hypothesis-generating – line of thought that leads to belief in God's reality: Let people muse on the universe and they will normally come to the belief that God is real.

Now it is clear that this belief in God's reality is not produced as a consequence of asserting definitely formulated premises. It is not as though one has some explicitly formulated beliefs P and Q and those beliefs entail that God is real. Peirce acknowledges as much. He distinguishes between arguments and argumentations. The latter are processes – or currents or lines – of thought that proceed on the basis of definitely formulated premises. The former are processes of thought that do not proceed on the basis of definitely formulated premises. But it does not follow from the fact that a process of thought does not proceed on the basis of definitely formulated premises that the process of thought is irrational.

Consider, for example, the mental lives of young adults – indeed, the mental lives of all adults. Take the example from the previous chapter: I need to go to the grocery store. One store is far away and another is nearby. The one far away has what I really want, but the one nearby has a suitable substitute. I am also pressed for time. I decide to go to the grocery store nearby. This is a process of thought issuing an action – and a reasonable process of thought to boot – but in typical cases we hardly bother to *definitely* formulate our premises. We just grasp the relevant items of information and choose a course of action. Similarly, the argument just presented – moving from musement to God's reality – does not proceed on definitely formulated premises. It does not thereby follow, however, that it is irrational or rationally unacceptable. To the contrary, Peirce thinks that this line of thought is rationally acceptable, though I will defer an exploration of why that is so for later.

Objections to the Argument as Commonly Understood

Now it may seem that what Peirce has offered us in the three steps presented earlier is an argument for the reality of God. I deny that for reasons I shall state later. But supposing that we are to take those steps as an argument for God's reality, we will see that the line of thought is obviously objectionable. First, it does not seem to produce the effects Peirce suggests it does. Second, Peirce's argument appears to be a case of special pleading. Third, the argument seems rather to be a case of some tender-minded sentimental daydreaming. Fourth, Peirce's own comments are contrary to the "common understanding" of the article.[2]

Christopher Hookway presents the first line of objection. He states, "I have to report that my own attempts to carry out Peirce's thought experiment do not have the effect he describes. It is just not obvious that a period of playful reflection upon one's experience does render the hypothesis of God's reality either plausible or compelling" (2000, 280). That is, Peirce's argument does not have the effect described. Either we do not hit on the hypothesis God is real or even if we do hit on the idea of God we will not find it compelling such that we begin to conform our conduct to it.

Peirce himself admits that some people will not be "ravished" by the idea of God. Thus, Peirce had limited the claim that people will be ravished by the idea to "any normal man" (EP 2:440). In particular, he

---

[2] In a particularly penetrating article on Peirce's "Neglected Argument," J. Caleb Clanton formalizes the arguments Peirce presents for each of his three steps and shows that each of those arguments is fallacious. My focus here is on objections to the common understanding of Peirce's general line of argument rather than to the specific arguments he develops. In fact, I believe Peirce would have resisted Clanton's efforts to formalize the arguments on the grounds that they are rather living processes of thought that do not have premises that can be explicitly formulated. Nonetheless, consistent with my own view, Clanton suggests that Peirce may have a more modest thesis in mind: "perhaps it is more charitable to say that Peirce, more modestly, means something like the following: if someone, after musing, is caused to believe that God is real, then that particular person is warranted in believing that God is real" (2014, 196). Clanton, though, does not develop this claim.

worries that the beauty of the idea of God's reality will not ravish pessimists and that they might constitute a goodly portion of the population. Hence, he denies that pessimists are normal: "It is out of the question to admit that both [optimists and pessimists] are normal, and the great majority of mankind are naturally optimistic. Now, the majority of every race depart but little from the norm of that race" (EP 2:449). Perhaps, then, Hookway is simply a pessimist or otherwise abnormal.

I have had the pleasure of meeting Hookway, and I must say that he strikes me as neither pessimistic nor abnormal. I have also met many other nonpessimistic, normal people who find the idea of God disturbing if not terrifying. This is true even of people who have thought long and hard about God. Moreover, I have met people who are pessimistic and who do find the idea of God ravishing. Peirce's "normal man" seems just to be a well-to-do, intelligent man from North America or Europe at the turn of the nineteenth to the twentieth century, and that man is far from the norm of humankind in general. And so with Hookway I am inclined to deny that any non-pessimistic normal person will be ravished by the idea of the beauty of God. Many people might have been ravished by the idea of God, be they normal or not. But the claim that any – perhaps even the claim that most – normal people would be so ravished can hardly be regarded as substantiated.

Furthermore, even people apparently ravished by the beauty of the idea of God do not always conform their conduct to it. Sometimes this is because of struggles in their own lives, perhaps because of addiction or emotional instability or a difficult upbringing. Whatever the cause may be, even if people find the idea of God enticing, they often struggle to live in accordance with the idea. Moreover, even people who apparently find the idea of God ravishing can be mean, manipulative, and immoral. If one is unfamiliar with examples from one's own life, I offer those of Jimmy Swaggart (a prominent married Christian evangelist who engaged the services of prostitutes), Ted Haggard (another Christian leader who abused drugs and cheated on his wife), and Mark Driscoll (a Christian leader who stepped down from his post after accusations of manipulation and unethical behavior). Perhaps Peirce would say such persons are not, properly speaking, ravished by the idea of God, but such a response is ad hoc.

A second but related worry is that Peirce's argument appears to be a case of special pleading, as M. H. Thompson has argued (1953,

143–154). Just because anyone – maybe even everyone – finds the idea of God ravishing, it does not follow that God is real. We cannot move directly from the claim that we find an idea enticing to the conclusion that it is true. That is, steps one through three may very well show that we will come to believe in God's reality, but it does not follow that God is real. At best, Peirce is only providing an account of how we come to believe that God is real and not an argument for the conclusion that God is real. By analogy, I (and I suspect nearly everyone) am ravished by the idea of having millions of dollars, but that does not mean I (let alone nearly everyone) have millions of dollars.

Peirce seems to have a sense of this problem. At one point, he suggests the manner in which we are ravished by the idea, its force and the way in which we are compelled to conform our conduct to it, is itself a sign of the truth of the hypothesis. He writes, "a certain altogether peculiar confidence in a hypothesis, not to be confounded with rash cocksureness, has a very appreciable value as a sign of the truth of the hypothesis. I regret I cannot give an account of certain interesting, and almost convincing cases. The N.A. excites this peculiar confidence in the highest degree" (EP 2:445).

Not only is this comment vague (what is this "peculiar confidence" that is to be distinguished from "rash cocksureness"?), it is both doubtful and fails as a response to the objection. With respect to being doubtful, on Peirce's own theory of abduction, abductive inferences do not merit the assertion of their conclusions. As Peirce states, abductive inferences "merely suggest that something [the conclusion of the inference] may be" (EP 2:216, 1903). In fact, in "A Neglected Argument" itself, he writes, "Retroduction [i.e., abduction] does not afford security. The hypothesis must be tested" (EP 2:441). Perhaps Peirce would respond that while the argument itself does not afford security, our confidence in the argument is a sign of the hypothesis's truth. Peirce states he has some examples in support of this claim, but he provides none. Moreover, it strikes me as doubtful. Consider, for example, the confidence that Socrates's interlocutors have in their theories and yet their confidence is entirely misplaced. Or consider how frequently we meet people who are convinced of patently false claims – for example, that ghosts exist or that the earth is only 6,000 years old – or of doubtful claims about politics, ethics, or history. Yet their confidence reaches a nearly fevered pitch, to the point that they are willing to sever friendships and belittle others in defense of them.

The confidence of all of these people cannot be a sign of the truth of their beliefs, especially when their beliefs are incompatible. Now Peirce may be correct that in specific domains where genuinely scientific investigators have had their beliefs and intuitions honed by intense study, the confidence they feel in their hypotheses may be a sign of the truth of the hypothesis. But this much qualified claim about genuinely scientific investigators in specific domains is utterly inadequate for Peirce's argument, as his argument depends on what "any normal man" would come to believe. With respect to Peirce's response failing as a defense of the Neglected Argument, the argument does not seem to excite the degree of confidence he suggests it does. Even if confidence in a hypothesis is a sign of its truth, people who believe in God's reality do not seem to have the confidence required to signify the truth of the hypothesis. Most religious people I know have reported having serious doubts and reservations about their beliefs even though they do believe them and even though they conform their conduct to those beliefs. In my (admittedly anecdotal) experience, confidence in one's religious beliefs is the exception rather than the rule.

Dennis Rohaytn succinctly states a third objection to the common understanding of Peirce's Neglected Argument. He writes, "even the best-intentioned reader is likely to see Peirce as performing a salvage operation on those of his private, sentimental, and 19th century beliefs which do not, in all honesty, survive the tests, if not of science then of tough-mindedness" (1982, 68). On the common understanding, Peirce's Neglected Argument does not even come close to being a respectable philosophical argument for God's reality, for respectable philosophical arguments (as Peirce well knew) do proceed on the basis of definitely formulated premises.

The final objection to this common understanding is textual. At least twice in the essay, Peirce states that he is not presenting a line of argument for God's reality. Rather, he is simply describing a line of thought that *might* lead one to belief in God, but there may be other such lines of thought. He writes, "different people have such wonderfully different ways of thinking that it would be far beyond my competence to say what courses Musements might not take" (EP 2:437). In an additament, he writes, "the theologians could not have *presented* the N.A.; because that is a living course of thought of very various forms. But they may and ought to have *described* it" (EP 2:448). In an answer to a questionnaire about his own religious beliefs, Peirce writes that he "meditates" while walking on an unlit path at night and that in the course of reflection during those walks, the idea of God occurs to him. He then states, "if [a person] allows instinct to speak, and searches his own heart, he will at length find that he cannot help believing [God is real]" but that Peirce himself "cannot tell how every man will think" (CP 6.501, c. 1906). Earlier, in 1896, he writes, "as to God, open your eyes – and your heart, which is also a perceptive organ – and you see him" (CP 6.493).

Peirce, then, is not offering an argument for God's reality. What he is doing is describing a line of thought that leads to belief in God's reality. The question with which the article is mainly occupied is whether the line of thought described is reasonable and so is, in fact, an *argument*, "*any* process of thought *reasonably* tending to produce a definite belief" (EP 2:435, emphases added), in this case a definite belief in God's reality.

Furthermore, even when Peirce proposes the article, he denies that the article was a proof of God's reality: "Properly speaking, it is not *itself* a proof, but is a statement of what I believe to be a fact, which fact, if true, shows that a reasonable man by duly weighing certain great truths will inevitably be led to believe in God" (quoted in Anderson 1995, 135). But even this, I think, is not quite an accurate characterization of what we get in "A Neglected Argument." Peirce is not arguing for the claim that a reasonable person will inevitably be led to belief in God by duly weighing truths. He is defending the claim that some lines of thought leading a person to belief in God – a real, living belief, that leads to action – are reasonable.

Finally, Peirce perhaps makes the clearest comment indicating that he had failed to convey the main gist of his argument in a letter to Lady Welby dated December 23, 1908. He writes, "I quite failed to convey my own sense of the value of the Neglected Argument, in that it does not lead to any theology at all, but only to what *I* mean by a purely religious *Faith*, which will have already taken deep root before the subject of it thinks of it at all as a belief" (SS 76). And earlier in the letter he states that by "faith," he means "trust" or "belief in something not as having any knowledge or approach to knowledge about the matter of belief, but . . . belief in it derived from one's belief that a witness who testifies to it would not so testify if it were not so" (SS 74). In short, Peirce's "A Neglected Argument" is only meant to support the claim that we may *trust* our abductively formed instinctive belief that God is real. But that is no more than to claim that it is *rationally acceptable* to adopt the conclusion of this abductive argument for God's reality. Moreover, as an abductive argument, it does not even show that God is probably real. It only suggests the hypothesis.

Sidestepping the Objections

If we understand Peirce's task in the way I am advocating, then we can easily sidestep the objections Hookway, Thompson, and Rohaytn raise. With respect to Hookway's objection that engaging in the sort of musement Peirce suggests does not have the presumed effect of shaping our action, we can concur that it does not always. Yet Peirce's claim is not that the specific line of musement he recommends is effective. In fact, Peirce may even deny that religious beliefs are typically formed by musement in the first place. Rather, they might more commonly result from processes akin to perception. At one point in the drafts, Peirce states that he will "now describe the Neglected Argument, not in the form it might take in the rudest mind, but as an ordinary man of intelligence might form it" (R 843:[1]12). But if the "ordinary man of intelligence" is modeled on Peirce, then probably every theist forms belief in God in a manner akin to how the rudest mind does. At any rate, all Peirce must maintain is that it is fairly common for people to hit on the hypothesis that God is real whether through a process of musement, through a quasi-perceptual experience, or through some other means. The question Peirce is tackling is whether their adopting that belief is rationally acceptable.

Thompson contends that Peirce's argument is really a case of special pleading. Certainly, as we have seen, Peirce suggests that the extreme plausibility of the hypothesis that God is real is a sign of its truth, and that claim is highly doubtful. However, if we read "A Neglected Argument" as a defense of the rational acceptability of belief in God's reality rather than as a defense of its truth, Peirce's argument is not a case of special pleading provided that holding that belief really does meet the conditions for rational acceptability. We shall explore whether it can in what follows.

Third and finally, Rohatyn criticizes Peirce's argument on the grounds that it does little more than reflect Peirce's own quaint nineteenth-century beliefs, beliefs that do not hold up to rigorous scientific scrutiny.

Rohatyn is surely correct that if belief in God's reality does not hold up to rigorous scientific scrutiny, we should abandon that belief just as we would any other. Moreover, he may well be correct that Peirce's own musings about the nature of the universe do not stand up to scientific scrutiny. Yet even so, it does not follow that belief in God's reality on some other basis cannot stand up to scientific scrutiny. Perhaps there is some other line of musement that would, or perhaps God's reality may, in some way, be perceived.

Abduction, Perceptual Judgment, and Rational Acceptability

As already indicated, in "A Neglected Argument" Peirce maintains that we come to believe in God by way of the formation of an abductive argument. In that essay, he describes us coming to the belief in God's reality by way of musement. But we have also seen that in an earlier passage from 1896, Peirce states we may come to the belief by way of a perceptual judgment made by opening our hearts. And in 1898, Peirce suggests that we may hear the call of our Savior. Also, in 1893, he writes, "when a man has that experience with which religion sets out, he has as good reason – putting aside metaphysical subtilities – to believe in the living personality of God as he has to believe in his own. Indeed, *belief* is a word inappropriate to such direct perception" (CP 6.436).

Accordingly, if I am correct that Peirce's "A Neglected Argument" is best read as a defense of the rational acceptability of belief in God, then the question of when it is rationally acceptable to believe in God's reality will be equivalent, on Peirce's view, to the questions of when it is rationally acceptable to adopt the conclusions of abductions and when it is rationally acceptable to believe perceptual judgments. As it turns out and for reasons I shall explain momentarily, Peirce thinks that perceptual judgments are just the conclusions of abductions – or, more precisely, from a logical point of view, the process that results in a perceptual judgment can be represented to have the form of an abductive inference. Thus, our question is really just one: Under what conditions is it rationally acceptable to adopt the conclusion of an abductive inference? To that end, we must first explore why Peirce thinks perceptual judgments may be logically treated as the conclusions of abductive inferences. Second, we will examine under what conditions Peirce thinks it is rationally acceptable to adopt the conclusions of abductive inferences. Peirce develops both of these themes in his works of 1903.

Perceptual Judgment and Abductive Inference

After delivering the seventh of his Harvard *Lectures on Pragmatism* – in which he presents three cotary propositions to "put the edge" on the pragmatic maxim – Peirce added to the manuscript what I shall call his fourth cotary proposition: The process that results in a perceptual judgment, and the steps that constitute that process, if subjected to logical analysis, would be found to have the form of an abductive inference.[3] Here are Peirce's own words:

On its side, the perceptive judgment is the result of a process, although of a process not sufficiently conscious to be controlled, or to state it more truly, not controllable and therefore not fully conscious. If we were to subject this subconscious process to logical analysis we should find that it terminated in what that analysis would represent as an abductive inference, resting on the result of a similar process which a similar logical analysis would represent to be terminated by a similar abductive inference, and so on *ad infinitum*. (EP 2:227)

Consider, for example, the process when I see a red apple and judge "That is red." We may schematize it as follows:

I. (visual sensorimotor coupling with the apple + intervening uncontrolled, unconscious process) → "That is red"

Here, → symbolizes what the visual sensorimotor coupling with the red apple and the intervening unconscious cognitive process yields, viz.

---

[3] What I call Peirce's fourth cotary proposition is importantly different from the preceding three. The three cotary propositions all concern perceptual judgment and intellection (be it conception or inference):

(1) There is nothing in the intellect that was not previously in the senses, and by "in the senses" he specifically means perceptual judgment (EP 2:226–27, 1903).
(2) "Perceptual judgments contain general elements" (EP 2:227).
(3) "Abductive inference shades into perceptual judgment without any sharp line of demarcation between them" (EP 2:227).

The whole weight of the seventh lecture consists in proving (3), for Peirce thinks that if it is proven, then the first two cotary propositions follow. In contrast with the first three, the fourth cotary proposition concerns that unconscious, uncontrollable process whereby perceptual judgments themselves are formed.

a perceptual judgment. Peirce's claim is that *if we treat the intervening uncontrolled process as having an inference form*, then we should find that it has the following form, which is an abductive inference:

(i)   Light stimulates my visual system in such-and-such a way (visual sensorimotor coupling).
(ii) If the apple were red, then it would not be surprising that my visual system were so stimulated.
(iii) Therefore, I have reason to suspect that the apple is red.

Peirce's fourth cotary proposition is quite far-reaching in at least three respects. First, it is not restricted to any particular sense modality. Hence, even this more general schema would have the form of an abductive inference if subjected to logical analysis:

II. (sensorimotor coupling + intervening uncontrolled process) → perceptual judgment

Second, Peirce indicates that if we divide II into parts, we shall find that the termination of each part has the form of an abductive inference. He grants that between sensory inputs and perceptual judgments are percepts: "The perceptual judgment professes to represent the percept" (CP 7.628, 1903). Thus, we should find that both

IIa. (sensorimotor coupling + intervening uncontrolled process)→percept

and

IIb. (percept + intervening uncontrolled process)→perceptual judgment

have the forms of abductive inference. Third, Peirce claims that this would be true if we divided the processes *ad infinitum*. I think these further qualifications are doubtful. What I wish to focus on here is merely that the process stated in IIb should be represented to have the form of an abductive inference rather than the form of a deductive or an inductive inference. To do that, I must first explain what Peirce thinks the form of an abductive inference is and then give an account of why on his view IIb may be represented to have the logical form of an abductive inference.

The Form of Abductive Inference: Importantly, Peirce's claim is that the process involved in IIb has the form of an abductive inference (or, as

Peirce puts it, that logical analysis would "represent" it as an abductive inference). The process is not in fact an abductive inference because on Peirce's view, all inference is self-controlled reasoning (see EP 2:463). However, as he states, IIb is not self-controlled; it is not even controllable.[4]

What is the form of an abductive inference? What is treated as Peirce's canonical statement is given in the same lecture as the fourth cotary proposition:

> The surprising fact, C, is observed;
> But if A were true, C would be a matter of course.
> Hence, there is reason to suspect that A is true.
>   (EP 2:231, 1903)

Yet immediately after making this statement, Peirce suggests that it is unsatisfactory as an account of how we arrive at a hypothesis. He writes, "A cannot be abductively inferred, or if you prefer the expression, cannot be abductively conjectured, until its entire content is already present in the premiss, 'If A were true, C would be a matter of course'" (EP 2:231). That is just to admit that this not an account of how we generate a hypothesis; it is only an account of how we come to suspect it is true. For this reason, Peirce comes to emphasize the instinctive nature of abduction, as explained in the previous chapter.

In their excellent essays on Peirce's theory of abductive inference, both Douglas Niño (2009) and Daniel Campos (2011) have argued that abductive inference is not the same as inference to the best explanation (which is regarded as a kind of induction on the accounts of Peter Lipton and Gilbert Harman), a position also suggested in an earlier essay by Daniel J. McKaughan (2008). Although Niño and Campos do not state it in quite this way, we can get to the heart of the issue by distinguishing between two senses of "inference to the best explanation." The first sense is inference *as a guess at* the best explanation. The second is inference *as a discernment of* the best explanation. Inference as a guess at the best explanation merely proposes a plausible hypothesis to tentatively adopt.

---

[4] This is an important, but little noted, change from Peirce's position in 1868's "Some Consequences of Four Incapacities," where he claims not just that it has the form of an inference but it is an inference (see W 2:214 and 223). There is another question, not broached here, of how abduction can be both inferential and instinctual. For a discussion of the issue and survey of different views, see Paavola (2005).

This is abduction. Inference as a discernment of the best explanation concludes that some hypothesis is probably true because it predicts the phenomena better than any competing hypothesis. This is a species of induction. Campos argues that Lipton's theory involves a conflation of these two sorts of inference, a conflation that "blurs an important distinction between the tentative, exploratory inference that first suggests a plausible explanatory hypothesis and the probabilistic inductive inference that admits or rejects a hypothesis as scientifically tenable" (2011, 440–441).

Following Niño and Campos, three points are particularly helpful for getting a handle on what form abductive inferences take, especially in contrast with inductive inferences: (1) Abductions, like all forms of inference, have some – perhaps not explicitly formulated – premises and a conclusion. The conclusion interprets the premises. (2) Abduction provides us with hypotheses to test, whereas induction tests those hypotheses. For example, I might see a black bird that looks much like a swan, whereas every other swan I have ever seen has been white. If not all swans were white, that surprising fact would be a matter of course. Now I have a reason to suspect that not all swans are white; that is the hypothesis I shall test. To do so, I perform an induction. I predesignate that I shall study swans with respect to their color and then I set about determining whether that black bird was in fact a swan. (3) Abductive inferences do not merit the assertion of – they do not assume responsibility for the truth of (see CP 5.546, c. 1908) – their conclusions (see EP 2:287, 1903). An abduction "merely suggests that something [the conclusion] *may be*" (EP 2:216, 1903). In contrast, induction yields conclusions that are probable and assertible.

Peirce's claim is that when the intervening process of IIb is treated as an "inference," we should find that (1) the perceptual judgment interprets the percept; (2) the perceptual judgment provides us with a hypothesis of the way the world is, a hypothesis that may be tested; but (3) the perceptual judgment does not, in and of itself, assert that the world is in fact the way it is presented in the percept. It only suggests the world is that way. To more fully appreciate this view, we must turn to Peirce's theories of the percept and perceptual judgments.

Percepts and Perceptual Judgments

In 1903's "Telepathy and Perception," Peirce endorses a dual-function theory of perceptual judgments.[5] First, a perceptual judgment interprets a percept. This process of interpreting a percept is what can be represented to have the form of an abductive inference. I call this the *interpreting function* of a perceptual judgment. Second, a perceptual judgment serves as a sign – or a first premise – of reasoning. I call this the *premising function* of a perceptual judgment.

The distinction between percepts and perceptual judgments is common enough even to us now: Percepts have some determinate phenomenal content (e.g., I see *the red apple*), whereas perceptual judgments have propositional content (e.g., I see that *the apple is red*). Peirce nicely characterizes the percept when he writes,

> Let us say that, as I sit here writing, I see on the other side of my table, a yellow chair with a green cushion. That will be what psychologists term a "percept" (*res percepta*). They also frequently call it an "image." With this term I shall pick no quarrel. Only one must be on one's guard against a false impression that it might insinuate. Namely, an "image" usually means something intended to represent, – virtually professing to represent, – something else, real or ideal. So understood, the word "image" would be a misnomer for a percept. The chair I appear to see makes no professions of any kind, essentially embodies no intentions of any kind, does not stand for anything. It obtrudes itself upon my gaze; but not as a deputy for anything else, not "as" anything. It simply knocks at the portal of my soul and stands there in the doorway. (CP 7.619)

Peirce underscores that the manner in which the percept is constructed from our sense impressions is a psychological question and the process by which it is constructed is nonconscious: "A visual percept obtrudes itself upon me in its entirety. I am not therein conscious of any mental process by which the image has been constructed. The psychologists, however, are able to give some account of the matter" (CP 7.624).

Peirce proceeds to discuss perceptual judgments. He proposes the word "percipuum" to identify perceptual judgments when they are serving their interpretive function. "I might be permitted to invent the term *percipuum* to include both percept and perceptual judgment" (CP 7.629), he writes. But include them both how? He clarifies that, "I propose to consider the percept as it is immediately interpreted in the perceptual judgment, under the name of the 'percipuum'" (CP 7.643). That is, the percipuum is the

---

[5] For more on this view, see Atkins (2014).

perceptual judgment understood as an interpretant of the percept. The percipuum is the perceptual judgment when it serves its interpreting function.

Peirce recognizes three ways in which something might interpret something else or be a representation of it. The first way is graphically or iconically. For example, a painting of a war scene is an iconic interpretation of the war. The second way is indexically. The height of the mercury in a thermometer's tube, for instance, is an indexical interpretant of the room temperature. The third way is logically. Peirce claims that the conclusion of an argument is an interpretation of the premises of that argument. Clearly Peirce has a broad notion of interpretation; it is not something that simply goes on inside of the head. But placing that aside, we might wonder in what manner a perceptual judgment is an interpretant of the percept. First, the interpretation is clearly not iconic or graphic. As Peirce states, the perceptual judgment "cannot be a *copy* of it; for ... it does not resemble the percept at all" (CP 7.628, 1903). The word "red" in "the apple is red" does not at all look like the color red. Second, the interpretation is clearly not logical. The percept is not propositional and so nothing can be inferred from it. He writes, "the percept cannot be a premiss, since it is not a proposition; and a statement of the character of the percept would have to rest on the perceptual judgment, instead of this on that. Thus, the perceptual judgment does not represent the percept *logically*" (CP 7.628, 1903).[6] If there are only three manners of interpretation and if the perceptual judgment does not interpret the percept graphically or logically, it follows that the perceptual judgment must represent the percept indexically. This is precisely the conclusion Peirce reaches:

There remains but one way in which it can represent the percept; namely, as an index, or true symptom, just as a weather-cock indicates the direction of the wind or a thermometer the temperature. There is no warrant for saying that the perceptual judgment actually *is* such an index of the percept, other than the *ipse dixit* of the perceptual judgment itself. And even if it be so, what is an index, or true symptom? It is something which, without any rational necessitation, is forced by blind fact to correspond to its object. (CP 7.628, 1903)

We are now in a position to understand why Peirce claims that IIb can be represented to have the form only of an abductive inference. For

[6] This is prefigures Donald Davidson's objection that sensations cannot *justify* propositions (see 1986/2001).

it is clear that the perceptual judgment could not possibly be deduced from the percept, as deduction requires that the conclusion necessarily follow from the premises. However, nothing necessarily follows from an image, which the percept is. The percept cannot logically entail the perceptual judgment. Neither can the perceptual judgment be inductively inferred from the percept. While it is clear that our ability to make correct judgments is learned through a process of language acquisition that might be likened to induction, we also make perceptual judgments about things we have never seen before or about events that surprise us. But in these cases, there is no predesignation of what we shall observe since the event is surprising. Neither is there any sort of sampling if it is the first time we have seen some object. Thus, the relation of the perceptual judgment to the percept cannot be represented inductively. Granted that there are only three sorts of argument forms by which we might logically represent the relation of the perceptual judgment to the percept – viz. deduction, induction, and abduction – it follows that we can only represent the relationship as an abduction. Peirce, then, maintains that perceptual judgments interpret our percepts indexically and that from a logical point of view the relationship may be represented as an abduction.[7]

Yet one issue that arises from this account is that we can have inconsistent perceptual judgments. For example, suppose that in dim lighting I judge that my solid-colored pants are gray, whereas in bright lighting I judge that they are brown. Obviously my solid-colored pants cannot be both brown and gray. Hence, one of my perceptual judgments must be false.

It is here that the premising function of perceptual judgments comes into play. Our involuntarily formed perceptual judgments cannot all be true provided that they are sometimes inconsistent. For creatures like us who care about the truth, who can aim to believe the truth and hope to discover it, this means that we must have some way to adjudicate among our involuntarily formed perceptual judgments. That is, we must inquire into them. As our perceptual judgments are but caused by our percepts *and* as the process of forming our perceptual judgments can at best be represented to have the form of an abductive inference *and* as abductive

---

7   Another possibility Kenneth Boyd once suggested to me is that it might be represented to have the form of an invalid (in the Peircean sense) induction, but then we should be committed to the view that it is unreasonable to believe our perceptual judgments.

inferences only give us a reason to tentatively suppose their conclusions, it follows that at most we can only have a reason to tentatively suppose that any given perceptual judgment is true. Consequently, Peirce thinks that we must avail ourselves of a theory of good reasoning to address occasions when our involuntarily formed perceptual judgments are inconsistent with each other. Providing a comprehensive account of such a theory is clearly beyond the purview of this book, but a brief of sketch of it is in order.

First, our involuntarily formed perceptual judgments are such that they "permit a simple theory of the facts" (EP 2:204, 1903). However, they do not furnish a theory of the facts. Those judgments are but hypotheses, abductions, about how the world in fact is. Second, we adopt, as regulative assumptions of inquiry, logical principles, such as the principle of bivalence and the principle that there is a simple theory of the facts that we can discover. It cannot be true, for example, that something is both entirely gray and entirely not gray. Moreover, we set aside the skeptical option that we cannot discover the truth or that there is no truth of the matter to be discovered. These are, though, merely regulative assumptions. As Peirce says – and as Misak (2011) has made clear – we hope they are true but they may not be. Third, we deduce what would follow from our hypotheses were they true. For example, if my solid-colored pants are gray, then if I hold them next to other gray things, they will appear similar in color. Fourth, we perform experiments, based on the deduction, to confirm or disconfirm the hypothesis. This is induction. For instance, I predesignate that I shall study my pants with respect to being gray. I then set about studying their color. Finally, based on the experiment, we either adopt the hypothesis as probable or approximately true (an induction) or we reject it.

This is, of course, a highly idealized, simplified account. First, the process just described need not be conscious. Second, there may be times when bivalence fails, as with failed presupposition, vagueness, or propositions about the future.[8] Third, deductions and experiments might be quite difficult to draw or design. The hypotheses in question may be complex theoretical matters, such as questions about the basic constituents of the universe. What I have said here about inference and inquiry is obviously a gross oversimplification. But the key point Peirce

---

[8] Peirce explicitly claims that "the Indefinite is not subject to the Principle of Contradiction" (R 641:24⅔) but denies that this means bivalence is false with respect to Indefinites since that would imply that the principle applies to them. See also Lane (1999).

wants to drive home is this: The scientific method if conducted rightly and persisted in indefinitely will eventually hit on the truth and root out error, supposing our hope to discover the truth is not itself misplaced. The application of that method is exceedingly complex and nuanced, in a way that I could not possibly explore here. But Peirce himself was as close to this method as one could be; he was not by profession a philosopher but a scientist. He did not view the scientific method as a straightforward endeavor of hypothesis formation, deduction, and induction. He was familiar, firsthand, with the complexities of inquiry. But he knew through his own work that the method, if persisted in, eventually arrives at the truth and extirpates error.

To sum up, Peirce does not think that perceptions merely cause our beliefs; rather, perceptions supply or contain some of our beliefs in the form of perceptual judgments. Second, those judgments are the "starting-point[s] or first premiss[es] of all critical and controlled thinking" (EP 2:227, 1903). They are "first" in two senses. One, they are the foundations for our reasoning; they are what will *permit* a simple theory of the facts. Two, they are where our reasonings that *furnish* a theory of the facts begin. In these senses, Peirce is a foundationalist – or, better, a quasi-foundationalist – as he regards our theories to rest on our perceptual judgments. Third (and this is why the "quasi-"), those first premises are mere hypotheses. They need to be confirmed in future experiments and experiences. Consequently, what matters for Peirce is not the coherence of our beliefs but the recalcitrance (or lack thereof) of our future experiences.

When Is Adopting the Conclusion of an Abductive Inference Rationally Acceptable?

The previous section aimed to show why, on Peirce's view, the question of when it is rationally acceptable to adopt a perceptual judgment is equivalent to the question of when it is rationally acceptable to adopt the conclusion of an abductive inference. That is because the process that results in a perceptual judgment can be represented to have the form of an abductive inference even if, strictly speaking, it is not an inference because it is not self-controlled and so not subject to logical criticism. This, though, raises our next question: Under what conditions is it rationally acceptable to adopt the conclusion of an abductive inference?

In 1903, Peirce delivered a lecture titled "Pragmatism as the Logic of Abduction." In that essay, he develops a theory of under what conditions it is rationally acceptable to adopt the conclusion of an abductive inference.[9] Of course, rational acceptability as such falls far short of justification. We have already seen that Peirce denies abductive inferences merit the assertion of their conclusions. They only give us a reason to suspect that they are true, to adopt them tentatively as hypotheses that might be overturned by future evidence and that might merit rejection in the face of better hypotheses.

Rational acceptability is a weak epistemic notion, but it is not an insignificant one. Consider perceptual judgments: Not all involuntarily formed perceptual judgments are rationally acceptable to hold. If I have a good reason to believe that my involuntarily formed perceptual judgment is also false, it is not rationally acceptable for me to hold it. For instance, if I make a judgment about the color of my pants while knowingly wearing sunglasses in a dark room, I have a strong countervailing reason to think that my belief is false; so, it would not be rationally acceptable for me to endorse my involuntarily formed perceptual judgment.

Here, then, is one condition that must be met for it to be rationally acceptable to endorse the conclusion of an abductive inference: One must have no significant countervailing reasons to disbelieve the conclusion. But what other conditions must be met? Peirce succinctly states them in a passage from 1903:

> What is good abduction? . . . Of course, it must explain the facts. But what other conditions ought it to fulfill to be good? The question of the goodness of anything is whether that thing fulfills its end. What, then, is the end of an explanatory hypothesis? Its end is, through subjection to the test of experiment, to lead to the avoidance of all surprise and to the establishment of a habit of positive expectation that shall not be disappointed. Any hypothesis, therefore, may be admissible, in the absence of any special reasons to the contrary, provided it be capable of experimental verification, and only in so far as it is capable of such verification. (EP 2:235, 1903)

The clause "in the absence of any special reasons to the contrary" captures the first condition just mentioned.

A second condition is that it must explain the phenomena that lead to the conclusion of the abduction. Recall that abduction is the mode of

---

[9] See also Khachab (2013) on this topic.

argument that generates hypotheses. Accordingly, whatever the conclusion of the abductive reasoning – or what might be represented as having the form of an abductive reasoning – may be, it must explain the phenomena that generate the abductive conclusion.

We will do well here to remember Peirce's previously quoted form of an abductive inference, that some surprising fact is observed, if *A* were true then it would be a matter of course, and so we have a reason to suspect that *A* is true (see EP 2:231). When regarded as an argument form, abduction looks much like affirming the consequent. As already noted, this passage is probably better treated not as stating an argument *form* but as a description of how abductive conclusions come to be affirmed as suspicions we adopt for true: We observe some surprising phenomena and try to come up with a theory or belief that would make the phenomena unsurprising to us. In fact, this is precisely how Peirce introduces it: "The hypothesis cannot be admitted, even as a hypothesis, unless it be supposed that it would account for the facts or some of them" (EP 2:231, 1903). Accordingly, for the generation of the hypothesis to be valid, the hypothesis must actually render the surprising phenomena unsurprising by explaining or accounting for them.

This characterization, however, seems to run afoul of Peirce's claim that the generation of perceptual judgments has the form of an abductive inference. For there hardly seems to be anything surprising about seeing a red apple that a judgment like "the apple is red" explains. Here, two points are important. First, obviously, once we have a working hypothesis, the surprise is explained away and so the phenomena are no longer surprising. Second, on Peirce's view, the judgment that the apple is red is a hypothesis that explains the surprising phenomena of seeing something red. Namely, it is the hypothesis that the apple has some property – red – rather than, say, that the perceiver is suffering an illusion. That is, the judgment states that *being red* is a property of the very apple. In short, the idea of something being red is itself already a working hypothesis to the effect that there are things that have properties, that being red can be a property of such things, and that this apple has that property. Using a different example, Peirce makes this very claim in 1893: "When I say to myself the stove is black, I am making a little theory to account for the looks of it" (R 403:22).

We may put this in the context of Peirce's theory of hypostatic abstraction. Whereas, on Peirce's view, "red" is a general term in that it is predicable of many, he regards "redness" as a hypostatic abstraction.

Clearly, "red" is an abstraction, too, but the addition of "-ness" converts the property of being red to a secondary substance or *hypostasis* capable of investigation. Red is not merely a property but some *thing* to be investigated. Peirce is fond of using Moliere's joke in *La Malade Imaginaire* to illustrate this point. In the joke, a student asks his professor why opium makes people sleepy. The professor responds that opium makes people sleepy because it possesses dormitive virtue. The joke is supposed to be that the professor has not explained anything at all. He has only taken a predicate – *sleepy* – and treated it as a thing – *dormitive virtue*. It is grammatical trickery and not an explanation.

Peirce is in complete agreement that the professor's response is not a scientific explanation. Nonetheless, he thinks that the professor is making an important contribution to scientific research. Namely, the professor is making the claim that there is some *thing* about the opium that produces the sensation of sleepiness, a thing that is capable of investigation. Peirce writes of the fact that opium puts people to sleep, "surely there must be some explanation of this fact . . . it seems to me to be precisely this which is asserted in saying that opium has a dormitive virtue which explains its putting people to sleep. It is not an explanation; but it is a good sound doctrine, namely that *some*thing in opium must explain the facts observed" (PPM 133, 1903). Of course, today we would all recognize that "something" to consist in the fact that the opium molecules are structured in such a way that they can bind to receptors in our brains, the chemical reaction resulting in feelings of sleepiness.

The key point I wish to drive home here is that – to return to the prior example – the judgment "The apple possesses redness" is based on the prior perceptual judgment that "the apple is red." This latter judgment – that the apple is red – regards being red as a property of the apple rather than the observer. The former judgment – that the apple possesses redness – states that there should be something about the apple that we can identify with or correlate to its being red. In this case (assuming a realist theory of color), redness is the surface reflectance property of the apple's skin. The perceptual judgment is the hypothesis that the apple possesses the property of being red. The other judgment is the hypothesis that the property is identifiable with or can be correlated to some objective feature of the object, for example, its surface reflectance property. Both, though, are hypotheses since the perceived red might not be a property of the apple (if we are suffering an illusion) and the apple might have no such property that can be identified with its being red (if, for instance, an error theory about color were true). All of this is to say that involuntarily formed perceptual judgments even of the most basic kind are hypotheses – perhaps it is preferable to call them proto-hypotheses – nonetheless. In fact, Peirce had defended the claim that conception itself – the formation of concepts – is a consequence of hypothetical inference as early as 1868 (see W 2:226). As explained earlier, these hypotheses are not justified beliefs. A percept's causation of a perceptual judgment alone cannot justify beliefs. Rather, for a perceptual judgment to become justified, it must be taken up into a process of inquiry. Consequences from the hypothesis must be deduced and then the hypothesis must be put to the test in induction.

This indicates a third condition that must be met for an abductive inference to be valid: The hypothesis must be such that it can be taken up into a process of inquiry. It has to be "capable of experimental verification" and is admissible only insofar as it is. A hypothesis that has no practical consequences, a hypothesis that could not conceivably be put to the test, is not a hypothesis that it is rationally acceptable to adopt. This is the heart of Peirce's claim that pragmatism is the logic of abduction, where "logic" is the study of the conditions under which an inference is valid. Here is not the place for a lengthy treatment of Peirce's developing theory of pragmatism; Hookway (2012) has recently examined this topic with brilliance. What I shall note here is that Peirce's mature statement of the doctrine is that the intellectual purport of a symbol – in particular, a concept or a proposition – consists in its conceivable practical consequences for conduct. Consequently, for a hypothesis to have any intellectual purport at all, it must "be capable of experimental verification" and is admissible "only in so far as it is capable of such verification. This is approximately the doctrine of pragmatism" (EP 2:235). A hypothesis devoid of consequences that might be put to the test is not a rationally acceptable hypothesis.

There is, I think, one more condition that must be met for an abductive inference to be rationally acceptable to adopt but that Peirce neglected in the long quotation presented earlier, perhaps because he realized it only later. It is that the preferable hypothesis must be the one that instinct suggests. As Peirce states, "it is the simpler hypothesis in the sense of the more facile and natural, the one that instinct suggests, that must be preferred" (EP 2:444, 1908). Peirce conceives of our ability to form abductive guesses as being akin to "a divinatory power, primary or derived, like that of a wasp or a bird" (EP 2:445, 1908) for flying and building nests. As Peirce states, it is instinctive in "its so far surpassing the general powers of our reason and for its directing us as if we were in possession of facts that are entirely beyond the reach of our senses" (EP 2:218, 1903). Importantly, the claim here is not that we cannot try hypotheses that seem unlikely. As explained in Chapter 1, sometimes we must try unlikely hypotheses and doing so was necessary to decipher cuneiform inscriptions. Rather, the claim here is that we should prefer those abductive conclusions that are the suggestions of instinct. Such abductive inferences are more rationally acceptable than those that do not carry the mark of instinct.

Consider, for instance, the example of seeing the mast of an approaching ship before seeing its hull. This is a surprising phenomenon, but what is the more natural explanation? We might suppose that the earth is shaped like a hyperbolic plane. That would certainly explain the phenomenon. But for whatever reason, the hypothesis that the earth is round is more natural, I suppose we would all admit. After all, no one ever suggested that the earth is a hyperbolic plane. *Why* it is more natural to suppose the earth is a solid sphere rather than a hyperbolic plane is another question yet. Peirce does not pretend to answer that question, even stating that instincts are such that "in the present stage of science, [they are] not at once satisfactorily and fully explicable as a result of any more general way of mental action" (EP 2:465, 1913). Yet that we are naturally attracted to some hypotheses over others is hardly deniable. Those hypotheses that are more natural in this sense, Peirce claims, are to be preferred, are the ones that are more rationally acceptable to adopt compared to other hypotheses.

In sum, it is rationally acceptable to adopt a hypothesis if and only if (1) one has no significant countervailing reasons to deny it, (2) it explains some phenomenon, (3) it has experimental consequences such that it can be put to the test, and (4) it is natural in the sense that it is the one instinct suggests. But do abductively or involuntarily formed beliefs about God's reality satisfy these four conditions? I think so and that Peirce's "A Neglected Argument" is best understood as contending that they do. Let us, then, return to Peirce's "A Neglected Argument" with the aim of ferreting out his defense of the rational acceptability of endorsing the hypothesis that God is real.

Peirce's "A Neglected Argument"

In the preceding section, I developed Peirce's accounts of under what conditions it is rationally acceptable to adopt the conclusion of an abductive inference and of why Peirce believes that perceptual judgments are, from a logical point of view, equivalent to the conclusions of abductive inferences. In this section, I turn to an examination of "A Neglected Argument." We shall see that Peirce's line of argumentation in "A Neglected Argument" directly parallels his account of the rational acceptability of adopting the conclusions of abductive inferences.

Ground Clearing

Before we can make good progress in understanding Peirce's "A Neglected Argument," we need to clear some ground. As already indicated, the article is an enigmatic and multilayered text, and part of its enigmatic nature stems from Peirce's idiosyncratic word choice and peculiar (which is not to say mistaken) philosophical commitments. We also need to make some important distinctions that will help guide our examination of "A Neglected Argument."

Abbreviations

I begin with some abbreviations. In the first additament, Peirce states that "A Neglected Argument" consists of a "nest" of three arguments. I shall follow Anderson (1990) in referring to the first as the HA (the Humble Argument), the second as the NA (the Neglected Argument proper), and the third as the SA (the Scientific Argument). When referring to the whole nest of arguments, I shall use NAN (the Neglected Argument Nest). Very little should be staked on these names (especially in calling them *arguments* – as noted earlier, Peirce also calls them *premises* in a draft); they are mainly to fix reference.

Argument and Argumentation

In "A Neglected Argument," the first and most important point to clear up is Peirce's use of the words "argument" and "argumentation." Peirce is quite explicit that these should not be conflated and makes the distinction between them as follows: "An 'Argument' is any process of thought reasonably tending to produce a definite belief. An 'Argumentation' is an Argument proceeding upon definitely formulated premises" (EP 2:435,

1908). The first problem with this statement is that Peirce's word choice is, to put it mildly, infelicitous. Almost everyone uses the word "argument" in a philosophical context to indicate a line of thought that proceeds on definitely formulated premises, that is, for what Peirce calls an argumentation. Worse, I am unconvinced that Peirce even respects this distinction throughout "A Neglected Argument" and its two additaments. In fact, if my interpretation of "A Neglected Argument" is correct, then it turns out that the article itself is an argumentation of this form: (1) Abduction is a valid inference form under the conditions noted earlier. (2) Certain lines of thought that lead to belief in God's reality are abductive inferences that satisfy those conditions. So, (3) belief in God's reality is rationally acceptable.

Peirce is much better at capturing the distinction in "Answers to Questions Concerning My Belief in God." I quote a passage at length:

They [the scientific men of Peirce's age] generally make the matter worse by erroneous, not to say absurd, notions of the function of reasoning. Every race of animals is provided with instincts well adapted to its needs, and especially to strengthening the stock. It is wonderful how unerring these instincts are. Man is no exception in this respect; but man is so continually getting himself into novel situations that he needs, and is supplied with, a subsidiary faculty of *reasoning* for bringing instinct to bear upon situations to which it does not directly apply. This faculty is a very imperfect one in respect to fallibility; but then it is only needed to bridge short gaps. Every step has to be reviewed and criticized; and indeed this is so essential that it is best to call an uncriticized step of inference by another name. (CP 6.497, c. 1906)

In his later work, Peirce recognizes the need to distinguish between processes that can be represented as having an inferential structure even though they are not inferences and inference in the robust and proper sense. The key difference is that the former are uncontrollable whereas the latter are controllable, and for Peirce that means that the former cannot be criticized whereas the latter can be.

Peirce came to realize that this distinction between inference properly so called and mental action that can be represented to have an inferential structure or form is needed not only with respect to perception (as we saw previously) but with respect to thinking itself. We humans are often carried along on currents of thought. Reverie is a good example of being so carried away, and it frequently happens in conversation. We become aware that we have been carried along on such currents of thought when we begin to reflect on how we have arrived at some point in the current of thought. For example, I begin by thinking about what I had for lunch yesterday and end by thinking that I have a credit card bill to pay. But how did I get from the first to the last? I recall that I had lunch with my friend John yesterday, that several years ago I went with him to purchase his engagement ring, that he took out a line of credit to pay for the ring, that I have lines of credit, and that I have a bill due. Here I am carried along on a current of thought. It would be an abuse of the word to say that I *inferred* from what I had for lunch yesterday that I have a credit card bill to pay. It would equally be an abuse of language to claim that I had made an *argument* from the former to the latter. That is because not all currents of thought are reasonable or even have a pretense of reasonableness.

Yet now suppose that my current of thought is slightly different. As before, I begin by thinking about what I had for lunch yesterday and end by thinking I have a credit card bill to pay. But here my current of thought is as follows: I had lunch yesterday; I put the meal on my credit card; therefore, I have a credit card bill to pay. Here, the current of thought is perfectly reasonable, for the final thought follows from the first two thoughts. Note, though, that I can be carried along on this line of thought without consciously performing an inference. One thought leads to the next, and there is certainly a rational connection between the thoughts. However, the steps are not reviewed. They are not criticized. It is only in retrospect that I *realize* I have made an argument at all.

We must, then, distinguish among four senses in which we may "think." In the first sense, we are carried along on a non-reasonable (not unreasonable) current of thought. This is what happens when I begin by thinking about my lunch yesterday and then am led to think about my friend John, his engagement ring purchase, and then my own credit history. In a second sense, we are carried along on an unreasonable current of thought without much reflection on that current of thought. This might happen if, for example, I begin by thinking about lunch yesterday and that I put the bill on my credit card and then directly conclude that I do not have a balance on my credit card. In the third sense, we are carried along on a reasonable current of thought, but we are carried along on that current of thought with little or no reflection, perhaps without even realizing we are being carried along on a current of thought and much less that it is reasonable. This is what Peirce, in "A Neglected Argument," calls an argument – "any process of thought *reasonably* tending to produce a definite belief" – and what he calls in the quotation an "uncriticized step of inference." For a current of thought to be an argument in this sense, it must (1) produce a definite belief, (2) tend to do so, and (3) do so reasonably. In the fourth and final sense, we perform an inference (we are not simply carried along on a current of thought), drawing a conclusion from explicitly formulated premises. This is what Peirce calls an argumentation. This is inference properly so called, and of course such an inference may be valid or invalid, strong or weak.

Reality and Existence: A comment on Peirce's use of the word "reality" is in order. Peirce distinguishes between existence and reality on the grounds that existent things "react with the other like things in the environment" and that consequently to claim that God exists "would be fetichism" (CP 6.495, c. 1906). The real, in contrast, is "that which holds its characters on such a tenure that it makes not the slightest difference what any man or men may have thought them to be, or ever will have thought them to be, here using thought to include imagining, opining, and willing" (CP 6.495, c. 1906). In 1906, Peirce concedes that this distinction might be regarded as "overscrupulosity." Yet he does state in 1909 that "the proposition that God Exists, since this, being a contradiction *in terminis*, will not receive five minutes' consideration from any clear-headed person" (R 641:20). In my judgment, though, nothing in the "A Neglected Argument" especially hinges on Peirce's technical distinction between reality and existence.

The Three Universes: At various places in "A Neglected Argument," Peirce also makes references to three universes of experience. The conception of three universes is tied up with Peirce's categories of Firstness, Secondness, and Thirdness. Roughly, Firstness includes the Universe of feeling, Secondness includes the Universe of brute reaction, and Thirdness includes the Universe of thought. Again, nothing in Peirce's "A Neglected Argument" hinges on his peculiar metaphysical or categorial scheme. This categorial scheme mainly appears in the context of his discussion of a line of musement that leads to a belief in God. Yet I have already indicated in my previous comments that the hypothesis of God's reality need not be hit on by musing (whether or not on the three universes); we may arrive at it in a manner more akin to how we form perceptual judgments.

The Neglected Argument Nest (NAN)

Peirce's "A Neglected Argument" is widely regarded to consist of three separate but nested arguments, all of which together form the NAN. On the one hand, this interpretation is fair to Peirce's own comments, since he writes at the start of the first additament, "a nest of three arguments of the Reality of God has now been sketched" (EP 2:446, 1908). On the other hand, there is no mention of the three arguments in the main article. Although there are undoubtedly three steps in the main article, it is clearly a later *accoutrement* to Peirce's original work to regard each of these steps as a separate but nested argument. Moreover, as already noted at the start of this chapter, in a draft Peirce referred to his argument as consisting of two premises that he also referred to as arguments. Furthermore, in the main article, Peirce is quite clear that the third argument – the SA – is not part of the argument for the reality of God but a defense of the logicality of the argument: "There is my more poor sketch of the N.A., greatly cut down to bring it within the limits assigned to this article. Next should come the discussion of its logicality" (EP 2:440). Perhaps for this reason some scholars have preferred to call each of the arguments *stages*. I shall follow Peirce in calling each of these stages *arguments*, though I do not think they are all arguments and certainly do not think any of them is an argumentation for the reality of God.

Each of the three arguments is intended to show that the line of thought that leads to a belief in God satisfies one of the conditions for that line of thought to be reasonable and to be an argument. The HA shows that the belief God is real explains some phenomena. It also shows that it can produce a definite belief. The NA shows that the belief that God is real is instinctual; so if the line of thought is adopted, it *tends* to produce a definite belief. The SA shows that the belief God is real has deducible conceivable practical consequences. Following that, I shall also argue that Peirce believes there are no significant, strong countervailing reasons to disbelieve in God's reality. Taken all together, these show that the line of thought is rationally acceptable to adopt.

The Humble Argument (HA): The HA is the innermost nest of the NAN. Peirce begins the HA by recommending "a certain agreeable occupation of mind" that he calls musement or pure play (EP 2:436,

1908). He characterizes it as a "lively exercise of one's powers. Pure Play has no rules, except this very law of liberty" (EP 2:436). It should not be limited in the employment of any sorts of reasoning: "there is no kind of reasoning that I should wish to discourage in Musement" (EP 2:437).

Peirce then inserts an important claim, one we noted earlier: "Different people have such wonderfully different ways of thinking that it would be far beyond my competence to say what courses Musements might not take" (EP 2:437). Peirce is acknowledging that musement may lead one in many directions by many means. He is not claiming that the course of musement he describes in the article is the one that you, me, or anyone else exactly (or even inexactly) will follow. In a draft, he states that the argument "is not capable of statement in propositions, but arises directly from unformulated observations" (R 843:[1]2, c. 1908). Peirce's claim is that whatever path one takes, "the idea of God's Reality will be sure sooner or later to be found an attractive fancy, which the Muser will develop in various ways" (EP 2:439, 1908). However it be developed, though, Peirce claims that "the more [a man] ponders it, the more it will find response in every part of his mind, for its beauty, for its supplying an ideal of life, and for its thoroughly satisfactory explanation of his whole threefold environment [i.e., the entire universe]" (EP 2:439).

Peirce does describe one current of thought that leads to the idea of God's reality: "From speculations on the homogeneities of each Universe, the Muser will naturally pass to the consideration of homogeneities and connections between two different Universes, or all three" (EP 2:439). Divorced from his theory of the three universes, the idea here is simply that we will find it remarkable how the different facets of the cosmos – namely, mind and world – fit together in such a way that we can know the world.[10] But what I want to stress is his qualification that comes quick on the heels of this current of thought: "This is a specimen of certain lines of reflection which will inevitably suggest the hypothesis of God's reality" (EP 2:439). Peirce is not claiming that this just *is* the HA for God's reality. Rather, it *describes* one way in which one might come to the idea of God's reality. It is a *specimen* of the argument – even more

---

[10] This is the course of musement Peirce presents in the three paragraphs beginning on the bottom of EP 2:437 and continuing onto EP 2:438. We reflect on psychological phenomena, which leads us to metaphysical problems, and then we set about examining the truth of our interpretations.

precisely, it is a *description* of a specimen of the argument – and not the argument itself. As noted, in one additament, Peirce is explicit that the HA cannot be articulated in definitely formulated premises. After commenting that the theologians had not given the HA its due, Peirce writes, "the theologians could not have *presented* [the HA];[11] because that is a living course of thought of very various forms. But they might and ought to have *described* it, and should have defended it, too" (EP 2:448, 1908). In short, the HA as Peirce presents it is not really an argument. It is a description of an argument, a description of a current of thought that might lead one to the idea that God is real.

Moreover, in various passages Peirce suggests that this idea that God is real may be had not just as a consequence of musement but also by way of a quasi-perceptual experience. We have already seen this in various places: Peirce's report of his own mystical experience in 1892; his statement in 1893 that we can have religious experiences; his comment in 1896 that "as to God, open your eyes – and your heart, which is also a perceptive organ – and you see him" (CP 6.493); and his suggestion in 1898 that we might hear the call of our Savior. We have also seen that we can logically treat perceptual judgments based on these experiences as the conclusions of abductive inferences.

I have been arguing that the HA is not an argument but a description of an argument. But there is another reason we should hesitate to regard the HA as an argument. Recall that Peirce thinks that for the HA to be an argument, it must produce a definite belief, tend to do so, and do so reasonably. Does the current of thought described in the HA satisfy all three of these conditions? With respect to the production of a definite belief, according to Peirce living beliefs are habits of action. He states, "Religion is a life, and can be identified with a belief only provided that belief be a living belief – a thing to be lived rather than said or thought" (CP 6.439, 1893). Yet it is quite clear that one can

---

[11] Peirce actually refers to the NA here, but it is clear from the context that he means the HA, which is canvassed in the preceding paragraph. In point of fact, in these two paragraphs he does not clearly distinguish between the NA and HA. He writes, "It is that course of meditation upon the three Universes ... that I have throughout this article called the N.A.," but the "N.A." here clearly refers to the HA, and Peirce states as much: "This is the 'humble' argument" (EP 2:448, 1908). This is a cause of confusion throughout the essay, since he also fails to clearly distinguish between the NAN and NA: "Though this [the NA] is properly the neglected argument, yet I have sometimes used the abbreviation 'the N.A.' for the whole nest of three" (EP 2:446).

have an "attractive fancy" without it altering one whit how one acts or lives. Consider, for example, those who find utopian visions that involve ending world hunger and peace prevailing on earth an attractive fancy but do nothing to bring that attractive fancy about. Now on Peirce's view such persons lack definite beliefs with respect to their utopian visions since those visions do not cultivate habits of action. Yet it would surely be odd to deny that they find these utopian visions attractive fancies that are beautiful and supply an ideal for life.

Peirce apparently thinks that the process of thought described in the HA is different from such instances of Spanish castle building. He writes,

From what I know of the effects of Musement on myself and others, . . . any normal man . . . will come to be stirred to the depths of his nature by the beauty of the idea and by its august practicality . . . desiring above all things to shape the whole conduct of life and all the springs of action into conformity with that hypothesis . . . [which is] neither more nor less than the state of mind called Believing that proposition. (EP 2:440, 1908)

Peirce's reference to "any normal man" will play a role in in the next section; here, I want to note that not all people will be moved to alter their lives by the current of thought described in the HA. Nonetheless, for the most part, those who are so moved will find themselves transformed by the "beauty and august practicality" of the idea. Obviously, Peirce's assertion is an empirical claim that may well turn out to be false. Certainly, his evidence for it is anecdotal. Moreover, even if it should be true, it would not follow that God is real. It would only follow that the *hypothesis* God is real is such that it compels our belief.

So, even if the process described in the HA can produce a living belief in God's reality, the fact that it does so does not support the claim that God is real or even that it is rationally acceptable to believe it. In an additament, he tries to obviate the problem that the argument does not show that God is real by claiming that there is no good argument for the claim that such beliefs should compel our assent if they are false and so the stronger hypothesis is that they are true: "Metaphysics, however, cannot adapt the human race to maintaining itself, and therefore the presumption [is] that man has no such genius for discoveries about God, Freedom, and Immortality, as he has for physical and psychical science" (CP 6.491, 1908). But it is fairly obvious that such beliefs can help adapt the species by establishing an all-seeing enforcer of social rules, by compelling people to place their interests after those of the state or the Godhead (whose vicar has often been thought to be the chief statesman), and by providing an ideal that can unify and rally a people to accomplish great things (as Peirce himself states in his discussion of the method of authority in "The Fixation of Belief" – see W 3:251, 1878). So, this strategy falls short of securing the conclusion that God is real.

As indicated in response to the objection that Peirce's argument is a case of special pleading, the worry under consideration is no problem if we read "A Neglected Argument" as I am proposing. If Peirce is defending the rational acceptability of belief in God's reality rather than the truth of the proposition that God is real, then the fact the abductive inference does not establish the truth of its conclusion is no objection to the rational acceptability of that current of thought. And that current of thought will be reasonable so long as it satisfies the four conditions for an abductive inference being reasonable. However, if we read it the other way – viz. as a defense of the claim that God is real – we should probably throw in the towel right here. The abductive inference fails miserably to do that.

Now, with respect to the production of belief in God's reality being rationally acceptable, it is quite clear that the HA considered by itself might be no more than a bit of sham reasoning flavored with a *soupçon* of wishful thinking. In the iteration that Peirce describes, how is the hypothesis that God is real – which Peirce suggests is a "satisfactory explanation of his whole threefold environment" (EP 2:439, 1908) – any better than resolving the problem of interaction on versions of substance dualism by saying that God makes it so? In "Some Consequences of Four Incapacities," Peirce had maintained that there are some things "Cartesianism not only does not explain, but renders absolutely inexplicable, unless to say that 'God makes them so' is to be regarded as an explanation" (W 2:212, 1868). It is unclear – at least from the HA alone – how appealing to God in the context of "A Neglected Argument" does any better. Put another way, why isn't Peirce himself being a "colporting brocard [i.e., a peddler of legalistic religious tracts] ... bar[ring] off one or another roadway of inquiry" (EP 2:436, 1908)? It is the NA and SA, to which we shall turn momentarily, that address these concerns.

For the moment, let us note that HA does show that the hypothesis that God is real does explain some phenomena. In the case of Peirce's musements, it explains the "three-fold environment" of experience. In the case of involuntarily formed perceptual judgments generated by a religious experience, belief in God's reality is a hypothesis like any other perceptual judgment, for example, that the apple is red. It is a hypothesis that there really is a God that explains why we have had the religious experience at all.

To sum up, the HA does not present an argument for God's reality. What it does is describe one of many currents of thoughts that might lead to the hypothesis that God is real. It shows that the hypothesis does explain some phenomenon, whether that phenomenon is the connection of mind and matter in such a way that we can know the universe or the mere fact that one hears the call of one's Savior. However, even so, that current of thought must both tend to produce a definite belief and do so reasonably if it is to be an argument. We have seen that Peirce does think it can produce a definite belief in some cases. But does it tend to? And is the current of thought reasonable? To answer those questions, we must turn to the NA and the SA.

The Neglected Argument (NA): The NA is the second in the nest of Peirce's NAN. In the first additament, Peirce describes it as "showing that the humble argument is the natural fruit of free meditation, since every heart will be ravished by the beauty and adorability of the Idea, when it is so pursued" (EP 2:446, 1908). But this description of the argument is wanting in at least two ways. First, as already noted, the way of musement – which is what Peirce means by "free meditation" – is just one of the ways that one might be led to the hypothesis that God is real. Second, not every heart is so ravished by the idea. As noted earlier, Peirce had limited the claim to any normal person and denied pessimists are normal, apparently worried that they will not be ravished by the beauty of the idea of God's reality and that they might constitute a goodly portion of the population. Moreover, we might wonder why it matters to the reasonableness of the current of thought that "normal men" are ravished by the idea of God's reality. Perhaps normal men are simply unreasonable. What, then, does the NA contribute to Peirce's argument? I submit that the NA is meant to support the condition that a rationally acceptable abductive reasoning be instinctual.

As we saw in our fuller discussion of instinct from the previous chapter, in 1913 Peirce characterizes an instinct as "a way of voluntary acting *prevalent almost universally among otherwise normal individuals* of at least one sex or other unmistakable *natural* part of a race" (EP 2:464, emphases added). I have here emphasized the parts pertaining to normalcy and naturalness to underscore the point that an instinctual current of thought – and on Peirce's view thinking is a species of action – is one that would be found to be prevalent among most normal people. The NA shows that belief in God is instinctual because most people do arrive at the hypothesis that God is real, even if they do not end up endorsing that hypothesis. It is instinctual to hypothesize that God is real.

Peirce also believes that instinctual beliefs should be given great weight. We have already seen that Peirce endorses this view with respect to the conduct of life and his theory of sentimental conservatism. He also endorses it with respect to belief in God. In a draft for "A Neglected Argument," he writes,

Animals of all species rise far above the general level of their intelligence in regard to those performances which are their proper function, such as flying and nest-building is for ordinary birds; and what is man's proper function if it be not to embody general Ideas in art-creation, utilities, and, above all, cognition? To give the lie to his own consciousness of divining the reasons of phenomena would be as silly in a man, as it would be in a fledgling bird to refuse to trust to its wings and leave the nest, because it had read Babinet and judges aerostation to be impossible on hydrodynamical grounds. (R 843:[1 New] 61–62 and see EP 2:443)

We instinctually arrive at the hypothesis God is real, and it would be silly to refuse to trust that instinct just because of some philosophical difficulties that need adjustment.

Now it might be objected that belief in God's reality is merely a culturally inherited belief and so not instinctual. To be sure, it is culturally inherited, but that does not preclude it from being instinctual as well. We have culturally inherited beliefs regarding incest. What counts as incest varies among cultures. But the incest taboo is instinctual as well. In like manner, beliefs about God vary from culture to culture. However, it can hardly be denied that the vast majority of humans throughout history have believed in God's reality. What explains the fact that diverse, unrelated cultures have arrived at belief in the reality of some god even if their conceptions of those gods vary? Peirce would maintain that it is to be explained because the hypothesis that God is real is instinctual. This is supported by Peirce's statement in the second additament that the NA makes "use of the principle that

that which convinces a normal man must be presumed to be sound reasoning" (EP 2:449, 1908). "Sound" here is being used with greater latitude than we use it today, and in this context refers to the rational acceptability of abductive reasoning. An abductive reasoning that prevails among a goodly number of normal people – whether or not they end up endorsing the conclusions of that abduction – is instinctual and so may be presumed to be sound. Note, though, that this only gives us a *presumption* of the argument's rational acceptability.

It might further be objected that belief in God is on the wane, and this might be thought to indicate it is not instinctual. Certainly this is true in European and North American countries. But the conclusion that the belief is not instinctual does not follow from declining adherents to religion. Instincts are selected for, and the instinct of belief in God might now be selected against in our current environment. This, though, does not entail the belief is not instinctual; Peirce admits that instincts can undergo "strange fluctuations" (R 334:F3, c. 1909). Moreover, Peirce seems to have confused the claim that the abduction will lead to definite beliefs in some people with the claim that it must lead to definite beliefs in most normal people for it to be instinctual. To be valid, an abduction only needs to be instinctually *made*. It is not required that the people who instinctually are led to hypothesize that God is real in fact come to believe it and conform the conduct of their lives to it. For those who do come to believe it, the line of thought leading to God's reality will be an argument because it produces a definite belief. Moreover, if those who do adopt the line of thought generally tend to conform their conduct to it, the line of thought will tend to produce a definite belief. Nonetheless, for others, it may remain a mere musement.

To sum up, the point of the NA is to show that the current of thought leading to belief in God's reality is instinctual. That the current of thought be instinctual is essential, for if that current of thought is abductive, then for it to be a rationally acceptable abduction the belief must be the one instinct suggests, the more facile or simpler hypothesis, as Peirce puts it. If those who adopt the conclusion of the inference tend to conform their conduct to it, then the line of thought will satisfy one of the conditions for it to be an argument: tending to produce a definite belief.

The Scientific Argument (SA): The final nest of Peirce's NAN is what Anderson calls the "scientific argument." Peirce himself does not give a name to this stage of the NAN. It is the stage of the argument that fills most of the pages of "A Neglected Argument" as well as the additaments. A large portion of these pages are focused on distinguishing abduction from deduction and induction (section III, EP 2:440–442) and determining when each of the three modes of argument may be "valid," that is, reasonable or logically acceptable (section IV, EP 2: 442–445). Since I have already surveyed the key ideas, there is no need to repeat them here.

The heart of the SA lies in "apply[ing] these principles to the evaluation of the N.A." (EP 2:445, 1908), especially showing that the belief that God is real can be taken up in a process of inquiry. This task occupies but one page, the last, of Peirce's main article, and what he has to say is short and schematic. I quote it at length:

The [scientific] man ... will see that the hypothesis, irresistible though it be to first intention, yet needs Probation [i.e., inductive testing]; and that though an infinite being is not tied down to any consistency [Peirce's worry here is that the hypothesis may not have any deducible conceivable practical consequences], yet man, like any other animal, is gifted with power of understanding sufficient for the conduct of life. This brings him, for testing the hypothesis, to taking his stand upon Pragmaticism [Peirce's distinct version of pragmatism], which implies faith in common-sense and in instinct, though only as they issue from the cupel-furnace [a furnace used to separate the noble metals like gold from others] of measured criticism. In short, he will say that the N.A. is the First Stage of a scientific inquiry, resulting in a hypothesis of the very highest Plausibility, whose ultimate test must lie in its value in the self-controlled growth of man's conduct of life. (EP 2:445–46)

More succinctly, Peirce's claim is that the test of the hypothesis that God is real lies in the positive transformation of one's life by virtue of conforming one's conduct to what is demanded by God. Or, as he states in "Answers to Questions about my Belief in God,"

If a pragmaticist is asked what he means by the word "God," he can only say that just as long acquaintance with a man of great character may deeply influence one's whole manner of conduct ... so if contemplation and study of the physicopsychical universe can imbue a man with principles of conduct analogous to the influence of a great man's works or conversation, then that analogue of a mind ... is what he means by "God." (R 845:A32, c. 1906)

At first glance, this might sound like a bit of silliness. However, I think we can read between the lines and generate an interesting argument. Suppose there is a God, a being who providentially orders the universe. If so, then it should follow that that God has ordered the universe in such a way that conforming to what God desires, subjecting our own wills to the will of God, making our interests the interests of the divine, will result in our personal growth and flourishing. It may not make us wealthy. It may not make us famous. It may not make us more intelligent or better looking or stronger or more influential. But what it will do is make us better people and, as Peirce would say, weld us into the universal continuum, a topic we shall take up in the next chapter.

For Peirce, the ultimate aim will not be our own individual flourishing but the growth of reason or concrete reasonableness. As Peirce had claimed in 1902, "let us ask our own hearts what if anything, makes the human race worthy of preservation. The answer would seem to be, its promise of ultimately developing ideas and of rendering the arrangements of its sphere of influence reasonable" (R 1343:36–7). In a draft for "A Neglected Argument," he writes,

We have to suppose that He has breathed into Man His Own Spirit so far as to render him capable of advancing indefinitely towards the solution of any problem he can propose to himself although in respect to the totality of objects, characters, and principles, Man's understanding must ever remain at least as inadequate as [a creature wanting to taste an orange but inhabiting the surface of its peel]. (R 843:(1)35.6)

A consequence of God's reality is that the universe is rational, it is rationally ordered, and we are able to understand it. If we in fact find that it is rationally ordered and that we can advance toward the solution of our problems, that will be evidence for the reality of God.

Here, then, are two consequences that would follow from the reality of God. First, the world is rationally ordered in such a way that we can understand it. Second, in participating in that order, we will find our greatest calling. If that is, in fact, the sort of argument Peirce has in mind, it is hard not to think of his religious experience at Saint Thomas Episcopal Church as informing it. More importantly, it is also clear that the hypothesis God is real does have deducible conceivable consequences. The first, as already noted, is that the world should be intelligible and, ultimately, thoroughly so. No one would doubt the universe is intelligible, but whether it is thoroughly so only further investigation can reveal. Taking up the second consequence, if God is real, then the universe has a rational and providential order in which we will find it our greatest calling to participate. We can then prede-signate that we shall study ourselves and others with respect to everyone's greatest personal growth in submitting to God's providential order. If we find that we or they do in fact grow and develop by submitting to God's will, it confirms the hypothesis that God is, in fact, real.

Michael Raposa makes this same point. He writes, "since the meaning of the idea of God is revealed in human conduct, a test of the reality of that being might consist in a long-range assessment of the fruitfulness, the success of behavior that conforms to this hypothesis as an ideal. If God is real, then behaving as if God were real ought to be efficacious" (1989, 134). Raposa, though, continues to register the complaints that this is obscure and would require "the gathering of data ranging over the entire scope of human history" (134).

With respect to Raposa's second point, Hookway quite rightly replies, "we do not test an hypothesis concerning the properties of gold by trying to examine as many instances as possible ... While the study of human beings may not exactly parallel that of metal, it does not contravene the rules of scientific method to experiment on a few people (or even just on myself)" (2000, 278–79). With respect to a test on oneself, the improvement of one's life as a consequence of heeding the call of one's Savior may provide at least a presumptive test in favor of the hypothesis, much as spraying luminol at a crime scene provides a presumptive test for the presence of an oxidizing agent, often presumed to be blood and, more particularly, human blood. And, of course, should one's life become miserable, that might constitute a presumptive test against God's reality.[12]

Hookway responds to Raposa's first point – obscurity – by stating that it is a "little unfair" (278). But Peirce himself concedes that the idea of God "can only be apprehended so very obscurely that in exceptional cases alone can any definite and direct deduction from its ordinary abstract interpretation be made" (EP 2:447, 1908). That is, there is a significant challenge to determining whether one has in fact heeded

---

[12] In a discussion of James's "The Will to Believe," Jennifer Welchman (2006) has argued that James's view can be understood as defending a sort of autoexperimentation. I think a similar claim may be made here with respect to Peirce's "A Neglected Argument."

the call of the true Savior since the very hypothesis that God is real is so vague. Who – or what – is God?

Peirce thinks that this objection is "counteracted by . . . [the hypothesis's] commanding influence over the whole conduct of life of its believers" (EP 2:447, 1908), and how it can be counteracted is indicated in the line of argumentation given earlier. Indeed, it is precisely at this point in the first additament that Peirce launches into a rather obscure argument about God and the universe's "super-order." I suggest that this super-order is meant to be the providential order of the universe that, if we subject ourselves to it, ensures our personal growth and development, the fulfillment of our highest calling.[13] Peirce makes another important claim in "Answers to Questions Concerning My Belief in God." There, he writes, "all the instinctive beliefs . . . are vague" (CP 6.499, c. 1906) but that this is no grounds for impugning their scientific character. Although "every concept that is vague is liable to be self-contradictory" (recall here Peirce's comment in "A Neglected Argument" that an infinite being is not tied down to any consistency), Peirce maintains that "*no* concept, not even those of mathematics, is absolutely precise" (CP 6.496). Moreover, he states,

Some of the most important for everyday use are extremely vague . . . For instance, we all think that there is an element of order in the universe. Could any laboratory experiments render that proposition more certain than instinct or common sense leaves it? . . . Men who are given to defining too much inevitably run themselves into confusion in dealing with the vague concepts of common sense. (CP 6.496)

These claims may be directly applied to the concept of God. Even though the concept of God may be exceedingly vague, there is perhaps no need to define it more than the obscure gropings of common sense supply. What those obscure gropings do supply is that God is the one who orders the universe, is its *logos* in some sense of that term, and that the order that God has set in the universe is the *right* one.

Now what that order *is* is yet another question. It is one that must be worked out by the generations of rational beings to come, just as the

---

[13] Rohatyn reads this as an argument for God's reality. I disagree and think it is rather an argument for the claim that if God is real, then there should be some order to the universe. God, though, is not identical to that order. As Peirce states, it is a pragmaticistic definition of *Ens necessarium*, that is, a statement of what would conceivably follow were there such a being.

generations past have sought to work it out. As Peirce states in a draft
for an additament, of the meaning of the "Doctrine of the *Ens necessarium*," "I will not here attempt to sum up the whole of its meaning.
So far as it has such meaning, it is verifiable" (R 844). Peirce's task is
not to sort that question out, and a defense of the rational acceptability
of the current of thought described in the HA does not require him to
do so. It only requires that the hypothesis in fact have deducible consequences that may be put to the test – even if that testing must continue
indefinitely into the future.

Peirce does think that belief in God has experimental consequences.
First, belief in God – living belief in God – should lead us to fulfillment
in joyful submission to God's plan. Second, we should be able to
answer any question with any definite meaning, provided sufficiently
rigorous inquiry be persisted in. If neither of these be true, we may
conclude that either our conception of God contains an error or there is
no God at all. Consequently, the SA shows that belief in God does have
experimental consequences that can be verified, even if their verification may lie in the long run of inquiry.

Countervailing Reasons to Disbelieve in God's Reality?

I have been arguing that Peirce's "A Neglected Argument" is a defense
of the rational acceptability of certain lines of thought that lead to belief
in God. Perceptual cases of involuntarily formed beliefs about God or
certain instances of musement leading to belief in God satisfy
the second, third, and fourth conditions for the rational acceptability
of adopting the hypothesis that God is real: (2) explaining some phenomena (the HA); (3) being able to be taken up in a process of inquiry
(the SA); and (4) being the more instinctual belief (the NA). What I have
yet to show is that there are no significant countervailing reasons to
reject the hypotheses that God is real. It would clearly be impossible to
comprehensively discuss the various objections to religious belief in this
chapter or even in a book. I shall, though, comment on Peirce's own
views on two significant objections, the first that the belief God is real is
an unnecessary hypothesis and the second that God's reality is incompatible with the reality of evil.

Is That God Is Real an Unnecessary Hypothesis? One line of objection
to the hypothesis that God is real is to deny that there is any need to

hypothesize the reality of a God. The theories we currently have – most notably, the Big Bang and the theory of evolution – are sufficient to explain the world around us. Hypothesizing a God in addition to the natural order is an unnecessary theoretical addition. This objection to religious belief is not new or novel. Thomas Aquinas mentions it in his *Summa Theologiae*, writing, "if a few causes fully account for some effect, one does not seek more. Now it seems that everything we observe in this world can be fully accounted for by other causes, without assuming a God ... There is therefore no need to suppose that a God exists" (1964, 13). As a medieval friar, Thomas thinks God is needed to explain the origins of the universe, for he believes God is the first cause and the one who directs unintelligent creatures toward their ends. But we now explain these facts by the Big Bang (or some other suitable physical theory) and the theory of evolution.

Peter Atkins (1994) makes this point in his book *Creation Revisited*. What, he wonders, must God be supposed to do? Consider, for example, elephants. We might suppose that God created them. However, we need only suppose that God created the first pair of elephants, not all of them. Moreover, we need not suppose that God created the first pair of elephants if they might have evolved from other creatures. If we trace this back far enough, we need not suppose that God does anything at all, in which case we need not suppose there is any God at all. More recently, Richard Dawkins (2006) has given expression to the view that belief in God's reality is an unnecessary hypothesis in his book aptly titled *The God Delusion*. After contending that there is no good argument for God's reality, he proceeds to argue, first, that the hypothesis that God is real is itself improbable and, second, that there is no need to appeal to a creator God to explain the origins of life or of the universe.

With respect to the first point, Dawkins's strategy is to turn the irreducible complexity argument on its head. Some theists attempt to argue for the reality of God based on the claim that certain organisms or organs are so complex it is implausible they could have come about by chance or natural selection. A better explanation is that God created them. Hence, God must be real. Setting aside the acceptability of this argument, Dawkins uses the argument to turn the tables on the theist. God, Dawkins holds, is more complex than any of those organisms or organs. So, if their existence is improbable, it follows that God's existence must be even more improbable. Since these theists admit that the existence of those organisms and organs is improbable, it follows they must also admit God's existence is even more improbable. There is obviously a suppressed premise in Dawkins's reasoning. One way to construe the suppressed premise is that the more complex an organism or organ is the more improbable is its existence. But construed in this way, the argument obviously fails because God is not an organism or an organ. Dawkins needs a more general premise: that if Y is improbable and X is more complex than Y, then X is more improbable than Y. But this principle begs the question against the theist who holds that God is a necessary being. Even if the theist admits God is more complex than any given organism or organ, God is a necessary being. Accordingly, such a theist would hold that the existence of some organism or organ is improbable, that God is more complex than that organism, and yet that God is real is not more improbable than that organism or organ just because God is a necessary being.

With respect to the second point Dawkins makes, he contends that multiverse theory can do the same work for physics that Darwinism does for biology. Namely, we can let an appeal to chance and fittingness do the work. Particularly interesting in the present context is that Peirce both admits the theoretical complexity of the hypothesis that God is real and develops a cosmology according to which the origins of the universe are to be accounted for by chance habit taking. With respect to admitting the theoretical complexity of belief in God, Peirce states that the "hypothesis of God is a peculiar one, in that it supposes an infinitely incomprehensible object, although every hypothesis, as such, supposes its object to be truly conceived in the hypothesis" (EP 2:439, 1908). Peirce's worry here is not Dawkins's but a logical worry. God, however God may be, is supposedly beyond our comprehension. But a hypothesis is, by its very nature, an attempt to state something true about its referent. To resolve the worry, Peirce claims that the hypothesis of God's reality is "vague but true so far as it is definite" (EP 2:439, 1908). Analogously, the statement that "every pile of 4,000,000 or more grains of sand is a heap" is true so far as it goes but indefinite insofar as the concept of a heap is vague. Likewise, the statement "God is good, just, merciful, loving, the providential orderer of the universe, and so on" is true so far as it goes but indefinite insofar as the concept of God is vague.

With respect to attributing the origins of the universe to chance, Peirce is likely the first person to extend Darwinian accounts of life to the origins of the universe itself, just as Dawkins suggests we do. Peirce states, "my opinion [as regards the laws of physics] is only Darwinism analyzed, generalized, and brought into the realm of Ontology" (W 4:552, 1883–84). This is evident in his cosmology developed in the early 1890s. Peirce maintains, "the only possible way of accounting for the laws of nature and for uniformity in general is to suppose them results of evolution" (W 8:101, 1890). Having worked tirelessly to devise ways to make more precise measurements using pendulums, he writes,

Try to verify any law of nature, and you will find that the more precise your observations, the more certain they will be to show irregular departures from the law. We are accustomed to ascribe these, and I do not say wrongly, to errors of observation; yet we cannot usually account for such errors in any antecedently probable way. Trace their causes back far enough, and you will be forced to admit that they are always due to arbitrary determination, or chance. (W 8:118, 1891)

In one passage from c. 1909, Peirce writes that Darwin's work opened a line of investigation "which must in the future deeply modify our ideas of morality and perhaps even of metaphysics" (R 334:B2x). Whatever we may think of Peirce's cosmology – Peirce himself expresses doubts about it (see R 842:127–28) – it is clear that he would be amendable to the sort of "evolutionary" theory of the universe Dawkins proposes provided the theoretical difficulties can be worked out.

How then are we to handle Dawkins's objection? One solution might be to deny that belief in God is a hypothesis at all. Alvin Plantinga, for example, takes up this line of thought when he criticizes thinkers who assume that "theistic and Christian belief is or is relevantly like a *scientific hypothesis* ... a *theory* designed to explain some body of evidence and acceptable or warranted to the degree that it explains that evidence" (2000, 329–30). He continues to note that most religious believers do not regard their beliefs as hypotheses but more akin to perceptual beliefs and memory-based beliefs. This line of response, though, is entirely out of the question for a Peircean theory of the rational acceptability of religious belief. Peirce, we have seen, believes that whatever the deliverances of religious experiences are, they are to be logically treated as the conclusions of abductive inferences. As such, they have a hypothetical nature. Moreover, they must be capable of being taken up in a process of inquiry and put to the test. They must have deducible conceivable practical consequences. And so, even if Plantinga were right that involuntarily formed religious beliefs are akin to perceptual beliefs or memory-based beliefs in that they are not held as hypotheses, such beliefs must nevertheless be capable of being treated as hypotheses.

I have already tried to indicate that religious beliefs do have some explanatory power, but it does not follow from that that they are rationally acceptable. Perhaps some other set of beliefs has equally strong explanatory power and simpler hypotheses. And this is the heart of Dawkins's critique: We can explain all that we need to explain without an appeal to God's reality. His argument is rather an appeal to simplicity in hypothesis adoption: Between hypotheses of equal explanatory power, the simpler hypothesis is the one to be preferred. I want here to focus on two conceptions of simplicity in hypothesis formation. Setting aside the qualification of equivalence of explanatory power, the first is that the hypothesis that postulates the fewest *entities* is the one to be preferred. This is metaphysical simplicity. The second is that the hypothesis that involves the fewest possible *theoretical commitments* is the one to be preferred. This is logical simplicity.

The objection from metaphysical simplicity is the easier to discard for two reasons. First, God is not an entity or certainly not an entity in the way that you, I, tables, cats, books, and so on are. At the very least, we are not theoretically committed to claiming that God is an entity. God is, on some theological views, the source of being but not *a* being. Paul Tillich refers to God as the ground of being: "the being of God is being-itself. The being of God cannot be understood as the existence of a being alongside other or above others ... Many confusions in the doctrine of God and many apologetic weaknesses could be avoided if God were understood first of all as being-itself or as the ground of being" (1951, 235). However mystical Tillich's comments may sound, an enormous body of literature is devoted to critiquing ontotheology, the conception of God as somehow belonging to the order of being, as a being among other beings.

Second, the simplest metaphysical hypothesis is some variety of token monism, whether existence monism (that there is exactly one concrete object) or priority monism (that there is exactly one basic concrete object and all other objects are derivatives or parts of it). Without giving either of these views their due, I think it is safe to say that most theorists are not priority monists and existence monism flies in the face of experience, which presents us with a diversity of ontologically distinct beings. Consequently, anyone who embraces the principle of metaphysical simplicity is likely doing so inconsistently with her own metaphysical commitments and practical beliefs.

What, then, of the principle of logical simplicity? This is the sort of simplicity that Dawkins most likely has in mind: the God hypothesis is an unnecessary theoretical commitment. But Peirce criticizes this principle on three grounds. First, if we are to prefer the logically simplest theory, then the preferable theory is no theory at all. Having no theory at all certainly involves the fewest theoretical commitments. If we adopted this principle, then there would be "no support for any hypothesis" (EP 2:444, 1908). Second, Peirce contends that setting aside having no theory at all, the preferable theory would simply be the conjunction of observed facts. As Peirce writes, "we ought to content ourselves with simply formulating the special observations actually made" (EP 2:444). The theory that involves the fewest theoretical commitments is the theory that merely records what has been observed rather than a record of what has been observed *and* an explanation of that record. Finally, Peirce notes, "every advance of science that further opens the truth to our view discloses a world of unexpected complications" (EP 2:444). In other words, the logically simplest hypothesis is not any more likely to be true than the complex one. Nature is complicated; though our theories undoubtedly explain goodly portions of it, those same theories also lead us to recognize the enormous complexity of the natural phenomena we seek to explain. Consequently, if our aim in inquiring is the truth, we need not adopt a principle of logical simplicity since the logically simpler theory is no more likely to be true than the logically less simple theory.

Instead, Peirce thinks that the right methodological maxim is not that we should prefer the logically simpler hypothesis but the more natural one, the *instinctual* one. Consider, again, Christopher Columbus sitting on the dock of the bay and watching ships roll in. He may notice that he sees the mast of a ship before he sees the hull. This will surprise him, and so he will look for an explanation. The logically simplest explanation might be that the earth is a hyperbolic plane. This hypothesis requires the least bit of rejiggering of his other theoretical commitments. It will not, for example, require him to call into question the testimony of others that earth has an edge. But the more instinctual belief – even for Christopher Columbus back in the 1490s – was that the earth is spherical. That is the "more facile and natural" hypothesis, the "one that instinct suggests" (EP 2:444). So, even if Dawkins is correct that belief in

God's reality is not the logically simplest hypothesis, we have already seen Peirce argue for the claim that it is instinctual and so the one that *il lume naturale* recommends.

The Problem of Evil: A second major objection to the rational acceptability of belief in God is the problem of evil. It is now common to distinguish between two versions of the problem, the logical problem of evil (given its most well-known expression by J. L. Mackie) and the inductive problem of evil (given its most well-known expression by William Rowe). Mackie (1955) argues that the propositions God is all-good and all-powerful and evil exists are incompatible supposing that good eliminates evil as far as possible and there are no limits to what an omnipotent thing can do. Rowe (1979) contends that the sheer amount of apparently gratuitous evil and suffering in the world entails that it is improbable God exists.

Peirce, of course, was not familiar with these two distinct versions of the problem of evil. On his view, the challenge is rather to give some account of why God should allow evil. His most explicit solution is indebted to Henry James Sr. In 1892's "Evolutionary Love," Peirce writes,

God visits no punishment on them [those who do not believe in God]; they punish themselves, by their natural affinity for the defective. Thus, the love that God is, is not a love of which hatred is the contrary; otherwise Satan would be a coördinate power; but it is a love which embraces hatred as an imperfect stage of it, an Anteros – yea, even needs hatred and hatefulness as its object. For self-love is no love; so if God's self is love, that which he loves must be defect of love; just as a luminary can light up only that which otherwise would be dark. (W 8:184–85, 1892)

Peirce continues to approvingly quote James Sr.'s book *Substance and Shadow*. Yet this solution to the problem of evil, it must be admitted, is weak. All that is required is that something not be loving for God to embrace and love it. But the absence of loving is not the same as hatred and hatefulness. Richard L. Trammell, who has done the most to try to understand Peirce's comments in light of James Sr.'s work, writes: "The problem of evil is solved by recognizing what 'evil' is – namely, the blind and brute element *absolutely necessary* for reasonableness to have something to make reasonable" (1973, 210). But bruteness is not necessarily evil or hateful. That, on Peirce's cosmology, the universe evolves from chaos and indeterminacy to greater and greater reason-ableness does not imply that the original chaos and indeterminacy was evil in any meaningful moral sense of that word.

Moreover, James Sr. himself writes that God is

bound to allow all the evil and falsity which exist potentially in the created nature to come to the surface, to come to the creature's consciousness by becoming actual; otherwise the creature must forever remain destitute of distinctive consciousness ... [W]hen by an actual experience of life [the creature] perceives himself to be prone to all manner of iniquity; he becomes spiritually disengaged from his natural foundations, exchanges his native pride and obduracy for modesty and docility, and inwardly looks up to God for help. (1863, 443)

But a statement like this is even worse than what Peirce had claimed. Surely not *all* potential evil must "come to the surface" for us to turn away from our own pride and obduracy toward God. And even if *some* must, on this side of the world wars, it is hard to maintain that as much evil and falsity as have become actual had to become actual. Finally, as Rowe has pointed out in his statement of the inductive problem of evil, that humans should need to experience evil to avoid remaining forever "destitute of distinctive consciousness" does not excuse the suffering of nonhuman animals.

Here is not the place to engage the vast literature on the problem of evil. What can suffice in the present context, though, is this. A survey of the literature on the problem reveals that two strategies predominate for dealing with the problem posed, setting aside (what I think is patently absurd) the strategy of arguing that evil is not real. The first is the strategy of excuse. This strategy is to argue that God has some good reason for allowing evil and suffering to exist and so God is blameless for permitting them to exist. For example, God allows evil to exist to test us, to make us better, because some evil and suffering are necessary for the existence of higher-order goods such as freedom of the will, and so on.

A second strategy – I think the more promising one – is the strategy of exculpation. This strategy is to argue that given the information we have, we are not in the proper epistemic position to issue a verdict on whether God is blameworthy for permitting evil and suffering to exist and so we are at liberty to deny that God is to be blamed for the evil and suffering in the world. That is, God is innocent until proven guilty beyond a reasonable doubt. We may in the future find that the evidence supports the claim that God is guilty, only we now have no conclusive reason for asserting that God is blameworthy. One notable defender of this strategy is William Alston (1991). Also, Descartes employs this strategy in his fourth meditation when he contends that the study of final causes is useless. This is a double-edged sword, for Descartes cannot then claim that God has some purpose in mind when permitting evil and suffering but neither can his opponent claim that God does *not* have some purpose in mind. But this solution is first found in the book of Job when God states, "Shall a faultfinder contend with the Almighty? He who argues with God, let him answer it ... Will you even put me in the wrong? Will you condemn me that you may be justified" (Job 40:2, 8)? In the end, the translations state that Job repents in dust and ashes, but what the passage really states is that Job defers or yields the floor. He shall no longer bring accusations, but that is a far cry from claiming that one's accusations are mistaken.

Since religious persons often claim to have experienced God and since they regard God as a good friend or comforter in times of trouble, they may give God the benefit of the doubt and claim that God surely has some good reasons for allowing evil and suffering to exist even if we cannot now say what they are. This is not far removed from our relationships with others. If a good friend is arrested for stealing a car, for example, and that friend is unlikely to have done so given what we know of her character and there is no conclusive evidence linking her to the crime but also none exonerating her, we surely should give her the benefit of the doubt. We should *exculpate* her of the crime – hold her for blameless – even if we cannot *excuse* her of it, that is, prove her blameless.

The religious person – the one who has heeded the call of her Savior – is precisely in the right sort of position to exculpate God of evil and suffering. She may not be in a position to have "adjusted a philosophical difficulty" and excused God of evil and suffering. Unless she is an academic, she will not be able to devote herself to studying the problem of evil. Moreover, even if she is an academic, she may not be able to arrive at a satisfactory conclusion. But she may *hold for now* that God is blameless, that God has some reason for permitting evil and suffering, however inscrutable that reason may be to us now. And though she may with haste and energy search for evidence of God's blameworthiness or blamelessness, she is surely no more irresponsible for exculpating God than is a mother who bails her son out of jail for a crime she believes in her heart of hearts he did not commit.

Peirce makes this point quite nicely, though in a different context. After distinguishing between those who do not believe in God because they have never experienced God and those who do precisely because they have experienced God, he writes that those,

> who have undergone true religious experience, – such as once experienced remains forever as the most real of all experiences, do not care at all about reasonings which must skim the surface of the truth and which are abhorrent to them owing to their arrogant and insane pretension that God cannot expect to have a standing in their court until He has proved Himself submissive to their jurisdiction. (R 857:1, undated)

And this, I think, gets to the heart of the matter. The person who has heard the call of her Savior will not think that God must first be proven blameless for the evil and suffering in the world before heeding that call. God is not on trial and much less is God subject to our jurisdiction. She will instead act and leave it to future investigation – perhaps the investigations of others – to adjust this particular philosophical difficulty. She must conduct her life even while she awaits inquiry's final verdict, and in conducting her life she may – indeed, she *must* – rely on her instincts.

Conclusion

Peirce's "A Neglected Argument" is best understood as a defense of the rational acceptability of allowing one's conduct to be transformed by a living belief in God. The line of thought that leads to a living belief in God's reality explains some phenomena, is instinctual, and has deducible conceivable practical consequences. Moreover, in Peirce's judgment, there are no significant countervailing reasons to deny that God is real. This, though, will not prevent us from continuing to gather evidence as to whether or not God is real. That will be part of the philosophy of religion, and the results of the philosophy of religion may, as we saw in previous chapters, affect our conduct by a slow process of percolation.

Moreover, some people may believe on the basis of the evidence that they have gathered that there are significant countervailing reasons to disbelieve in God's reality. For those persons, it would not be rationally acceptable to believe that God is real because it would violate one of the conditions for the hypothesis to be rationally acceptable. They may, as Peirce suggests, have to wait until they hear their Savior's call, which will be further evidence in favor God's reality. For until then, their religious beliefs would be but a pretense.

Finally, it ought also to be clear from the preceding how different Peirce's defense of the rational acceptability of belief in God is from William James's defense in "The Will to Believe." James maintains that religious belief is permissible because it presents us with a genuine option that cannot be decided on intellectual grounds: "*Our passional nature not only lawfully may, but must, decide an option between propositions, whenever it is a genuine option that cannot by its nature be decided on intellectual grounds*" (WWJ 6:20). Peirce contends that religious beliefs are rationally acceptable precisely because they satisfy the conditions that must be met for any hypothesis to be intellectually respectable. In other words, even if we cannot now say that God's reality has been proven or demonstrated, on Peirce's view one's belief in God's reality is in no worse of a position than any other hypothesis that one might adopt though it has not yet been proven. And everyone would surely admit that there is nothing epistemically dubious about adopting undemonstrated hypotheses provided the conditions Peirce sets forth are met. Doing so is at the heart of all of our intellectual endeavors. Unlike in some of these intellectual endeavors, however, Peirce believes that the hypothesis that God is real begins to inform the religious person's conduct at the level of instinct and before theoretical inquiry ever begins.

4 | On Becoming Welded into the Universal Continuum

In the drafts for 1898's "Philosophy and the Conduct of Life," Peirce strikes a mystical note when writes, "the supreme commandment of the Buddhisto-christian religion is, to generalize, to complete the whole system even until continuity results and the distinct individuals weld together" (R 435:34/CP 1.673). He elaborates on this claim in another draft,

Thus it is that while reasoning and the science of reasoning strenuously proclaim the subordination of reasoning to sentiment, the very supremest command of sentiment is that man should generalize, should become welded into the universal continuum, which is what true reasoning consists in, as the logic of relatives demonstrates, and that this should come about not merely in his cognitions which are the surface of his being but objectively in the deepest springs of his life. In fulfilling this command man prepares himself for transmutation into a new form of life, the joyful Nirvana in which the discontinuities of his will shall have almost disappeared. (R 436:34, 27)

In the lecture itself, however, Peirce's claims about religion and sentiment are pushed into the background. After discussing the mathematician who "corrects the Heraclitan error that the Eternal is not Continuous," Peirce writes that the "end that Pure Mathematics is pursuing is to discover that real potential world" of the Platonist (RLT 121). He continues to note that "once you become inflated with that idea, *vital importance* seems to be a very low kind of importance, indeed" but that in our "workaday world" where we cannot all be mathematicians, we must rely on instinct which is also "capable of development and growth" (RLT 121). Note, though, that the same ideas appear here as are expressed in the drafts: There is some great continuum of which we become a part and both reason and sentiment or instinct can weld us into that great continuum.

This is exceedingly obscure, however. Moreover, Peirce's claims here appear to be inconsistent with what he states five years earlier. For whereas in the drafts for "Philosophy and the Conduct of Life," Peirce indicates that we are preparing for a new form of life and a joyful Nirvana, he earlier states, "we are all putting our shoulders to the wheel for an end that none of us can catch more than a glimpse at – that which the generations are working out. But we can see that the development of embodied ideas is what it will consist in" (CP 5.402n2, 1893). But the embodiment of *which* ideas? If we can but glimpse the end, Peirce's proclamation that it will consist in a joyful Nirvana wherein distinct individuals are welded together would be unfounded at best.

At worst, it is flat out wrong. For Peirce is thinking in evolutionary terms. Over successive generations, he indicates, we will be fused into the universal continuum. As Michael Raposa has claimed, according to Peirce "all of reality is continuous, gradually evolving towards an ideal state, under the gentle but ultimately irresistible influence of a divine love" (1989, 91) and "nature's teleology, history's teleology are most perfectly understood when conceived in religious terms" (83). But there is no reason to think that some greater unity will be the outcome of natural selection. There is even less reason to think that even if a greater unity were produced, it would be an ideal or a good. It would certainly be a change, but there is no reason to conclude that some state of affairs that is a consequence of natural selection is better than another.

That is, there is no reason to draw such a conclusion unless one already has in mind some religious notions in accordance with which, as Raposa suggests, nature is being understood. But what could possibly license understanding nature in those terms? For even in "Evolutionary Love," Peirce is compelled to concede that "if it could be shown directly that there is such an entity as the 'spirit of an age' or of a people . . . this would be proof enough at once of agapasticism [evolution by love rather than Darwinian sporting variation or cataclysmic evolution] and of synechism" but that he is "unable to produce a cogent demonstration of this" (W 8:203, 1892). The best that Peirce can offer us is the fact that many discoveries were made simultaneously and independently. But that only shows that persons countenancing the same questions and in possession of the same or similar evidence recognized the same solution. This might be an indicator favoring the truth of the solution; it does not favor Peirce's evolutionary cosmology. Later, Peirce even suggests that he rejects a portion of his evolutionary cosmology, namely, the thesis that the laws of nature evolved from a chance tendency toward habit taking. He notes, without dissent, that Edmund Montgomery objects to it on the grounds that Peirce's theory is not evolutionary but emanational, that

Ogden Rood objects to it on the grounds that there must have been some original tendency to take habits that did not arise according to his hypothesis, and that he is struck by the difficulty of explaining the law of sequence in time, since all laws on his theory must develop from single events, and an event already presupposes time (see R 842:127–128, c. 1907). In short, it is hard to see how Peirce's belief that the outcome of evolutionary processes will be that we are welded into the universal continuum could be any more than a religious faith. If so, the introduction of it into his philosophy would be inconsistent with Peirce's desire that philosophy be a strict science.

Recently, James Liszka (2014) has noted a tension in Peirce's thought. On the one hand, Peirce concedes we cannot now discern what is the greatest good or that toward which evolutionary processes are tending. On the other hand, Peirce states that there is some ideal end of evolutionary processes and it is the growth of concrete reasonableness, being welded into the universal continuum, a joyful Nirvana, and the outcome of God loving the world into greater and greater loveliness. The tension arises because Peirce appears to recognize both a positive esthetics – approximation toward an end – and a negative esthetics – wherein there is no predetermined end but good results from eliminating faults. Liszka tries to resolve the problem by appealing to Peirce's theory of scientific reasoning, but it is not clear how this is supposed to dovetail with our "supremest commandment," especially when we consider that we are mere cells in a social organism, busied in our workaday world.

We are clearly in the thick of a number of issues. Fortunately, we can make some headway in resolving them and bringing clarity to Peirce's ideas if we keep in mind the distinction between what Peirce has to tell us about philosophy as a science and what he has to tell us about how we should conduct our lives while we wait for the results of our scientific investigations. When it comes to scientific inquiry, Peirce must admit that he does not know what will be the result of evolutionary processes. However, he can tell us something about the *summum bonum* – the greatest good – with respect to reason. This concerns what Peirce calls the science of esthetics, which he stresses is not a science of sensuous beauty and art (EP 2:460, 1911). We can then extend what Peirce states about reason and the summum bonum to sentiment and instinct and, in turn, shed light on Peirce's rather mystical claims. Those claims, though, are not licensed in theoretical science; they rather concern the conduct of our lives. More specifically, they concern the conduct of life for those who have a theistic bent, as Peirce does. In other words, we can get some traction on Peirce's rather enigmatic, and occasionally inconsistent, claims about the summum bonum and the outcome of evolutionary processes if we keep what he has to tell us about theoretical philosophy separate from what he has to tell us about the conduct of life. Peirce's views on each are not inconsistent, but they are separately licensed. The main problem with this proposal, though, is that Peirce's comments on esthetics, the science of the summum bonum, are themselves very brief and enigmatic. We will first have to do some work to get them into shape.

Peirce's Esthetics

Esthetics in the Context of Peirce's Mature Theory of Inquiry

Peirce presents his theory of inquiry in the *Illustrations of the Logic of Science* papers of 1877–78, especially "The Fixation of Belief." On his early view, inquiry is the struggle to free ourselves from doubt by establishing beliefs not liable to be overturned by future experience. The aim of inquiry is not truth but settled belief. Nevertheless, Peirce does think that true beliefs will be those that do stand up to future experience. Consequently, we ought to establish our beliefs in accordance with a method that will result in the formation of true beliefs, and the method best for doing so is the scientific method since it presents an objective distinction between right and wrong and stays close to reality. Peirce holds that truth is the predestinate opinion of scientific inquiry and that reality is what is represented in a true proposition.

Peirce's conception of scientific inquiry develops from his *Illustrations of the Logic of Science* series and reaches maturity in the 1900s. Albert Atkin (2016, ch. 3) provides an admirable summary of what those changes are, and the account in this section is indebted to his account there. One key change is that Peirce began to conceive of philosophical inquiry architectonically and, by 1903, recognizes three general domains of philosophical inquiry, viz. phenomenology, normative science, and metaphysics. Most importantly for our concerns here, esthetics, ethics, and logic comprise the normative sciences. Although Peirce is clearly borrowing from the traditional classification of the normative sciences, he certainly does not have the same conception of them. He treats esthetics as a science that studies what is objectively admirable, ethics as the science of self-controlled conduct, and logic as the science of self-controlled thought (see EP 2:260, 1903). The theory of inquiry itself falls under logic as a subscience he calls *methodeutic*; in accordance with Peirce's method for classifying the sciences, it is supposed to employ principles found in esthetics. A primary task of this section is to identify what those principles are regarding *theoretical* inquiry. Crucially, those principles will account for why certain methods of inquiry are prescriptive: They are normative because they attain the aims of inquiry.

A second development in Peirce's mature conception of inquiry is his prizing truth and reality, as Atkin notes. Peirce concedes that there may be truths for which there are no corresponding realities, such as mathematical truths, and suggests that there may be realities for which there are no corresponding truths. Nevertheless, as he had in 1877's "The Fixation of Belief" (see W 3:248), Peirce continues to identify settled belief as the aim of inquiry and to regard true beliefs as those that will be settled, that is, stand up to future experience.

Third, Peirce begins to clarify the relationship between science and inquiry. First, he recognizes that not all inquiries demand the rigors of scientific investigation. This should already be evident from what has been said in previous chapters, especially Chapter 2. Second and as noted in Chapter 3, he maintains that a variety of regulative assumptions or *hopes* underwrite the scientific enterprise, such as that there is some answer to our questions and that we are able to discover the truth. Finally, since Peirce now identifies three distinct normative sciences and thinks that they bear orderly relations to one another – self-controlled thought (the subject matter of logic) is a species of self-controlled conduct (the subject matter of ethics) aimed at bringing about the summum bonum (the subject matter of esthetics) – inquiry itself is a way of realizing the greatest good. The problem is that we need an account of what the greatest good is, an account that Peirce's esthetics is supposed to provide.

The Received Conception of Peirce's Esthetics

Particularly puzzling with respect to the normative sciences is Peirce's theory of esthetics. Peirce maintains that esthetics is the study of the admirable and unadmirable. Drawing on Peirce's own comments, Peirce scholars understand esthetics to be the study of the greatest good, and so the admirable is to be identified with what is the greatest good.[1] They also concur that the greatest good is the growth of concrete reasonableness. Yet there are at least four worries about these claims.

The first problem is that in 1902, Peirce identifies ethics, not esthetics, as the study of the summum bonum: "the *summum bonum* ... forms the subject of pure ethics" (CP 1.575). In 1903, he writes, "ethics ... must appeal to esthetics for aid in determining the *summum bonum*" (EP 2:260). But this statement is ambiguous. Is esthetics the study of the summum bonum? Or do the results of esthetics merely aid ethical theorists in discovering what the summum bonum is? Peirce's comment in 1906 is similarly unclear: "ethics ... involves the theory of the ideal itself, the nature of the *summum bonum*" (EP 2:377). On the one hand, Peirce may mean that ethics derives the summum bonum from esthetics and so involves the summum bonum in that way. On the other hand, he may mean that ethics needs assistance from esthetics, but the discovery of the summum bonum is unique to ethics.

Second, it is not clear what the growth of concrete reasonableness is. Peirce writes, "the pragmaticist does not make the *summum bonum* to consist in action, but makes it to consist in that process of evolution whereby the existent comes more and more to embody those generals which were just now said to be *destined*, which is what we strive to express in calling them *reasonable*" (EP 2:343, 1903). This comment is obscure. What kind of evolutionary process? How are the generals embodied? In what does this destiny consist? Are we assured to reach this destiny? Or is it a mere hope? And why is that destiny reasonable? Peirce goes no further. Instead, he writes, "there is much more in elucidation of pragmaticism that might be said to advantage, were it not for the dread of fatiguing the reader" (EP 2:344).

Fortunately, Peirce scholars have endeavored to clarify what he means by the growth of concrete reasonableness. Unfortunately, they articulate Peircean esthetics either in the context of Peirce's evolutionary metaphysics or through his logic (which he also calls semiotics). Patricia Turrisi (1986), for example, elucidates the growth of concrete reasonableness through Peirce's evolutionary metaphysics and the notion of divine creative love. C. M. Smith (1972) endeavors to understand Peirce's esthetics through his semiotics. Beverly Kent (1976) uses

---

[1] For a smattering of examples among many, see Potter (1967, 33), Turrisi (1986), Parker, (1998, 129–130), and Lefebvre (2007, 326).

Peirce's pragmatism and his considerations on the problem of evil to elucidate his esthetics.

The problem though – and this is our third – is that these attempts to explicate Peirce's esthetics violate his commitment to the order of the sciences. Peirce maintains that the sciences are organized according to whether they lend or borrow principles from one another, and these dependence relations are derived from Peirce's categories of Firstness, Secondness, and Thirdness (see Kent 1987 and Atkins 2006). Here is not the place for an exposition of Peirce's classification of the sciences or the classification of the sciences in general. The essential point is simply that in Peirce's classification of the sciences, esthetics appears before logic and metaphysics. Consequently, esthetics can lend principles to metaphysics and logic. However, esthetics cannot derive principles from them. Peircean esthetics must derive its principles from elsewhere than these sciences, for by Peirce's manner of classifying the sciences, the doctrine that the growth of concrete reasonableness is the summum bonum cannot be ascertained in esthetics if the proof for it lies in logic or metaphysics. Yet, if this is so, no one has succeeded in showing how the doctrine that the summum bonum is the growth of concrete reasonableness is established independently of Peirce's logic and metaphysics. None of this is to deny that turning to logic and metaphysics can helpfully elucidate Peircean esthetics. In an early classification of the sciences – the very classification in "Philosophy and the Conduct of Life" – Peirce maintains that the sciences are to be organized not only by their dependence relations but also by data relations: The lower sciences provide data to the higher sciences. Accordingly, theorists of Peircean esthetics might look to logic and metaphysics for data. From which it would also follow that Turrisi, Kent, and Smith may all shed important light on Peircean esthetics. Nonetheless, the present claim is that Peircean esthetics must be established on its own grounds and in accordance with his classification of the sciences.

Finally, in 1903 Peirce acknowledges that he is "a perfect ignoramus in esthetics" (EP 2:189) and that he does "not feel entitled to have any confident opinions about it" (EP 2:200). He is even hesitant to consider esthetics a science: "I am inclined to think that there is such a normative science; but I feel by no means sure even of that" (EP 2:200). In 1904's "Reason's Conscience," Peirce indirectly reveals that he is uncertain as to how esthetics informs the system of the sciences. He proposes to show that "the problems of logic cannot be solved without taking advantage of the teachings of Mathematics, of Phenomenology, and of Ethics" (NEM 4:193). Curiously, of the sciences prior to logic in his classification, Peirce omits only esthetics, suggesting either (a) he has no clear conception of how esthetics informs logic or (b) esthetics does not importantly contribute to solving logic's problems. However, (b) is implausible because esthetics is the science of the greatest good and logic is the study of good reasoning. Hence, esthetics must, in some way, lend principles to logic. Rendering (a) more plausible as a reason for the omission is the fact that Peirce's comments on esthetics are brief, enigmatic, and occasionally inconsistent, as Kent herself notes (1976, 263). This is not to deny that he has a genuine insight into the normative sciences, but whatever insight Peirce does have is exceedingly dim. We can, though, shed some light on Peirce's theory of esthetics with the help of Kant's *Critique of the Power of Judgment,* for there can be little doubt that Peirce had been studying Kant's aesthetics as he developed his own theory of esthetics.[2]

Kant's Critique of the Power of Judgment

Although Kant discusses art in the third critique, even a cursory reading of it reveals that his comments on art are secondary to the larger problem he addresses in the book. Kant's primary interest is in the nature of reflecting judgments. Reflecting judgments are distinguished from determining judgments, which are those in which one is in possession of a concept and then applies that concept to intuitions (presentations of a sensory manifold). Or, to state it slightly differently, in making determining judgments, one is subsuming a particular under a concept already in possession. Kant addresses the nature of determining judgments in his *Critique of Pure Reason.* Reflecting judgments, in contrast, occur when one has an intuition but must *create* a concept on its basis. In making reflecting judgments, one is creating a concept to subsume a particular.

Kant makes this distinction between determining and reflecting judgments because he recognizes that numerous concepts mediate between

---

[2] Compare, for instance, what Peirce says at EP 2:201 to the following comments on aesthetic judgment and Kant's comments on the dynamical sublime at 5:260–61 (2000).

his universal categories and intuitions. These mediating concepts are the ones employed in the empirical sciences. For example, the metaphysical concept of causality derives from the form of a conditional (or, as Kant says, hypothetical) judgment. However, there are various kinds of causes. Both hand production of an object and generation are kinds of causes. Also, there are various kinds of generation, among them sexual reproduction and crystallization. Yet, how does one discover these intermediary concepts? They are not known *a priori* but only *a posteriori* by means of reflecting judgments. The creation of these concepts is a technique or an art. Kant explains, "the reflecting power of judgment thus proceeds with given appearances ... not schematically, but **technically**, not as it were merely mechanically ... but **artistically**, in accordance with the general but at the same time indeterminate principle of a purposive arrangement of nature in a system" (20:214). These concepts enable the inquirer to find his or her way in the labyrinth of intuitions and the empirical laws that govern nature. The doctrine of intermediate forms is a necessary presupposition for the power of judgment and the progress of inquiry. The progress of empirical knowledge presupposes that nature can be understood. Consequently, the power of judgment is based upon the principle that "**Nature specifies its general laws into empirical ones, in accordance with the form of a logical system, in behalf of the power of judgment**" (20:216). Only on the supposition that nature can be rationally understood according to determinate laws and concepts is reflecting judgment possible.

Kant maintains that one is enabled to know intermediate forms through the faculty of the imagination brought into agreement with the understanding in an act of judgment. He writes, "the imagination (as a productive cognitive faculty) is ... very powerful in creating ... another nature, out of the material which the real one gives it" (5:314). The imagination is able to apprehend the intuitions, which are synthesized in an act of comprehension about which a judgment is made (20:220). Such judgments are made possible by the free play of the imagination and the understanding, as they are not bound by any determinate rules of cognition (5:217). They are unbound because they are reflecting judgments aimed at creating a concept. That is, no concept is already in place to govern the play of the imagination and the understanding.

At this point, a further distinction between two kinds of reflecting judgments, aesthetic judgments and teleological judgments, is necessary.

Aesthetic judgments are reflecting judgments that are merely subjective. They require no determinate concept of an object. In aesthetic judgment, the mere agreement of imagination and understanding suffices. Therefore, aesthetic judgments are not cognitions but feelings (5:203). However, in teleological judgments, the agreement is judged objectively. Consequently, teleological reflecting judgments are about a natural end, the purposive intermediate forms of nature's specification (20:221). In teleological judgments, although the creation of the concepts is not subject to any rules, it is nevertheless required that future intuitions of nature be recurrently consistent with those concepts. Thus, such judgments are cognitions (20:221).

The agreement of the imagination and the understanding in either kind of reflecting judgment results in pleasure. Pleasure is the maintenance of agreement between the imagination and the understanding: "**Pleasure** is a **state** of the mind in which a representation is in agreement with itself, as a ground, either merely for preserving this state itself ... or for producing its object" (20:231). Such pleasure is brought about by the genius: "the mental powers, then, whose union (in a certain relation) constitutes **genius**, are imagination and understanding" (5:316). Genius is the power to imaginatively create concepts in reflecting judgments that bring the imagination into agreement with the understanding. One is liable to make the mistake of thinking that pleasure is a feeling. Kant stresses, however, that pleasure is a state.

When the imagination and the understanding actively reach agreement, there is no tension between them. This results in a judgment of beauty, in the case of aesthetic judgments. The maintenance of this agreement may be called aesthetic pleasure. In the case of teleological judgments, in which there must also be an agreement with the natural object, there is astonishment (in the incompatibility of intuitions and concepts) or admiration (in the continual recurrence of their compatibility) (5:365). The continual recurrence of the agreement with the natural object may be called intellectual pleasure. With intellectual pleasure, one is in a state in which there is no shock, no astonishment. Kant understands the architectonic of knowledge – the fully articulated specification of the natural forms – as a regulative ideal of systematic knowledge (5:381). The sciences must proceed on the assumption of systematicity, and the continual admiration of the agreement of concepts and intuitions grounds the adequacy of empirical scientific claims. In this way, normativity resides ultimately in pleasure (keeping in mind Kant's specific understanding of pleasure as the maintenance of agreement between the imagination and the understanding).

Peircean Esthetics in a Kantian Light

Peirce understands esthetics to be a positive science. It contributes something to our knowledge of the universe that no other science does. The key lies in identifying what that positive contribution is. For Peirce, esthetics is the first science that mediates between what merely manifests itself to the mind (phenomenology or phaneroscopy, the observation and description of what is manifest) and what is real regardless of whether or not anyone thinks it (metaphysics and the special sciences). Consequently, esthetics plays a crucial role in the systematicity of knowledge. Only with assistance from esthetics can anyone hope to arrive at knowledge of the real.

Here we glimpse the first significant overlap between Peircean esthetics and Kant. For Kant, the primary principle of the power of judgment is that nature itself specifies its general laws into empirical ones in such a way that the power of judgment can know them. This affirms that nature must be such as to be amenable to one's judgments if one is to have any knowledge of nature. As Peirce notes, one would never be able to detect the regularity of nature (and hence engage in the scientific enterprise) "if there were not an affinity between our mind and Nature's" (EP 2:24, 1895). Peirce would later articulate the same point in terms of *il lume naturale*: "unless man have a natural bent in accordance with nature's, he has no chance of understanding nature, at all" (EP 2:444, 1908).

The second significant point of overlap is between their two theories of pleasure. In 1902's "Minute Logic," Peirce connects esthetics and pleasure. He writes, "in order to state the question of esthetics in its purity, we should eliminate from it, not merely all consideration of effort, but all consideration of action and reaction, including ... our receiving pleasure, everything in short, belonging to the opposition of the *ego* and the *non-ego*" (CP 2.199). Peirce clarifies his conception of pleasure in 1903's Harvard *Lectures on Pragmatism*. He moves from a consideration of esthetics to a clarification of the nature of pleasure. Peirce rejects a conception of pleasure as a feeling: "it is a great mistake to suppose that the phenomena of pleasure and pain are mainly phenomena of feeling" (EP 2:189). Rather, he maintains that pleasure and pain are instances of the striving for a state of *quietus*: "They mainly consist (Pain) in a Struggle to give a state of mind its *quietus*; and (Pleasure) in a peculiar mode of consciousness allied to the conscious-ness of *making a generalization*, in which not Feeling, but rather Cognition, is the principal constituent" (EP 2:190).

Three points are relevant here. First, Peirce identifies pleasure as cognitional. On the surface, this may seem inconsistent with Kant's theory of aesthetics, which he maintains is not cognitional. But that is true only of aesthetic judgments; teleological judgments are cognitional. Specifically, they are cognitions of the intermediate forms into which nature is specified. This fits with Peirce's conception of esthetics. As has already been noted, Peirce distances his conception of esthetics from the "silly" science of sensuous beauty. Second, Peirce understands this mode of consciousness to be allied to *making* a generalization. This accords with Kant's understanding of reflecting judgments as creating generals under which to subsume particulars. This act of creating a general with the aim of making objective claims about nature is cognitional. Specifically, it is a teleological reflecting judgment. The third point is that Peirce understands pleasure to be a state of *quietus* that emerges from a struggle. This struggle must be between the mind and some putative reality, as is evident in the previously cited quotation from "Minute Logic." Esthetics, purely, is divorced from the struggle between mind and world. What it must mean for the mind to reach a state of *quietus* with reality, in the context of inquiry, is that there is an agree-ment between the judgments one makes and the way the world is. This is an important point of overlap between Peirce's work in esthetics and 1878's "The Fixation of Belief." Inquiry is the struggle to free ourselves from doubt, and that "when doubt ceases, mental action on a subject comes to an end" (W 3:248). Yet the scientific method alone is the one that can fix belief well because it alone presents a real distinction between wrong and right and it alone stays close to the facts.

One apparent problem with this account is that it appears to be psychologistic. In fact, Peirce makes this criticism in 1903 when he writes,

My original article carried this [his proof of the principle of pragmatism] back to a psychological principle ... I do not think it satisfactory to reduce such fundamental things to facts of psychology. For man could alter his nature, or his environment would alter it if he did not voluntarily do so, if the impulse were not what was advantageous or fitting. (EP 2:140)

Peirce is not here objecting to making generalizations about inquiry based on our observations of humans. He is, though, objecting to an account of the summum bonum based solely on generalizations from our observations of human nature. Those observations may supply data for our general theory, but we will want our general theory of the summum bonum not to be merely based on abstractions from psychological observations.[3] Peirce's esthetics will be grounded not simply on the basis of these observations about human nature but also on the nature of teleological reflecting judgments and under what conditions they are admirable. In theoretical inquiry, our judgments are admirable when they are in agreement with, or correspond to, their objects. To be certain, when those judgments are true and would stand up to future experience, the struggle to end doubt ceases. Mental action comes to an end. This is what Peirce had claimed in "The Fixation of Belief." But that mental action ceases is rather a consequence of our beliefs being true and cannot support the claim that the good of inquiry simply is the cessation of mental action. Rather, for the later Peirce, the esthetic state is that in which one has reached *quietus*, or pleasure, just because the judgment is true and not because of the peculiarities of human psychology. This doctrine is akin to Kant's affirmation that pleasure is a state of continually recurring agreement between the imagination and the understanding in judgment. As noted earlier, in teleological reflecting judgments this also requires agreement with the natural object.

The third significant overlap between Kant and Peirce is that both identify the esthetic state as admirable. Kant understands teleological reflecting judgments to be admirable if they are pleasurable (i.e., if there is agreement among the imagination, the understanding, and nature) and astonishing if there is no such agreement. The study of admirableness is also how Peirce describes esthetics. In 1905, he considers replacing his science of esthetics with the science of axiagastics, the science of the admirable. In 1911, when he rejects the silly conception of esthetics as the science of sensuous beauty, Peirce defines esthetics as "passionate *admiring* aspirations after an inward state that anybody may hope to attain or approach, but of whatever more specific complexion may enchant the dreamer" (EP 2:460, emphasis added).

---

[3] See Kasser (1999) for a defense of the claim that Peirce's early work is not, at root, psychologistic. See also Stjernfelt (2014, ch. 2) and Hookway (2012, ch. 5) for studies on Peirce's anti-psychologism.

We have now identified three significant points of overlap between Peirce's esthetics and Kant's account of the power of judgment (especially of teleological reflecting judgments). First, they both aim at the systematic articulation of the categories and forms as a comprehensive theory of nature. Second, they both aim at the agreement of the mind and reality in reflecting judgments, and they identify the continual recurrence of this agreement as a state of pleasure. Third, they both identify the state of reaching this agreement as admirable. These overlaps are sufficiently significant as to merit the claim that Peircean esthetics can be significantly modeled on Kant's critique of the power of teleological judging. In short, Peircean esthetics is the science of the admirableness of generalizations based on their continually recurrent agreement with the objects or features of reality, and the maintenance of their agreement is a state of pleasure. The first portion of this section's task is now complete: to show that there is such a significant overlap between Peirce and Kant on esthetics that the former can be modeled on the latter. Now, the second task must be addressed: Can this view clarify the received conception of Peirce's esthetics while remaining faithful to esthetics' place in Peirce's classification of the sciences?

Clarification of the Received Conception of Peirce's Esthetics

As noted, the received conception of Peirce's esthetics is (a) that esthetics is the science of the summum bonum and (b) that the summum bonum is the growth of concrete reasonableness. Now if the concepts utilized in reflecting judgments were already known to be true, then inquiry would not be necessary. That is so because all of our concepts would already be adequate to reality. Whatever we wish to know would already be known, and so there would be no *quietus* to achieve. The task of inquiry is to develop theories sufficiently general to explain diverse phenomena. Setting about this task, though, presupposes that not all phenomena have been adequately explained theoretically. Consequently, the summum bonum only becomes a summum bonum in the context of the inadequacy of our concepts to reality. Achieving *quietus* only becomes a goal for us when we are in a state of doubt.

This helps clarify Peirce's apparently ambiguous comments that, on the one hand, ethics looks to esthetics for the summum bonum but, on the other hand, the summum bonum is the subject of ethics. On the one hand, the struggle of inquiry aims to reach a state of *quietus* in which mind and reality are no longer at odds; that is, our cognitions are in agreement with the object of our cognition. That this state of *quietus* is admirable in itself is discovered in esthetics. On the other hand, this *quietus* is not achieved in esthetics. To the contrary, for inquiry, only in rational conduct is it realized that this ideal state is an *ideal* at all. That is to say, only in rational conduct do we treat a state of *quietus* – conformity to reality – as the goal of our self-controlled thinking. This is what Peirce means when he claims that the dualism of the normative sciences is "softened almost to obliteration in esthetics" (EP 2:379). In the admirable esthetic state, our concepts are adequate to reality and so we have reached a state of *quietus*. No occasion for doubt will arise precisely because our judgments about the object are true; that is, they conform to their object. Since our judgments are true, they are not liable to be overturned by future experience; they will not be cast into doubt.

This insight is not grounded in any psychological propositions. Rather, it is rooted in the very function of teleological reflecting judgments. As Peirce states in another context, "the question of the goodness of anything is whether that thing fulfills its end" (EP 2:235, 1903). The end of a teleological reflecting judgment is to accurately express the intermediate forms into which reality is specified. If one is to have knowledge of reality, then there must be an "agreement" – a correspondence or conformity – between our judgments and reality.[4] When there is no such agreement, a struggle between mind and reality – a struggle to *understand* reality – ensues. This is the origin of inquiry. Furthermore, this account of the admirableness of the state of *quietus* is not justified by any insights from evolutionary metaphysics or logic. Rather, the account is justified by

---

[4] This comment touches on Peirce's theory of truth. Although some theorists today attempt to fuse Peirce's pragmatic elucidation of truth as what would be believed after a sufficiently long and rigorous course of study with a deflationary analysis of truth, there can be little doubt that Peirce actually endorsed a variety of the correspondence theory of truth, which I call the conformity theory of truth. Here are some representative quotations: "truth is the conformity of a representamen [=sign] to its object – *its* object, ITS object, mind you" and what a sign must do to make an object its object is "to seize its interpreter's eyes and forcibly turn them upon the object meant" (EP 2:380, 1906), and "the purpose of every sign is to express 'fact,' and by being joined with other signs, to approach as nearly as possible to determining an interpretant which would be the *perfect Truth*" (EP 2:304, 1904).

the purpose of teleological reflecting judgments as aimed at making our conceptions adequate to reality. Hence, the present account remains true to Peirce's classification of the sciences and to his categories.

These claims elucidate Peirce's position that the summum bonum is the growth of concrete reasonableness. We should not understand the achievement of concrete reasonableness as a state of inactivity. Rather, concrete reasonableness grows and is maintained through the agreement of our judgments with the objects of our judgment. First, it is reasonable, for our concepts are accurate and are adequate to understand reality. In this state, the struggle of inquiry reaches a minimal intensity, is softened to oblivion. Second, it is concrete, for not only do our beliefs withstand the test of future experience, but we will also use them to regulate our future inquiries. We *embody* the ideas in our theorizing. As Peirce writes in a letter to James, "the individual deed [is] the only real meaning there is [in] the Concept, and yet ... it is not the mere arbitrary force in the deed but the life it gives to the idea that is valuable" (CWJ 8.244, 1897).

Finally, the present account sheds light on how esthetics grounds the other normative sciences in Peirce's classification of the sciences. As Peirce notes, his theory is exactly contrary to hedonism (EP 2:189, 1903), which locates normativity in the *feeling* of pleasure. In contrast, Peirce is clear that the feelings of pain and pleasure are mere accompaniments, or "symptoms," of the activity between the ego and the non-ego (EP 2:379, 1906). His own conception of normativity is grounded in the struggle for a *state* of pleasure. This is the agreement of the faculties of understanding and imagination in reaching determinate concepts by which to subsume (and hence understand) reality. Esthetics recognizes the state of *quietus* to be what is admirable in itself. In theoretical inquiry, what is admirable is to have true judgments, for true judgments accurately represent their objects, and, therefore, future experiences will not bring about occasions for doubt.

Welding into the Continuum

With an explanation of Peircean esthetics with respect to theoretical inquiry in place, we are now in a position to give an account of how we can be welded into the universal continuum, as Peirce mystically states. The focus thus far has been on our theoretical endeavors, and so I begin with Peirce's conception of how reason can weld us into the universal continuum. Recall, though, that Peirce thinks this sort of welding is only superficial. What "penetrates through the whole being of the soul" is our sentimental and volitional welding into the universal continuum. Accordingly, we shall use our account of cognitive welding into the universal continuum to shed light on how we can be sentimentally and volitionally welded into the universal continuum.

Cognitive Welding

In the preceding, I gave an account of Peirce's esthetics according to which the good of teleological reflecting judgments is the correspondence of a proposition to reality such that in believing the proposition, one's mind is brought into conformity with the way the world really is. This is what it means to be cognitively welded into nature or reality: We believe what is true and in this sense – in our beliefs and cognitions – we are of a piece with the reality itself. Indeed, Peirce's theory of facts entails just this view, for Peirce claims that a fact is "so highly a precissively abstract state of things, that it can be wholly represented in a simple proposition" (EP 2:378, 1906) and that facts "hav[e] the structure of a proposition, but [are] supposed to be an element of the very universe itself" (EP 2:304, 1904). On Peirce's view, facts are real, propositional features of the universe. When our judgments are true, their propositional content represents the fact itself. Yet the only difference between a true proposition and a fact is that a true proposition is supposed to be relative to mind, whereas a fact is supposed to be relative to reality. Abstracting away from these relative characteristics, a true proposition just *is* a fact.[5]

There are, moreover, two other ways in which we can become cognitively welded. The first, as just noted, is that we can be welded to reality by having true beliefs. The second is that having true beliefs about the way the world is welds us to other people who have those same beliefs. In a probing essay on Peirce's theory of personhood, Robert Lane (2009) draws our attention to Peirce's distinction between internal and external thoughts. An internal thought is a thought that some specific person has, an individual human's mental state. An external thought is the content of

---

[5] In this respect, Peirce anticipates the view of Jennifer Hornsby (1997). Unfortunately, Peirce's theory of facts has not received due attention from Peirce scholars.

an internal thought, such that the external thought can be instantiated in the minds of different people. Just as a proposition can be expressed in many languages, so the same external thought can be had by many minds. When, for example, two people both believe that triangles are three-sided figures, they have the same external thought even though, insofar as they individually think it, they have different internal thoughts. Abstracting away from who has the thought, it is the same (external) thought. But considered relative to who has the thought, it a different (internal) thought.

Moreover, insofar as two people have different internal thoughts with the same content – the external thought – those two people, Lane maintains, overlap. He writes, "persons in their animal aspect are physically distinct from one another, and in that respect each has a separate identity from the rest. But in their semiotic aspect, persons are not distinct in this way. A person overlaps with others, in that the thought-signs that constitute who she is are shared with others" (2009, 10). In their semiotic aspect – in their beliefs, their conceptions, their lines of thought – persons can share the same external thought even though that thought is instantiated in different organisms. It is in this sense persons become cognitively welded to each other: They have the same external thought. Peirce makes this point when, in 1906, he writes, "signs require at least two Quasi-minds; a *Quasi-utterer* and a *Quasi-interpreter*; and although these two are at one (*i.e., are* one mind) in the sign itself, they must nevertheless be distinct. In the Sign they are, so to say, *welded*" (CP 4.551). Distinct minds are cognitively welded together when their external thoughts are the same.

Of course, individual persons might have the same false belief. Such persons would be welded to each other. They would not, however, be welded into nature, for their beliefs would not be in conformity with the way the world really is. Their judgments would not state the facts just because the propositional content of those judgments would not *be* a fact. To be welded into the universal continuum, it will not be sufficient for all humans to have the same external thoughts; they will also have to have true beliefs about how reality is, about the facts.

This leads us to a third sort of cognitive welding. Raposa (1989, 7–9) quite rightly notes that Peirce inherits his father's belief that in knowing what is true, we are in essence reading the book of nature, which God has written. What God believes – in whatever sense God may be said to have beliefs – is the way that the world is. As we saw in the previous chapter, on Peirce's view the world is rationally ordered, and he believes

God to be the one who rationally orders the universe. He regards this as a consequence of the hypothesis that God is real. Accordingly and in a manner analogous to how persons can be cognitively welded by having the same external thoughts, if there be a God, then we can be welded to God by believing as God believes. That is, so long as we have true beliefs about how God has rationally ordered the universe, we are cognitively welded to God insofar as our beliefs and God's beliefs – again, in whatever sense God has beliefs – overlap. That said, a word of caution is in order here. Peirce, as I argued in the previous chapter, does not provide us with an argument that proves God is real, and he certainly does not think it to be scientifically demonstrated that there is a God. So, the claim that having true beliefs cognitively welds us to God cannot be understood as licensed *theoretically*.

Furthermore, Peirce believes that this sort of cognitive welding into the universal continuum is superficial. He writes, "sentiment also generalizes itself; but the continuum which it forms instead of being like that of reason merely cognitive, superficial, or subjective is ["entitative" and "existential" are crossed out] penetrates through the whole being of the soul" (R 435s). Like conceptions, our sentiments generalize, and, on Peirce's view, the discontinuities of our wills can disappear. The next section aims to make sense of these claims by extending the account of cognitive welding just given to volitional and sentimental welding.

Sentimental and Volitional Welding

In the preceding sections, I developed an account of the summum bonum in Peirce's philosophy by drawing on Kant's *Critique of the Power of Judgment*. However, that account of the summum bonum was restricted to scientific inquiry alone and the manner in which one may be said to be cognitively welded to reality, to others, and to God (should there be a God). Yet in his 1898 lecture and as noted in previous chapters, Peirce concedes that in this "workaday world," we cannot all be engaged in this sort of inquiry. In c. 1905, Peirce writes, "I wish philosophy to be a strict science, passionless and severely fair. I know very well that science is not the whole of life, but I believe in the division of labor among intellectual agencies" (CP 5.537). We cannot all be scientists, let alone philosophers or mathematicians who become cognitively welded into the universal continuum by discovering and believing what is true. So, in this life, if we are to be welded into the universal continuum, we will have to do it in a different way.

It is here Peirce's evolutionary account of the origins of sentiments and instincts and his religious commitments – examined in the previous two chapters – come to the fore. If we cannot all be mathematicians who study the Continuous Eternal, we must instead hope that we shall be welded into the continuum in a process of evolution that brings about a union with nature, with others, and with God. *That* we will be welded together in this way is a claim that is licensed not theoretically but practically, in the conduct of our lives. Let us, then, turn to Peirce's evolutionary account of sentimental conservatism and then to his conception of God and the Absolute.

Sentimental Welding with Nature: As we have seen, in an important but rejected passage from "Philosophy and the Conduct of Life," Peirce maintains that sentiment generalizes. Peirce's claim is that sentiment is also capable of reducing a manifold to unity. In Chapter 2, I gave an account of how this is so. A rabbit, for example, that feels fear when it sees a fox comprehends noncognitively but sentimentally that the fox is a thing to be feared. The rabbit that has no such feeling of fear will be selected against because the fox will eat it. The rabbit that has such a feeling of fear even with respect to nonpredators will be selected against because it will not venture out of its rabbit hole.

This way of sentimentally *comprehending* phenomena is very much akin to cognitively *understanding* phenomena by grouping them under concepts. However, sentimentally, the fox, for instance, is grasped as fearsome by the emotion of fear and not by the concept *being fearsome*. Sentiments help us comprehend the world, as concepts do, but they help us comprehend the world in a noncognitive way. Sentiments do not help us understand the world – to identify laws and gather diverse phenomena under a concept – but they do help us comprehend the world, to grasp diverse phenomena as the same sorts of things. Insofar as our sentiments do this, they weld us into the way nature really is. The fox, to use the previous example, really is something for rabbits to fear.

These sentiments, though, need not be restricted to sentiments that concern survival. The feeling of disapproval we have when we see acts of injustice, for example, is a way of grasping or comprehending injustice in a noncognitive way. Moreover, it is a feeling we may have even when we learn of instances of injustice never before personally encountered and instances of injustice that emerge as a consequence of changes in one's social condition. As an example of the first, consider orthodox Jewish women who seek a divorce but their husbands refuse to grant one. Such women are not permitted to remarry or to date. As someone who is not Jewish and is unfamiliar with Jewish customs, I nevertheless have a feeling of disapproval when I hear about these circumstances and that feeling of disapproval helps me understand that the woman is being wronged. I have this feeling even if I can give no account of what, precisely, is wrong with such customs and can give no account of what, precisely, justice is. As an example of the second – changes in one's social condition – consider worries about persons tampering with electronic voting machines. We feel that it would be an injustice were one to tamper with machines to affect the outcome of a vote. However, worries about such tampering could arise only with the digitization of voting.

Our sentiments about these cases do not help us understand the world conceptually, but they do help us comprehend the world sentimentally. Without understanding the complex ethical questions pertaining to Jewish divorce rights and to the design, programming, and possible manipulation of voting machines, I can nevertheless comprehend the wrongness of these actions by way of my sentiments. Moreover, I can comprehend the wrongness of these actions without having a robust – or even anemic – ethical theory. Peirce is merely noting a feature of sentiments: They help us comprehend diverse phenomena. This might be true even if there are no moral facts independent of our beliefs or feelings about them. Peirce is not making a claim about the nature of moral judgments. Sentiments can be a way of comprehending diverse phenomena regardless of whether or not moral judgments express our beliefs about what the moral facts are.

To be certain and as we saw in Chapter 2, Peirce believes that some sentiments are mere prejudices we inculcate from our society. Other sentiments, though, are based on instincts. Those sentiments that are mere prejudices will likely shift depending on what is advantageous for the person or group who has them. The ones that are instinct based, in contrast, are selected for in evolutionary processes. For instance, a human who is not disgusted by the prospect of eating animal waste is less likely to survive than the one who is. Note that this feeling of disgust tracks a real feature of the universe: The consumption of animal waste really is disadvantageous to one's survival.

Sentimental and Volitional Welding with Others: I have followed Lane in distinguishing between internal and external thoughts, where the former are the thoughts of distinct organisms, whereas the later are the contents of those thoughts, which can be instantiated in any number of organisms. I submit that there is a similar distinction to be made between internal and external sentiments and internal and external volitions.

To begin with the sentiments, consider again the example concerning Jewish divorce rights. Even if a Jewish woman and myself have never met, if we both comprehend the wrongness of the woman's situation according to a sentimental feeling of injustice, we have two different internal sentiments but our external sentiments overlap. We both feel that the action is wrong. Even though we each have our individual feelings (the internal sentiment), our sentiments have the same content (the external sentiment). That content is the noncognitive comprehension of the woman being wronged, a content that is felt rather than believed. Of course, these instances of sentimental overlap need not be restricted to sentiments concerning injustice or morality. Two persons might hope for the same thing, regret the same event, dread the same possible outcome, rejoice in the same good, and so on. I may hope for your success just as you hope for your success, and in this respect our hopes overlap. We can rejoice and mourn for each other, and when we rejoice and mourn for the same things our external sentiments overlap. A musical composition may elicit the same sentiments in us; insofar as it does, we are sentimentally welded. This sort of overlap occurs whenever two people feel the same way about the same thing.

Interestingly, this account of sentimental welding need not be limited to humans alone. Suppose, for example, that I go for a jog with my dog in Southern California. As we are jogging along a path, we come on a mountain lion and both feel fear upon seeing it. This is a sort of sentimental welding insofar as we have the same emotional response to the same (or sufficiently similar) experience of the mountain lion. Our sentimental states overlap (externally) even though we have our distinct feelings individually (internally).

Furthermore, persons and animals may not only feel the same thing but may will the same thing. This occurs, for instance, when two people work together for a common goal. If two people are on a boat in the middle of a lake and wish to make it to shore, they each individually will to row, but they also will that the other person rows. Insofar as the individual person wills that she rows and the other person wills that she rows, they have the same external volition (viz. for her rowing) even though they have differing internal volitions. With respect to animals, if I will that my dog run from the approaching mountain lion and my dog wills the same, then we are volitionally welded.

Because of such sentimental, volitional, and cognitive welding, Peirce states, "your neighbors are, in a measure, yourself, and in far greater measure than, without deep studies in psychology, you would believe. Really, the selfhood you like to attribute to yourself is, for the most part, the vulgarest delusion of vanity" (EP 2:2, 1893). Insofar as our internal thoughts, sentiments, and volitions have the same content – they are the same external thoughts, sentiments, and volitions – we are one with each other. Two people (or, in some cases, animals) who have the same thoughts, sentiments, and volitions would obviously not be the same *organism* and so have distinct internal thoughts, sentiments, and volitions; they would nevertheless overlap with respect to their external thoughts, sentiments, and volitions. In this sense, they are welded together.

Sentimental and Volitional Welding with God: As we saw in Chapter 2 and I have mentioned again here, Peirce believes that our sentiments and instincts have been selected for over successive generations, and it is for this reason that they are trustworthy. Peirce does not believe that human instincts are limited to base survival instincts. As noted in Chapter 2, in 1902 he claims that in addition to the suicultural instincts for self-preservation and the civicultural instincts for the preservation of the stock, we also have specicultural instincts for the embodiment of ideas. Also as noted in the previous chapters, in 1909, he states that humans have instincts for beauty, for morality, and for just reasoning and that these instincts have undergone "upward growth" overall (R 334:F3). Peirce believes that these three instincts both have been selected for over the course of human history and have continued to evolve over the past several thousand years.

Yet as noted at the start of this chapter, Peirce's assertion that these instincts have undergone an "upward growth" is suspicious. It would seem rather that Peirce should claim these instincts have merely undergone change. For growth implies progress, but natural selection has no goal, no end point. It is merely selection for attributes that are more favorable for survival. While survival is certainly a good for the organism or for the species, it makes no sense whatsoever to claim that it is good *full stop*. That the growth can be regarded as upward growth, in any sense that implies progress toward a definite and singular good, is doubtful. Also as noted previously, Liszka has argued that there are really two Peirces when it comes to his conception of the greatest good. The first Peirce believes that the greatest good is the growth of concrete reasonableness and that this is the end point of evolutionary processes. The second Peirce believes that we cannot say in advance what the outcome of evolutionary processes will be. We can only wait and see.

While I concur with Liszka that there are these two strains of thought in Peirce, my view is that they are not in tension. They rather reflect Peirce's distinction between theoretical philosophy and the conduct of life, as I have been indicating. On the one hand, from a theoretical perspective, Peirce cannot claim to know what the outcome of evolutionary processes will be. All we can say is that the good of science, the good of inquiry, is the growth of concrete reasonableness, where concrete reasonableness consists in the admirability of our judgments – their conformity to reality – and their use in regulating and guiding our inquiries. But when it comes to evolutionary processes themselves, we have no power over them; if we did, it would not be evolution. As he had written to James in 1897, "there really is no evolution in the proper sense of the word if individuals can have any arbitrary influence on [what evolves]" (CWJ 8:245). We cannot foresee what will evolve; perhaps even tomorrow will see the total extirpation of life of earth. This is not to deny that we might exert self-control and that this might result in evolutionary development. Peirce writes, "in its higher stages, evolution takes place more and more largely through self-control" (EP 2:344, 1905). Nonetheless, how self-control is exerted must itself be selected for, so that the individual does not exert *any arbitrary* influence over what evolves.

When it comes to the conduct of life, however, Peirce is a theist. His theistic commitments lead him to believe that the ultimate aim of creation is unity with God. God is loving the world into greater and greater degrees of perfection. This process, being worked out in evolution, will ultimately result in the unity of all things with God. In the previous chapter, we saw that Peirce concedes he has no demonstration of this claim (see W 8:203, 1892). Peirce has no strictly scientific and philosophical grounds to believe that becoming welded into the great continuum – into an Absolute in which we have our union with God – will be our joyful Nirvana. He does, though, think that his philosophical position leaves room for it.

Nevertheless, granted that there is a God, we are now in a position to understand how we can be welded together with God not only cognitively but also sentimentally and volitionally. For just as our beliefs can overlap one with those of another insofar as they are the same external thought, so also what we will be done and what we feel can overlap. Likewise, should God be real, we can will to do what God would have us do and feel as God would have us feel. When God and we will that the same thing be done, our external volitions overlap in a manner analogous to how two people in a boat who both will to make it to shore have overlapping wills. Moreover, our sentiments can overlap when we have the same feelings about certain proposed or past courses of action as God. We can take joy in doing what God wills just as God takes joy in us doing as God wills. We can regret our past misdeeds, just as God can regret our past misdeeds. When we have the same sentiments as God – in whatever way God can be said to have sentiments – our sentiments overlap in a manner analogous to how our external thoughts can overlap.

This notion of sentimental and volitional welding with God and with others is a rather mystical view, but it is one Peirce almost certainly gleaned from the work of Henry James Sr. As noted at the end of the previous chapter, Peirce maintains that James provides the "everlasting solution" to the problem of evil when he argues that God needs hatred to love the world into greater and greater loveliness. While this claim does little to solve the problem of evil, it does reveal how Peirce thought of the process of creation. It is a process of growth in which God loves this world into greater degrees of perfection. In a fine essay exploring what Peirce may have gleaned from the work of James Sr., Richard L. Trammell I has pointed to the centrality of community in both of their works. He writes, "the unity of all life is for James the ultimate reality of the universe, before which all shallow individualisms must perish" (1973, 213). Trammell then notes that for Peirce, too, community is of central importance and that this is so is reflected in Peirce's idea "of the continuity of mind, a continuity which extends not just from one person's mind to another person's mind, but also from reason in man to reason in nature" (214).

Trammell, though, cautions against carrying this parallelism too far: "In Peirce's thought, the justification of the primacy of the community is more logical than theological or social" (214). While from a purely philosophical point of view Trammell is surely correct, we also have seen that Peirce thinks that philosophy, as a science, is only part of life. As he states in his drafts for "Philosophy and the Conduct of Life," "the complete generalization, the complete regeneration, of sentiment is religion, which is poetry, but poetry completed" (R 435:35/CP1.676) and "poesy is the universalization and regenerative metamorphosis of personal emotion. As such it fulfils [sic] in a better and objective way the purpose of reasonings. Now a religion is a deeper sort of poetry; and a carping criticism of it is equally odious" (R 436:31). From a religious point of view, God is drawing the universe into a greater harmony, a joyful Nirvana, and this is not brought about solely or even primarily in our intellectual lives but also in our sentiments and instincts developed according to God's providential plan. When all of our external cognitions, wills, and sentiments overlap with God's, then we will all be welded into the universal continuum. This unity is not yet understood in our sciences but can be comprehended in poetry and in religion.

Donna Orange brings out this point in her work on Peirce's developing conception of God. She writes that beginning in his drafts for the Cambridge Conferences Lectures in 1898, Peirce had argued that nature itself syllogizes (see RLT 161). Peirce then began "to endow the fully real with the same religious meaning that Hegel gives to the highest and fullest development of Reason" and that Peirce would "soon begin to speak of creation as the evolution of concrete reasonableness, the growth of reason in nature or God" (1980, 131). Ultimately, Peirce would begin to regard evolutionary processes as part of God's creative operations. Orange notes that for Peirce, creation "is the gradual progress, by means of sporting variation and of the tendency toward habit taking, from chaotic nothingness to concrete reasonableness, the summum bonum. God's creative functions are to introduce the chance variations, and, as Ideal, to draw the world forward toward its full actuality as God's creation" (190). God, though, is not identical to the outcome of evolution: "As ideal end of evolution, God is more than any world of mere facts, possibilities, or finite minds" (191).

The religious person has faith – a *trust* – that God will bring about this ideal of evolution, of growth and development. Philosophers *qua* scientists, though, cannot admit this ideal end. As Peirce writes c. 1902, to use the name of God in philosophy is "like inviting a man to see the body of his wife dissected" (CP 8.125). Religious faith is a living thing. As we saw in the previous chapter, Peirce believes that it is rationally acceptable to allow religious beliefs to guide the conduct of our lives. But that is not to assert that those beliefs are now rationally *well supported*. They are, for Peirce, only suggested as the conclusions of abductions and meet the conditions for being good abductions. Though Peirce does not deny that there can be a philosophy of religion, a science that dissects the idea of God, that is to be kept largely separate from how we conduct our lives. As a science, the philosophy of religion should affect the conduct of life only by the "slow process of percolation" (RLT 106).

Finally, if God does draw the world into a greater and greater unity with God's self, it also follows that individual persons will be brought into a greater and greater unity with one another. We will all come to believe what God believes, will what God wills, and feel as God feels. And insofar as we all have the same content of thought, will, and sentiment, we will be welded not merely with God but with one another. This ultimate unity of all things is that universal continuum into which, on Peirce's view, we all hope to be welded. It is the Absolute. This Absolute is none other than that absolute unity *qua Grenzbegriff*, the monism part and parcel of Peirce's synechism and of which his tychism is a corollary, as explained in Chapter 1.

Conclusion

To conclude this chapter, let us turn to Peirce's 1901 classification of ends, which he develops in his review of Karl Pearson's *The Grammar of Science*.[6] Most broadly, Peirce identifies the ends of action as falling into seven classes. First, one may aim to satisfy a momentary desire, such as when one aims to avoid feelings of blame or to placate another person. Second, one may aim to act according to some rule, such as to satisfy as many desires as possible or to conform to the rules of one's society. Third, one may aim "at bringing about an ideal state of things definitely conceived," such as the maximum possible amount of

---

[6] In the review, he calls it a classification of motives, but in 1903 he corrects himself and states that it is a classification not of motives but of ends (see CP 1.585 and 1.574).

pleasure for all beings (EP 2:59). Fourth, one may aim to bring about some "result not otherwise known in advance." One example of this is sentimentalism, wherein one aims to bring about that state of affairs of which the human heart may approve or disapprove. A second example is evolutionism, where the aim is merely "whatever the operation of cosmical causes may be destined to bring about" (EP 2:59). Fifth, one may aim to act only in accordance with what we pronounce to be true or what is reasonable. Sixth, one may aim to "generaliz[e] or assimilate[e] elements in truth" (EP 2:59). Seventh, one may aim to act in accordance with that "living reason for the sake of which the psychical and physical universe is in process of creation" (EP 2:59). Peirce calls this religionism.

By now it should be clear that on Peirce's view, not all of these ends are inconsistent with one another, and we might endorse several of them depending on the context in which we are thinking about the end of our actions. That context is whether we are considering the summum bonum from a purely theoretical point of view or from the point of view of the conduct of our lives. Patently, the aim of the sciences is the sixth, to generalize and to assimilate elements in truth. This is what I have been arguing for in my discussion of Peirce's esthetics viewed in light of Kant's *Critique of the Power of Judgment*. Yet, as Peirce states, this is not the whole of life. Independently of our scientific endeavors, the universe is evolving and changing. This introduces Peirce's fourth class. With respect to evolutionary processes and from a purely theoretical point of view, it is true that we do not know in advance what the outcome will be. When it comes to the conduct of our lives, however, the purely theoretical view does not preclude our faith that evolutionary processes embody some living reason, a purpose for which the universe in all of its respects is in a process of creation, Peirce's seventh class. Moreover, as our sentiments are selected for in evolutionary processes, the hope is that these too will embody that living reason for creation. And finally, that leaving reason for creation, Peirce believes, will bring about an ideal state of things definitely conceived, his third class. That ideal state is not the mantra of utilitarianism but his own mathematical and mystical vision in which we are prepared for a joyful Nirvana, when our individuality melts away and we are welded into the universal continuum, a perfect union of our cognitions, sentiments, and will with the Divine Love.

5 | Self-Control and Moral Responsibility

The drafts of Peirce's 1898 lecture "Philosophy and the Conduct of Life" reveal his bitterness at being shut out of academia as well as a deeply critical attitude toward those who think what ultimately matters in life is comfort and making money. He complains that Harvard was established so "that the *élite* of her youths may be aided to earning comfortable incomes and living softly cultured lives" (R 435:2/CP 1.650). He sarcastically remarks, "when I received the honor of a call to lecture so near the sacred precincts of Athletics ... I thought there was no more needful word that I could utter than a solemn warning against any harmful overstraining of the reasoning powers" (R 436:1). In the lecture itself, he says, "I do not want to hold forth the slightest promise that I have any philosophical wares to offer you which will make you either better men or more successful men" (RLT 108).

When we compare these comments to Peirce's assessment of his own life's work, the difference is striking. At the very end of the Cambridge Conferences Lectures, he remarks that if anyone in his audience should decide to "select for his life's explorations a region very little trodden" (RLT 268), he will make great discoveries. However, "he will find that he has condemned himself to an isolation like that of Alexander Selkirk. He must be prepared for almost a lifetime of work with scarce one greeting" (RLT 268). Selkirk was a Scottish sailor who lived for four years marooned on an uninhabited island of the South Pacific. Such did Peirce regard his own condition: a castaway, isolated in Milford, Pennsylvania, and marooned on an uncharted island of ideas for which he could find no audience. This was not a comfortable life; Peirce was absolutely destitute. Nonetheless, he regarded his sacrifices as for a greater good. He thought that his self-sacrifice would yield great benefits for humankind in some indefinite future. Indeed, peeved that for the Cambridge Conferences Lectures of 1898, James had asked him not to lecture on logic, Peirce wrote arrogantly in reply,

Soon your engineers will find it better to leave great works unbuilt rather than go through the necessary calculations. And Harvard is only a little in advance of the rest of the country on this road, & this country a little in advance of Europe. The Japanese will come in & kick us out, and in the fullness of time *he* will come to the questions which my philosophy answers, & with patience he will find the key, as I have done. (CWJ 8.330)

Yet we might be suspicious of this characterization. Is not Peirce himself ultimately doing what he wants to do? To be sure, Peirce does not desire to live in penury. But he does desire to spend his time studying logic and philosophy and, presumably, he would prefer that to wealth. Furthermore, in "Philosophy and the Conduct of Life," Peirce claims that "Reason is of its very essence egotistical" and that people "fancy that they act from reason when, in point of fact, the reasons they attribute to themselves are nothing but excuses which unconscious instinct invents to satisfy the teasing 'whys' of the *ego*" (RLT 111). This would seem to open Peirce's view to an objection: Perhaps all we are ever able to do is to pursue our own pleasures and avoid personal pains. In that case, whether we are Harvard men aiming to live lives of comfort or Peirceans toiling away in obscurity with the dim hope of being welded into the universal continuum, we are at root always motivated by the desire for our own pleasures and avoiding any unnecessary pains.

This is the theory of psychological hedonism (PH): All of our actions are ultimately motivated by a desire for our own pleasure or an aversion to our own pain. The philosophical rise of PH coincides with the rise of the mechanical philosophy, which Peirce characterizes as Boyle's "doctrine that 'the phaenomena of the world are physically produced by the mechanical affections of the parts of matter, and that they operate on one another according to mechanical laws'" (R 435:19). It is not hard to understand why these two theories should coincide philosophically: If what motivates us to act is pleasure and pain, we can understand all action as a consequence of mechanistic causes. Namely, we are moved toward those things that cause pleasure and are moved away from those things that cause pain, keeping in mind that a complex set of causes might be acting on us at any given time. As we shall see momentarily, Peirce maintains that the mechanical hypothesis also sought to explain all motion in terms of "attractions and repulsions."

Here we touch on another theme found in the letters and drafts for "Philosophy and the Conduct of Life" but ultimately omitted from the lecture itself. If the mechanical hypothesis is true, it would seem that PH is the best account of motivation. But is the mechanical hypothesis true? As early as 1892, Peirce understood that it is not, as most of us believe now given the discoveries of quantum physics. But allowing for randomness is nature – as Peirce's tychism does – does not preserve freedom of the will (or whatever sort of freedom is necessary for moral responsibility). Peirce, then, will need a separate account of what sort of freedom is required for moral responsibility. Matters are further complicated when we consider his theism. In a 1905 letter, Peirce maintains, "the God of my theism is not finite. That won't do at all. For to begin with, existence is reaction, and therefore no existent can be *clear supreme*" (CP 8.262). Yet this raises questions concerning divine foreknowledge and freedom. For if God foreknows all that we shall do, then it would seem to follow that we have no choice in the matter. Psychological hedonism, the mechanical hypothesis, and God's fore-knowledge, then, would all seem to foreclose freedom of the will and moral responsibility. Whatever we do, we must do. And if we must do it, then we cannot be held morally responsible for it.

The Mechanical Hypothesis and Divine Foreknowledge

James's "The Dilemma of Determinism"

As I argued at length in Chapter 1, Peirce's "Philosophy and the Conduct of Life" was written with James's *The Will to Believe* in mind. Although the issues of the mechanical hypothesis and God's foreknowledge do not make an appearance in that lecture, they do appear in the letters and drafts for the lecture. As noted in the first chapter, Peirce's contentious claim in the lecture that belief has no place in science is first made in the drafts at the end of a long discussion of why scientists are coming to conclude that the mechanical hypothesis is false.

William James had taken up the problems posed by the mechanical hypothesis and divine foreknowledge in "The Dilemma of Determinism," published in *The Will to Believe*. In objecting to determinism, James maintains,

The world must not be regarded as a machine whose final purpose is the making real of any outward good, but rather as a contrivance for deepening the theoretic consciousness of what goodness and evil in their intrinsic natures are. Not the doing of good or of evil is what nature cares for, but the knowing of them. Life is one long eating of the fruit of the tree of *knowledge*. (WWJ 6:128)

He proceeds to deny the mechanical philosophy. James, though, offers no reason to think that the mechanical philosophy is false; he only rejects the metaphor of nature as a machine.

James is, moreover, struck by one problem in particular: reconciling God's foreknowledge with free will. To resolve the problem, he conceives of God as finite and in time and as coping with events beyond God's control. He writes,

Belief in free-will is not in the least incompatible with the belief in Providence, provided you do not restrict the Providence to fulminating nothing but *fatal* decrees. If you allow him to provide possibilities as well as actualities to the universe, and to carry on his own thinking in those two categories just as we do ours, chances may be there, uncontrolled even by him, and the course of the universe really ambiguous; and yet the end of all things may be just what he intended it to be from all eternity. (WWJ 6:138)

James proceeds to liken God to an expert chess player who makes moves in response to those of novices (us) to ensure the end that God intends. In a footnote, James concedes that this entails that God is in time. He proceeds to argue that if God were not in time, then God would have to see all things, past and future, as actual and hence this would be a block universe: "Is not the notion of eternity being given at a stroke to omniscience only just another way of whacking upon us the block-universe, and of denying that possibilities exist" (WWJ 6:139n10)?

Peirce on the Mechanical Hypothesis and Divine Foreknowledge

The Correspondence: Although James had originally published "The Dilemma of Determinism" in 1884, when he reprints it in *The Will to Believe* he adds a footnote mentioning Peirce's *Monist* series of the 1890s as being consistent with his own view and shedding important light on the topic of determinism. Accordingly, Peirce's letter of March 13, 1897, ends with him noting that he is "much encouraged at your thinking well of 'tychism.' But tychism is only a part and corollary of the general principle of Synechism" (CWJ 8:245). I discussed this in Chapter 1 in the context of James's pluralism and Peirce's monism. He writes again on March 18, 1897, stating that he has "been much struck with the *Dilemma of Determinism*" (CWJ 5:247). Peirce is especially struck by how James makes the question of determinism and free will amount to whether possibility is a mode of being. He is in agreement but thinks that James has failed to perceive that treating the question of determinism as the question of plurality is the same as treating it as the question of possibility.

Peirce continues to note that he "cannot admit the *will* is free in any appreciable measure" for reasons he states in 1892's "Man's Glassy Essence." Chance may occur only with an approximation to an unstable equilibrium, but "in the act of willing there is no such state of things. The freedom lies in the *choice* which long antecedes the will. *There* a state of nearly unstable equilibrium is found. But this makes a great difference in your doctrine" (CWJ 8:248). It is not the *will* that is free; by the time we will something, we are already determined to do it. If Peirce is correct that there are such unstable equilibria, it follows that the mechanical hypothesis is false. This, though, does not clearly suffice to preserve the sort of freedom necessary for moral responsibility. For if the unstable equilibrium is a state of randomness, then we cannot be held morally responsible for our actions either. I can be no more responsible for actions that are random than I can be for actions that are determined. In neither case do I have control over what I do.

Peirce is also critical of James's comments on God and time, writing "as for the note about God being out of time, it seems to me probable that it was hastily penned." Peirce maintains both that if God is out of time "the difficulty is removed" and that by putting God into time "there is no contradiction between Foreknowledge and Free Will" (CWJ 8:248). Hence, whether or not God is in time, foreknowledge is consistent with free will. Peirce, though, does not elaborate on these claims.

The Drafts: In R 435, Peirce returns to these criticisms of James. Peirce writes that "the last book [of Boethius's the *Consolation of Philosophy*] which [crossed out: most strongly] resembles a modern essay much more than all the rest [n.b. the last six words are a later insertion], is a mere diet of bran for the hungered soul" (R 435:16). Peirce follows this comment with a very long excursus on the origins of the mechanical philosophy and why it is false.

With respect to the first comment, there can be no question of Boethius's final book resembling any modern essay in form, and so Peirce must mean that it resembles *some* modern essay in content. I think it is clear he means James's "The Dilemma of Determinism." For the final book of *The Consolation of Philosophy* is an examination of fate and free will, especially with respect to divine foreknowledge. Boethius contends that God is out of time and so it is a mistake to claim that God has beliefs at any given time. Rather, God has the whole of reality before God's mind atemporally and to say that God has the universe before God's mind "at once" is metaphorical. James's position is not Boethius's in good part because, as Peirce complains in his letter, James does not fully grasp the Boethian view that God is outside of time. Nonetheless, James's essay does resemble Boethius's in claiming that the question of determinism "slides into the question of optimism or pessimism, or, as our fathers called it, 'the question of evil'" (WWJ 6:127). Similarly, Boethius worries that if God foresees all, then all human deeds and desires will have been ordained by God, even the evil ones.

That Peirce has James in mind is made more evident from his long excursus on the mechanical hypothesis. Peirce concludes his discussion of it with the statement that "to a person who, like myself, has been a student of physics for the last 50 years, it seems that the mechanical philosophy, if not refuted, has at any rate been sinking in importance during the greater part of that period" (R 435:23). James, in contrast, has not been a student of physics for 50 years, and so all he can give us is a diet of bran. He does not understand the origins of the mechanical hypothesis or why it has come into doubt. Peirce proposes to offer us a full meal by *showing* that the evidence now weighs against the mechanical hypothesis. It was merely a provisional belief taken up into the cart of inquiry. However, in Peirce's judgment, the evidence is now weighing against the mechanical hypothesis and so it should be kicked off the cart.

Why does Peirce believe the mechanical hypothesis should be kicked off the list of propositions scientists propose to use? As Andrew Reynolds has argued (2002, especially ch. 2), Peirce's primary objection is that the mechanical hypothesis cannot make sense of irreversible natural processes, such as the expansion of a gas to fill the increased volume of a container. On Peirce's view, the position that the *entire universe* is a conservative system in which processes are reversible is overturned by the results of thermodynamics and, in particular, the law of entropy. Accordingly, Reynolds writes, "Nonconservative actions tend to work ... irreversibly toward some final end. As an example of such a final end ... [Peirce] offered the case of thermal equilibrium" (44). As Reynolds argues, Peirce also regards the evolution of the entire universe as non-conservative, flowing from a state of disorder or chaos to a state of perfect regularity and "reasonableness." As discussed in the previous chapter, our aim is to be welded into that reasonable, rational order of the universe.

Peirce also maintains that evolutionary processes are irreversible. He writes in "Evolutionary Love" that *The Origin of Species* found a sympathetic audience in part because the kinetic theory of gases had been developed in the decade immediately preceding its publication in 1859 and so "the idea that fortuitous events may result in a physical law, and further that this is the way in which those laws which appear to conflict with the principle of the conservation of energy are to be explained, had taken a strong hold upon the mind of all who were abreast of the leaders of thought" (W 8:190, 1892). Consequently, Peirce is critical of theories of evolution that treat it merely as a mechanical process. Carl Hausman notes that Peirce likely had Herbert Spencer in mind "as holding a view according to which evolution is explained by mechanical principles" and "the irreversibility of evolutionary developments is central to Peirce's own theory" (1993, 174; see also Reynolds 2002, ch. 4). This is precisely right. Spencer, Peirce maintains, is only a "half-evolutionist" (W 8:102, 1890) because he "makes the evolution of the world depend exclusively upon the principles of mechanics; while according to other evolutionists there are two factors, force and the effect of accidental variations" (W 5:260, 1885). When he criticizes Spencer's theory in 1890, Peirce notes that if evolution "is only a secondary result ... of the conservation of energy" (W 6:398), then "if the directions of motion of all the bodies in the world were at one instant all to be reversed while the velocities remained the same" then the bodies would pass back through all its previous configurations (W 6:399). However, "eggs grow to birds, not birds back to eggs. Yet this cannot be a mathematical consequence of the persistence of force" (W 6:405). As Peirce says, it would "not be evolution, but counterevolution – not growth, but ungrowth, one would think" (W 6:399).

In the drafts for "Philosophy and the Conduct of Life," we find a more detailed, historically oriented criticism of the mechanical hypothesis but still drawing on scientific work involving collisions in ideal gases. Here, he identifies the beginnings of the rejection of the mechanical hypothesis with debates over "the number of constants required to express the elasticity of perfectly elastic bodies" (R 435: 21). To get there, he begins by noting that "the mechanical philosophy in its pre-Newtonian stage is first that the universe is a geometrical diagram with moveable parts [i.e. akin to a clock], and second that it is a purely mechanical automaton not able to develope [sic] any idea or purpose or mode of action that is not put into it at the beginning" (R 435:19). Newton's *Principia*, Peirce maintains, gave the mechanical philosophy "a more precise definition. For what came then to be understood by it was that all the forces and qualities of nature are attractions and repulsions" (R 435:20). These principles were taken to apply not merely to solid bodies such as celestial objects but to atoms themselves. Peirce notes that in John Dalton's memoirs "he never speaks of [atoms] as anything new or of doubtful existence" because Boyle had already adopted the "corpuscular hypothesis" so that he could "conceive chemistry as an application of rigid dynamics" (R 435:18, n.b. this page was not renumbered and so there are two page 18s in R 435). Nonetheless, Peirce maintains that the "full significance" of the mechanical philosophy "was not thoroughly understood until Helmholtz in 1847 published his celebrated paper on the conservation of force" (R 435: 21). Yet Helmholtz, Peirce asserts, had retracted this view by 1881 because he sided with those who claimed that a larger number of constants are requisite to express the elasticity of a perfectly elastic solid body: "[Helmholtz] substantially retracts the proposition that the forces of the universe are attractions and repulsions between pairs of particles, evidently because that is inconsistent with the larger number of elastic constants" (R 435:22).

Although Peirce had rejected a discussion of the mechanical hypothesis for the first lecture of the Cambridge Conferences, he does return to the topic in his sixth and seventh lectures. In the seventh, he notes that the nonconservative laws that "seem to violate the law of energy" (RLT 220) have two characteristics. First, they are finious, that is, they "tend asymptotically toward bringing about an ultimate end state of things" (RLT 220), such as thermal equilibrium in the case of thermodynamics. Second, they are irreversible. Notably, though, Peirce acknowledges that these characteristics may not be "*criteria* of the conservative or nonconservative character of an action" and so apparently non conservative action might possibly be explained by conservative action. As Kenneth Laine Ketner and Hilary Putnam explain, Peirce hedges his claims here because he is aware that Ludwig Boltzmann had given an "explanation of irreversibility [that] makes irreversibility fully compatible with the time-reversible causation of Newtonian physics" (1992, 88). Nevertheless, Peirce thinks that the better explanation is that there is such nonconservative action. After all, he believes that evolution is also nonconservative. As he states in the rejected portion of R 435, "it is true that a pretty seriously modified form of the mechanical philosophy is still tenable; but nobody has succeeded in imagining how solid bodies can be constituted" (R 435:22).

Moreover, in the seventh lecture, he argues that *mental* action is nonconservative. He defends this claim by developing an account of the association of ideas. He maintains that ideas decrease in vividness but that associated ideas become more vivid or dimmer "according to the strength of the associations" (RLT 236) so that dim ideas that become associated with vivid ideas become more vivid, for example. The connections among ideas, though, are undergoing continual changes. As a consequence of these connections being made, a vivid idea connected with a dimmer idea makes it more likely that the dimmer idea will be called up on the next occasion the vivid idea is had. This, though, weakens the associations of these ideas with other ideas. Peirce concludes, "that the mental action, as so described, is upon the surface, at least, causational and not conservative is quite obvious" (RLT 237). Peirce's claim that this is "obvious" is surely based on a superficial analogy between how ideas become associated and how molecules interact, for he admits "it would be possible to suppose that it was a conservative action affected to such a degree by resistances, that the momentum had no sensible effect" (RLT 237). Clearly, Peirce did not think that the final nail had been put in the mechanical hypothesis's coffin. What he did foresee was that the advancements in the sciences were calling the mechanical hypothesis into question such that a better strategy might be to kick the hypothesis off the cart of science, to strike it from the list of propositions scientists propose to use. Whatever we may think of Peirce's own arguments against the mechanical hypothesis, there can be little doubt today that he was on the right side of the debate.

In sum, Peirce rejects the mechanical hypothesis in favor of his theories of tychism and synechism. As explained in Chapter 1, Peirce regards his tychism as a corollary of synechism. Moreover, he believes we can reconcile belief in an infinite God with human freedom by putting God outside of time, as Boethius does. But, of course, it does not follow from the falsity of the mechanical hypothesis that psychological hedonism (PH) is false as well. Furthermore, as I have indicated, endorsing tychism does not give us the sort of freedom necessary for moral responsibility. In 1903, Peirce would provide an extensive critique of PH, and it is his criticism of it to which we turn now. Peirce's rejection of PH is unique in that it is based on a detailed descriptive analysis of self-controlled action, and he maintains that his account preserves moral responsibility.[1]

Psychological Hedonism

We saw in Chapter 4 that Peirce's own theory of pleasure is that pleasure is a state and not primarily a feeling, though the state of pleasure is typically accompanied with feelings of pleasure. We also saw in Chapter 2 that Peirce is critical of hedonism – understood to be the view that we ought to seek out those things that bring us feelings of pleasure and shun those things that cause pain – on the grounds that pain and exertion are "the safeguards of our race." Consequently, those who endorse hedonism are "disseminators of the seeds of racial extinction" (R 334:B2). And yet the theory of psychological hedonism – that all of our actions are ultimately motivated by a desire for our own pleasure or an aversion to our own pain[2] – would seem to imply that we are all hedonists, whether or not we wish to be so. Moreover, the truth of PH is often thought to have important implications for ethics. In particular, it would call our commonsense notions of morality into question. C. D. Broad writes,

For, if Psychological Hedonism were true, a desire to do what is right could not be ultimate, it must be subordinate to the desire to get or prolong pleasant experiences and to avoid or cut short unpleasant ones.

Now it is plain that such consequences as these conflict sharply with commonsense notions of morality. If we had been obliged to accept Psychological

---

[1] There is, to my knowledge, only one essay discussing Peirce's views in relation to egoism, and it is Gary Bedell's essay of 1980, but his focus is on rational and ethical egoism.

[2] A variant of PH is that all of our actions are motivated by a belief that the course of action will cause pleasure or avoid pain. We shall set that variant aside for our present purposes.

Egoism, in any of its narrower forms, on its merits, we should have had to say: "So much the worse for the common-sense notions of morality!" (1950, 114)

PH states that our ultimate motivation is our own pleasure or our own pain. It does not deny we may have nonultimate motivations that are other directed. For example, if I cook a pie, my ultimate motivation is the pleasure it brings me (perhaps either in the act of cooking or in the act of eating it), but that does not preclude a nonultimate motivation, for example, the pleasure my friends will take in the pie, too (which is not to be conflated with the pleasure I take in my friends taking pleasure in the pie). Elliott Sober (1989) makes this clear in his distinction between the extreme and moderate egoist. The extreme egoist's sole motivation is her pleasure, such that the interests of others in no way figure into her preference structure. The moderate egoists *ultimate* motivation is her pleasure, such that while the interests of others figure into her preference structure, when her pleasure is at odds with another's interests the moderate egoist opts for her pleasure. More briefly, PH is not the theory that our *sole* motive is pleasure. Furthermore, PH does not claim we will in fact enjoy some pleasure or avoid some pain when we act. I may jog out of the motivation to reap the pleasures of good health but be struck by a car and suffer permanent, debilitating injuries before I have taken 10 strides. I was ultimately motivated by the pleasures of good health even though I will not in fact enjoy such pleasures.

Peirce's Account of PH

In 1903's "What Makes a Reasoning Sound?" Peirce succinctly articulates PH thusly:

We find in some of the old writers a fallacious argument to prove that there is no distinction of moral right and wrong. The argument runs as follows:

The distinction between a good act and a bad one, if there be any such distinction, lies in the motive. But the only motive a man can have is his own pleasure. No other is thinkable. For if a man desires to act in any way, it is because he takes pleasure in so acting. Otherwise, his action would not be voluntary and deliberate. Thus, there is but one possible motive for action that has any motive; and consequently, the distinction of right and wrong, which would be a distinction between motives, does not exist. (EP 2:244)

With his phrase "action that has any motive," Peirce apparently means to exclude what, today, are regarded as behaviors. Note also that Peirce's characterization of PH here is overly strong, treating PH as the theory that the desire for pleasure is the sole motive of action. Nonetheless, in this passage, Peirce presents PH, presents an argument for PH, and indicates that if it were true it would call our commonsense notions of morality into question.

Peirce refers to some "old writers," and he surely has at least Thomas Hobbes in mind. This particular interpretation of Hobbes's moral theory owes itself to Théodore Jouffroy's *Introduction to Ethics*, which was a popular work in Peirce's time (see Liszka 2012, 45) and which Peirce acknowledges to be one of the texts on ethics he studied early in his life (see EP 2:189, 1903). Here is what Jouffroy writes of Hobbes:

[Hobbes] asserts that the end of *every* action is the pursuit of pleasure, or the escape from pain; and, generalizing his observation, he thus expresses the formula which is the principle of his system – *well-being is the end of man.*

... If the end of every act is pleasure, it follows necessarily that the universal motive of every act is the desire of pleasure.

... There may be, therefore, as many modes of right conduct as there are persons, because every one may have his own way of conceiving of happiness and of the modes of attaining it, and all modes are in themselves equally good. (1851, 281 and 286)

Here we see the same ideas we find in Peirce: The ultimate motive to action is one's own pleasure or the avoidance of one's own pain. Consequently, every action is equally good; that is, there is no distinction of right and wrong. Two other thinkers Peirce may have had in mind as endorsing PH are Bernard Mandeville, whose *The Fable of the Bees* maintains that vice and self-love are necessary for the flourishing of civil society, and Claude Adrien Helvétius, whose *Treatise on Man* reduces all of the virtues to self-love and contends that self-love is the passion that excites all action. Peirce mentions Mandeville's *The Fable of the Bees* at W 8:189 and makes passing reference to Helvétius at W 8:185, both references being made in 1892's "Evolutionary Love."

Setting aside Peirce's historical reference, his statement of the argument for PH and its implication for morality is this:

(1) A person adopts a line of conduct only if she takes pleasure in so acting.
(2) If the person takes pleasure in so acting, then her ultimate motive to action is her own pleasure.
(3) Therefore, if a person adopts a line of conduct, then her ultimate motive to action is her own pleasure (PH).
(4) If pleasure is the ultimate motive to every action, then there can be no distinction between a good act and a bad one.
(5) Therefore, there is no distinction between a good act and a bad one.

The conclusions (3) and (5) are prima facie implausible. In fact, accepting (5) would threaten the entire enterprise of normative ethics, not to mention our commonsense notions of morality.

But what is wrong with this argument? Though it is not Peirce's, our immediate inclination may be to reject premise (2). Just because pleasure accompanies every act, it does not follow that the ultimate motive of action is one's own pleasure. In like manner, just because salivating accompanies every act of eating, it does not follow that the ultimate motive of eating is one's own salivation. This strategy is wanting, however. For one, it is obvious that we sometimes are – perhaps predominantly are – motivated by pleasure. As Sober writes of such a claim, "The idea behind this analogy is that pleasure is an artifact, not a cause, of deliberative action ... [I]t presents an altogether unreal picture of human motivation. The idea that pleasure is a mere epiphenomenon does not characterize people of flesh and blood" (1989, 91). Importantly, Sober's comment is not meant as a defense of premise (2) – for that it would fall far short – but to show that an appeal to pleasure as a mere accompaniment of action offers an implausible account of motivation.

More importantly, there is a reason to think premise (2) is true, and that reason follows directly from a defense of premise (1). To begin that defense, it is obvious that we sometimes have conflicting and mutually unsatisfiable first-order desires. For example, I may desire to spend my morning (a) drinking beer, eating donuts, and watching television; (b) exercising; or (c) volunteering at a charity. Suppose I can spend my morning in only one of these ways (in this fictional example my exercise routines are lengthy) but desire to do all three. At this level, I am in something like the quandary of Buridan's ass. Halfway between water and food, equally hungry and thirsty, it is strung on the bow of two desires. However, I will not die as Buridan's ass does. For I have a second-order desire (so a defender of PH might tell us) to satisfy some one of my first-order desires rather than to satisfy none of them at all. I at least have the second-order desire to be pleased by the satisfaction of one of my first-order desires. Hence, I will act in some way, perhaps even choosing (c) to volunteer at a charity. What will ultimately motivate me to choose (c), though, is the desire to please myself by satisfying at least some one of my first-order desires.[3]

Now comes the generalizing step: Granted this is the correct account of motivation when we have conflicting and mutually unsatisfiable first-order desires, it is also the right account whenever we act at all. For if we act, then we will to so act. If we will to so act, we have both the first-order desire to so act and the second-order desire to satisfy that first-order desire. Hence, if we act, then we desire (second order) to satisfy a desire (first order). Now, the satisfaction of our second-order desires brings us pleasure, since it pleases us to satisfy at least one of our first-order desires rather than none at all. Hence, if we act, then we are enjoying the second-order pleasure of so acting. That is the defense of premise (1).[4]

Furthermore, we now see why premise (2) is true given this defense of premise (1). The pleasure we desire is the pleasure that comes from satisfying a second-order desire to satisfy a first-order desire. But that pleasure itself is a second-order pleasure. Indeed, doing the action involved in my first-order desire – volunteering at a charity, say – may bring me no pleasure whatsoever. Perhaps I will end up hating the volunteer work. Perhaps I will despise the people with whom

---

[3] Sober makes a related point when he notes, "people who are first-order altruists may wish to remain so. They thereby have second-order preferences that are self-directed . . . Seen only from the point of view of their first-order wants, their actions are altruistic. But if we interpret their actions from the vantage point of second-order preferences, the diagnosis may seem to change. They wish to remain altruists . . . In choosing to act altruistically, they are satisfying their self-directed preference to remain the kind person they are (1989, 98–99). A similar point applies to those who wish to become altruists, such that "people aiming above all at becoming first-order altruists are themselves second-order egoists" (98).

[4] This line or argumentation may suggest the criticism of Butler's Stone (that desires only have for their objects external things and not the pleasure arising from the satisfaction of the desire), but for a critique of Butler's Stone, see Sober (1992).

I volunteer. In that case, I gain no first-order pleasure. Nevertheless, I still gain the second-order pleasure of having satisfied my first-order desire. In fact, ultimately, that is why I chose to volunteer in the first place. I wanted to satisfy some one of my first-order desires rather than none at all. Hence, my own second-order pleasure is the ultimate motivation of my action, which is what premise (2) states.

The picture, then, is as follows: I have first-order desires. But just because I desire to do something, it does not follow I do it. After all, I desire to do all sorts of things I do not do. Rather, for me to do some action voluntarily, I both have to desire (first order) to do it and desire (second order) to satisfy that desire (first order). Now doing the action – that is to say, satisfying my first-order desire – may or may not bring me a first-order pleasure. Yet whether or not it does, I always do get a second-order pleasure from satisfying my second-order desire, since it pleases me to satisfy some one of my first-order desires rather than none at all. As Harry Frankfurt (1971) has rightly explained, there are many more complexities to be ferreted out here. For example, one may have a second-order desire to have a first-order desire without desiring that the first-order desire be effective. Also, one may have third-order desires pertaining to her second-order desires. I shall set these complexities aside, for if Peirce's descriptive analysis of self-controlled action is accurate, then there is no need to appeal to second-order desires at all.[5]

The previous discussion also enables us to gain some clarity with respect to the argument Peirce discusses in favor of PH. For with respect to premise (1), it turns out that if I do an action, it is not because I expect the action itself to bring me pleasure. Rather, it is because I expect the pleasure accompanying the satisfaction of my second-order desire to satisfy a first-order desire. What satisfies my first-order desire

---

[5] Of course, Frankfurt's second-order volitions are themselves second-order desires, and so it also follows that if Peirce's descriptive analysis is correct, then Frankfurt's theories of selfhood, free will, and free action are doubtful. However, an examination of Peirce's views on these topics, especially in contrast with Frankfurt's, is outside of the purview of the present book. See Holmes (1966), Petry (1992), Hookway (2000), and Pape (2012) for studies on Peirce's theory of self-control and Colapietro (1989) and Lane (2009) for examinations of Peirce's theory of the self. Most of the work on Peirce's theory of self-control has focused on what Peirce calls logical self-control, that is, self-controlled reasoning. None of them has explored Peirce's theory of self-controlled action in relation to psychological hedonism. Perhaps more curiously, neither do they explicate Peirce's descriptive analysis of self-control.

is doing the action. That may or may not be pleasurable. What satisfies my second-order desire is satisfying a first-order desire. That always is pleasurable, and it is that second-order pleasure that ultimately motivates every action I do.

It is important to note that this is not the so-called argument from our strongest desires. The argument here is not that we always act on our strongest desires, so we always do what we most want to do, which means we are always pursuing our own interests. To the contrary, the argument here is more modest. It takes as its premise that we always act on some desire (first order), whether or not it is our strongest. Since acting on a desire (first order) requires that we also desire (second order) to so act, we will always at least derive the second-order pleasure of satisfying a second-order desire, and that second-order pleasure is what ultimately motivates us to act at all.

Peirce's Descriptive Analysis of Self-Controlled Action

With the preceding in place, we are now in a position to understand why Peirce begins his criticism of the argument for PH with the otherwise cryptic (because it is neither introduced nor explained) comment, "it is so far from being true that every desire necessarily desires its own gratification, that, on the contrary, it is impossible that a desire should desire its own gratification" (EP 2:245, 1903; see also EP 2:166 and 169, 1903). The suggestion Peirce is rejecting is that if I have a desire, then I also have the desire to satisfy the desire. My desire (first order) desires (second order) – or at least arouses a second-order desire for – its own satisfaction. Perhaps the position Peirce intends to echo is that of Francis Hutcheson. Hutcheson writes, "Desire does never arise from a View of obtaining that *Sensation of Joy*, connected with the Success or Gratification of Desire; otherwise the strongest Desires might arise toward any Trifle, or an event in all respects indifferent" (1756, 16–17). If desires arose out of the promise of the pleasure attendant on satisfying the desire (if desires desired the pleasure of their own satisfaction), we could arouse any desire at all simply by contemplating the pleasure attendant on satisfying the desire.

Although there can be little doubt Peirce was familiar with Hutcheson's views – he controversially claims that Hume's *Principles of Morals* "merely modified Hutcheson's doctrine" (EP 2:71, 1901) – it must also be admitted that Peirce does not even attempt to prove it is impossible that a desire should desire its own gratification. Moreover, as I have presented the argument, it does not hinge on desires desiring their own gratification but on having a second-order desire to satisfy a first-order desire. Whether that second-order desire arises from a first-order desire is a different question. In fact, to claim that second-order desires do arise from the first-order desire would seem to threaten an infinite regress if we have conflicting and mutually unsatisfiable first-order desires. For then we should have corresponding second-order desires to satisfy each of our first-order desires, third-order desires to satisfy each of our second-order desires, and so on. At any rate, what Peirce does show is what he needs to show: The desire (second order) to satisfy a desire (first order) is not necessary for voluntary action. As we shall see, his account also entails that premise (1) and PH are false. Peirce's argument against premise (1) is unique in that it takes its cue from a descriptive analysis of what is involved in self-controlled action. Peirce thinks that if we carefully attend to all of the elements that go into typical cases of self-control, we will find that action is not a consequence of a second-order desire to satisfy a first-order desire but of a **determination** to act in some way.

What are the elements involved in self-controlled action? Note that this question is different from the question of what a self-controlled action is. The question is not asking for a set of necessary and sufficient conditions that define self-controlled action as opposed to other sorts of actions. Rather, the question asks for a description of what is involved in self-controlled action. To draw an analogy, we might think of a self-controlled action as a molecule that is the result of a chemical reaction. The posed question asks for the elements that make up a self-controlled action and how they interrelate. Peirce's aim in ascertaining the elements that go into self-controlled action is to discern which element is a necessary spring to action. That element, whatever it may be, is the motivation for our actions. As we have already seen, the person who endorses PH as defended earlier maintains the necessary element is a second-order desire, the satisfaction of which is pleasurable. However, Peirce will give us a reason to doubt that account.

The preceding comments call for an account of what Peirce understands by a motivation. I have just suggested that Peirce thinks motivations are springs to action, the gears and pulleys that give rise to action. This account is fitting with the view of Hutcheson, who characterizes motives as springs of action (1753, 159 and 201) and of Peirce's contemporary, Henry

Sidgwick (see *The Methods of Ethics*, Book III, Chapter XII), who acknowledges his indebtedness to Hutcheson. Yet here we encounter a textual issue in understanding Peirce's position. For in 1903, Peirce refers to 1901's "Review of Pearson's Grammar," stating that he there "enumerated a number of ethical classes of motives, meaning by a motive, not a spring of action, but an aim or end appearing to the agent" (CP 1.585). We examined this list of ends in the conclusion of Chapter 4. But in 1906, he writes that we should not confuse "an ideal of conduct with a motive to action. Every action has a motive; but an ideal only belongs to a line [of] conduct which is deliberate" (CP 1.574). I think we should read Peirce as stating in 1903 that in 1901 he did confuse motives and ends or ideals. In 1903, he clarifies that when he spoke of motives in 1901, he really meant ends. However, come 1903 and 1906, he does think of a motive as a spring of action.[6] Every action has some spring. Yet just because it has some spring, it does not follow it accords with an ideal. For example, a person yelling "Fore!" in conjunction with my desire or determination not to be struck by a stray golf ball motivates me to duck. It is a spring of action. However, my action is not deliberate or performed in accordance with some ideal. It misdescribes the experience to say that I have the ideal not to be struck in the head by a stray golf ball, even though obviously I do not want to be struck in the head. Clearly, to describe motivations as the springs of action is highly metaphorical. Nevertheless, the metaphor is quite appropriate for Peirce's purposes. For a motivation is, on Peirce's view, an efficient – even mechanistic – cause. A motivation causes an action, and it can cause an action without any reference to an ideal. Consequently, motivations are not final causes, even if acting toward a final cause requires some motivation.[7]

Let us now move to Peirce's description of self-controlled action. We are all sufficiently familiar with self-controlled actions so as to differentiate them from actions or behaviors that are not self-controlled. For example, my heartbeat is not self-controlled. I do not exercise control over my dreams (though some people can). If a stranger grabs my arm and forces me to punch him in the face, my punch is not self-controlled, though it is controlled by another self. In contrast, my action of cooking a meal rather than ordering in is self-controlled. My action of writing this

---

[6] On these points, see also Liszka (2012, 58–59).
[7] For more on Peirce's view of final causality, see Short (2007, 91–151) and Liszka (2012, 55–58).

chapter is self-controlled. My future action – planned for this afternoon – of repairing a crack in my sidewalk will be self-controlled.

Peirce thinks that in typical cases of self-controlled action, eight elements interact to make up the resultant molecule of self-controlled action, though Peirce stresses that not all of them are involved in every case of self-controlled action:

1. The first element is an **ideal**. Ideals describe the sorts of conduct befitting "a rational animal in his particular station in life" (EP 2:245, 1903). Peirce states that ideals are "in the main ... imbibed in childhood. Still, they have gradually been shaped to his personal nature and to the ideas of his circle of society rather by a continuous process of growth than by any distinct acts of thought" (EP 2:246).

2. The second is an **intention** to make one's own conduct conform to those ideals. It is important to note that this is an intention and not a desire. I can intend to act in accordance with an ideal even though I do not desire to do so. For example, I may intend to volunteer at a charity even though what I desire to do is drink beer, eat donuts, and watch television.

3. The third is a **formulation of rules of action**. The formulae may be quite vague, but such rules are "convenient and serve to minimize the effects [of] future inadvertence" (EP 2:246). As we shall see momentarily, these rules of action are what become our moral beliefs.

4. The fourth is **foreseeing** that there will be an opportunity to put one's rules of action into effect. "Thereupon," Peirce writes, "a certain gathering of his forces will begin to work, and this working of his being will cause him to consider how he will act" (EP 2:246).

5. The fifth element is a **resolution** to act in a certain way on the foreseen occasion. This resolution is a plan of action. This is one element that Peirce explicitly notes is sometimes lacking from self-controlled action. It may be lacking just because there is insufficient time to form a resolution.

6. The sixth element is the **process of imprinting the resolution** on one's nature, so to speak. Peirce writes that it is "similar to" that of impressing a lesson on one's memory (EP 2:246).

7. The seventh element is a **determination**. The determination is a consequence of imprinting the resolution on one's nature. Nonetheless, one can be determined to act in some way even if one has not had the

opportunity to imprint a lesson on one's own nature, as is the case when we are determined to act in some way because of our upbringing. In either case, the determination is what makes a person act as he or she does. Peirce writes that it is "a really efficient agency, such that if one knows what its special character is, one can *forecast* the man's conduct on the special occasion" (EP 2:246).

8. The eighth and final element is a **capacity for comparing** the results of the action to the ideal.

Peirce's account is most readily grasped with an example. Consider that as a naturally introverted person and a philosopher, I am quite socially awkward and can be rather boorish. Nevertheless, from various media such as television, books, and movies as well as from my interactions with others, I have imbibed an **ideal** of extroversion and joviality. I **intend** to act in a manner conforming to that ideal. I begin by **formulating rules of action**. For example, I make it a rule not to talk about philosophy outside of professional contexts. I adopt the rule of always doing whatever plans my (reasonable) friends propose. I make it a rule to always have on hand some joke or story to tell.

Peirce states that reflecting on these rules of actions modifies our moral habits: "Reflection upon these rules, as well as upon the general ideas behind them, has a certain effect upon his disposition, so that what he naturally inclines to do becomes modified" (EP 2:246). That is, these rules become living beliefs through reflection on them and on our ideals. As early as 1877 (and likely much earlier), Peirce adopted the position of Alexander Bain that beliefs are dispositions – or more precisely, habits – of action: "Belief does not make us act at once, but puts us into such a condition that we shall behave in a certain way, when the occasion arises" (W 3:247, 1877). Later, he suggests a distinction between beliefs that are mere sayings or thoughts and beliefs that are living, as when he writes of religion that it "can be identified with a belief only provided that belief be a living belief – a thing to be lived rather than said or thought" (CP 6.439, 1893). In the present context, Peirce maintains that the formulation of rules of action and reflection on them produce in us new *moral beliefs*, new habits of action. Accordingly, on Peirce's view all moral beliefs are habits of action, though of course not all habits are moral beliefs. Cheryl Misak (2000, 73–76) draws out the normative implications of these rules becoming moral beliefs. If formulating these rules of action produces new beliefs, it also follows that they entail certain normative commitments. For example, for one to believe or to assert p entails that the person is committed to the consequences of p's being true, to defending p, to giving it up on the basis of future evidence, and so on. This insight has important consequences for moral discourse and deliberation, which Misak masterfully explores. The key point here is that these rules of action imply normative commitments that can be subject to criticism.

As explained in Chapter 2, Peirce distinguishes between inherited habits and acquired habits. The former are instincts. The latter are acquired either by repeated action or imagination. He writes, "multiply reiterated behavior of the same kind, under similar combinations of percepts and fancies, produces a tendency, – the *habit*, – actually to behave in a similar way under similar circumstances in the future" and that "*reiterations in the inner world, – fancied reiterations, – if well-intensified by direct effort, produce habits*, just as do reiterations in the outer world [i.e., repeated action]" (EP 2:413, 1907). That is, as noted, reflection on our rules of conduct and ideals produces a tendency to act in accordance with our rules of action when occasions in which they may apply arise. As noted in Chapter 2, inherited habits are also subject to a degree of control. Both inherited and acquired habits are general in the sense that they inform how we *would* act in sufficiently similar circumstances.

To continue with the example, I **foresee** that there will be some occasion to put some of my rules into practice. Suppose, for example, that a friend has set me up on a date. I know that dating can be a rather disappointing affair for the other person given my introverted and boorish personality. I realize that on my date I will need to put my plan of action into practice. At this point, there is a summoning of my powers. I **resolve** to act in accordance with my rules of conduct and begin to **imprint on my nature** a plan of action. My plan is this: When I meet my date, I shall smile broadly, give her a hug, and tell her how happy I am to see her. This is in contrast to what I usually do: say hello and uncomfortably stare at my shoes while I ask if she is ready to go. When she talks, I shall lean in, look into her eyes, and nod regularly. I shall do everything in my power not to lean back, fold my arms, and glance out the window, even though prolonged eye contact makes me uncomfortable. I shall come up with jokes to tell, questions to ask, lines of conversation to pursue. When she begins discussing topics tangentially related to philosophy, such as the themes of the recent book she read or the movie she watched, I'll do everything in my power to avoid mentioning how it relates to C. S. Peirce or psychological hedonism. I replay the anticipated events of the evening over and over in my head. I picture myself smiling. I imagine myself leaning in, rapt with attention. I think over all the questions I will ask her. I write down my jokes and memorize various lines of conversation to raise when awkward silences begin to creep in. I practice being extroverted and witty with my friends. I have conversations with myself in the mirror.

It bears mentioning that since moral beliefs or habits are tendencies to act in a similar way in similar circumstances, I might imprint any one of several plans of action on my nature. Peirce has a complex theory of modality, but one important feature of it is that Peirce is a realist about possibilities. As we saw earlier, Peirce rejects the doctrine of determinism and maintains that the future is contingent. This (he believes) obliges him to maintain that possibility is real or objective (see EP 2:358, 1907). Moreover, Peirce writes, "the only controllable conduct is Future conduct" (EP 2:359, 1905). Accordingly, when we imprint a plan of action on our natures, we are deciding upon really possible courses of action and thereby determining that we do act that way. Forster (2011, esp. 189–94), Lane (2007), and Noble (1989) ably examine Peirce's theory of possibility.

All of these efforts instill in me a **determination** such that I will in fact act in the way resolved and planned, provided of course that I am not thwarted by events outside of my control. It might be worthwhile to note here that Peirce was a stickler about the concept of determination or "being determined" even in his early work. As early as 1867, he writes, "['determined' means] fixed to be *this* (or *thus*), in contradistinction to being this, that, or the other (in some way or other)" (W 2:155–56). This occurs in the context of a discussion of Hegel, and so he also appeals to the etymology of *bestimmt*: to be settled by vote. Accordingly, if one is determined to act thus and so, one will act thus and so, barring events outside of one's control. It is settled or decided that one will so act. These determinations differ from our moral beliefs or habits in that they are particular. A determination is how one will act in this circumstance; a moral belief or habit is how one *would similarly* act in *similar* circumstances. Accordingly, I will now be caused or determined to act in some specific way when the situation arises precisely by the force of my resolution and by imprinting the lesson on my nature.

Finally, I do act according to my determination. After having done so, I **critically reflect** on my actions: Did they in fact attain my ideal of not being introverted and boorish? If so, wonderful! Perhaps a second date is in my future. If not, I realize I must alter my plan of action or, perhaps, abandon my ideal or my intention to act according to it. This capacity for critical reflection on our ideas, our intentions, our rules of action, and our resolutions is what preserves moral responsibility on Peirce's view. "What would be requisite in order to destroy the difference between innocent conduct and guilty conduct?" he asks. He asserts that the "one thing that would do it would be to destroy the faculty of effective self-criticism" (EP 2:249, 1903). So long as we possess a faculty for effective self-criticism, we can modify our ideals, our moral beliefs, and so on.

Note that these elements appear not merely in the present example. They are found in all sorts of self-controlled action. Consider, for example, a police officer who may be called on to respond to a real and significant threat with lethal force. He has an **ideal**: to nullify the threat with minimal risk to himself and others. He **intends** to act according to the ideal and **formulates rules of action**: observe my surroundings; draw my pistol; position myself protectively; warn the threatening person of my intention to use lethal force; communicate with others who may be present; and so on. He **foresees** that there will be some occasion when he will have to implement his plan. After all, that is part and parcel to his job. He forms a **resolution** to act according to his rules and **imprints that lesson** on his nature. His rigorous training, practice, and preparation are precisely that process of imprinting the lesson. He is now **determined** to act according to his plan. When he responds to a threat called over the radio, he acts accordingly, as if it is second nature. Finally, following the event, he **critically reflects** on the experience to ascertain whether he could have done anything differently to attain his ideal.

These are the eight elements, Peirce maintains, that typically go into a self-controlled action. However, there is something quite peculiar about Peirce's account, especially given the context of his discussion of PH. It is that none of the eight elements are desires. In his description of self-controlled action, Peirce does mention desires once. He writes, "we may become aware of the disposition [i.e., the determination to act in some way], especially if it is pent up. In that case, we shall recognize it by a feeling of *need*, of *desire*" (EP 2:246, 1903). But this comment is not particularly helpful, since it is about the feeling of a desire and not desire itself.

Peirce's most detailed comments on desire are in 1902's "On Science and Natural Classes."[8] Peirce identifies three characteristics of desires. First, a desire is always for some *"kind* of thing or event" (EP 2:118). Desires are general, not particular. Peirce illustrates this claim with desiring a light. Suppose I am writing at night. I desire light, but there are diverse ways to get it. I may turn on an electric light. I may light a candle. I may light a fire. I *desire* some general kind of thing: a light. However, I *decide* on some specific thing: this electric light. Second, desires are variable. Peirce's example is of a man who prefers veal to pork. Such a man typically desires veal. However, he will prefer the "occasional spare rib [to] having cold boiled veal every day" (EP 2:118). As Peirce notes, variety is the spice of life. Third, desires are longitudinal. Desires are fully satisfied at an ideal state, but they can be satisfied at less than ideal states. There is longitude to what will satisfy a desire. Peirce's example, again, is a light. He desires a bright light for writing at night. However, his wallet and lungs would prefer a more economical – and hence less bright – option. (Peirce, recall, was quite poor and so concerned with the cost and quality of his lighting.) He must strike a compromise among his desires such that they are all satisfied to some degree, even if none of them fully.

In what will be important for what follows, we are now in a position to see how desires differ from determinations. First, determinations are not general. They are efficient agencies to act in some particular way. For example, a determination is not simply a *desire* to tell a story when an awkward silence creeps in. I might desire to tell the story but fail to do it. Rather, a determination is the *efficient agency* of telling a story when an awkward silence creeps in. Second, determinations are not variable. When a person is determined to act in a particular manner, he or she does so act when the situation arises. If a man is determined to eat cold boiled veal, he will eat cold boiled veal, even if he desires a spare rib. Finally, determinations are not longitudinal. Either one does or does not so act.

We are also in a position to see how desires differ from moral beliefs or habits. Whereas both desires and habits are general, they are general in

---

[8] It may seem strange that Peirce should discuss this in a text on classification, but see Stephen B. Hawkins (2007) for an examination of Peirce's account of desire in relation to Aristotle, classification, and final causality.

different ways. Desires are for some general kind of thing or event, but having a desire for something does not imply that one will tend to act on that desire. For example, former smokers may well desire to smoke without tending to smoke. In contrast, habits are general in the sense that they are habits of action. Desires are not effective in the sense of informing how we would act, whereas moral beliefs or habits are. Also, desires are variable, and though our habits may change they are not variable in the way that desires are. Whereas one might desire some variety in the foods she consumes weekly, it would not be a habit were one to treat people well on most days of the week but poorly on a few others. Habits are constant and enduring tendencies to act in some way, whereas our desires may well change from day to day.

The question now arises: Where do desires appear in Peirce's account of self-control? The answer is that they can appear in four ways. First, we may desire that some **ideal** be realized. However, we can have ideals without having a desire for their realization. Indeed, the ideals we imbibe in childhood do not always have attendant desires. For example, a happily introverted person may nevertheless have an extroverted ideal. Moreover, much of adolescence seems to be a process of trying to reject ideals we do have precisely because they do not comport with our rebellious desires. Second, we can desire ideals without having an intention to realize them. For example, many people desire that this be a world where no one suffers from hunger even though they have no intention of doing anything to realize that ideal. Nevertheless, we may both desire and **intend** to conform our conduct to some ideal. Yet, as just noted, we can have intentions to conform our conduct to ideals without desiring to do so. Third, in **foreseeing** that a special occasion will arise when we can implement our rules of action, we may also desire that the occasion arises. However, we need not desire such an occasion. For example, a police officer likely desires that an occasion to use lethal force does not arise. Fourth, when we **resolve and are determined** to act in in some way, we may also desire to act in that way. When the opportunity to so act does not arise, we may become conscious of the fact that we want to act in that way and so have a feeling of need or desire. However, we may not desire to act in the way we are resolved and determined to act. For example, I may resolve and be determined to exercise even though I do not desire to do so. What role, then, do desires play in self-controlled action? They are often attendants of our ideals, intentions, anticipations, resolutions, and determinations. However, they are not necessary components of any of them or of self-controlled action in general.

Peirce's Rejection of Premise (1) and of PH

With our accounts of desire and self-controlled action in place, we are now in a position to understand Peirce's rejections of premise (1) and of PH. Recall that premise (1) is best understood as the claim that if we act, then we take some second-order pleasure in so acting, a second-order pleasure we enjoy by satisfying a second-order desire to perform some first-order action. However, if Peirce's account is correct, this premise confounds desire, pleasure, and determination. A determination is an efficient agency. A desire is not an efficient agency to do some particular thing but a general, variable, and longitudinal mental formulation for some *kind* of thing or event. Likewise, the pleasure consequent on satisfying a desire is not an efficient agency.

To return to the example from before, I may well have the first-order desires to (a) drink beer, eat donuts, and watch television; (b) exercise; and (c) volunteer at a charity. I may even have the second-order desire to do some one of those things rather than nothing at all. However – and this is the key point – that second-order desire is not sufficient to get me to do any of them in particular. The second-order desire is only that some *kind* of thing be done – that one of (a)–(c) be done – it does not determine that in fact (c) (for example) is done. What, then, leads me to choose (c) over (a) or (b)? The answer is a determination to do (c). It is the determination and not the promised pleasure consequent on the satisfaction of my second-order desire that compels me to do (c). Thus, Peirce says, it is "moral self-control" (by which Peirce means self-controlled action in contrast with rational self-control, which is self-controlled thought) that "insures us against the quandary of Buridan's ass" (EP 2:347, 1905) and not a second-order desire. Moreover, those determinations can change as a consequence of critical reflection.

We are also in a position to understand why Peirce rejects PH. The defender of PH maintains that desires for one's own pleasure or for the avoidance of one's own pain are the ultimate motivations to action. But, on Peirce's account, the true springs of action are not desires but determinations. Desires are general; they are for some kind of thing or event. They cannot alone determine how one will act; rather, we make *decisions* or *choices* about what particular thing we will opt for. Also, desires, unlike determinations, are variable and longitudinal. Rather than being our desires, it is our determinations that are the truly efficient agents of action. Peirce writes,

What is the element which it is in truth unthinkable that deliberate action should lack? It is simply and solely the determination. Let his determination remain, as it is certainly conceivable that it should remain although the very nerve or pleasure were cut ... and he will certainly pursue the line of conduct upon which he is intent. (EP 2:249, 1903)

Lastly, Peirce immediately follows this with the comment that,

those who have reasoned in this fallacious way have confounded together the determination of the man's nature, which is an efficient agency prepared previously to the act, with the comparison of the conduct with a standard, which comparison is a general mental formula subsequent to the act, and having identified these two utterly different things, placed them in the act itself as a mere quality of feeling. (EP 2:249)

It is important to note that this is not a gloss on why Peirce rejects premise (1) and PH in particular. It is a gloss on why he rejects the entire line of reasoning (1)–(5). It is those who claim the truth of PH calls into question our commonsense notions of morality who conflate the determination with the comparison of conduct to a standard and the defender of premise (1) who conflates the determination with the pleasure of so acting. The appearance of this comment in the paragraph criticizing PH and premise (1) makes one liable to conflate this comment with his reason for rejecting PH and premise (1). But I have not here treated Peirce's surprising denial that the truth of PH would call into question our commonsense notions of morality because I doubt that he is correct, for the truth of PH might make it such that we do not engage in critical reflection precisely for fear of "incur[ing] the sting of conscience" (EP 2:249). That might suffice to render our faculty of self-criticism ineffective and so destroy the one thing necessary for there to be a distinction between good and bad conduct. If Peirce is correct that PH is false, however, the point is moot.

Conclusion

In conclusion and in sum, the mechanical hypothesis, God's foreknowledge, and PH each call into question freedom and moral responsibility.

Peirce rejects the mechanical hypothesis by maintaining that some action is nonconservative and there is randomness in nature. This, though, does not suffice to preserve moral freedom. He contends that by placing God outside of time, we can preserve freedom and moral responsibility. Though he does not develop this claim, he appears to be content with Boethius's response to the problem. Moreover, Peirce thinks that the defenders of PH have conflated determinations with the desires and the feelings associated with action. What is unique about Peirce's account is that his reply to defenders of PH is to provide a descriptive analysis of self-controlled action and by doing so show that desires are not the springs of action. Moreover, his descriptive analysis entails that it is our capacity for critical reflection that is at the heart of moral responsibility. Perhaps it will be argued that Peirce has misdescribed self-controlled action. If he has, I fail to see where. Much to the contrary, it is the defender of PH who finds herself turning every which way in the winds of redescription and reinterpretation to make the facts fit her theory.

6 | *Peirce and Practical Ethics*

Throughout this book, I have been urging that Peirce's sentimental conservatism – the twin theses that we ought not to trust too much to our own ethical theories and reasonings in the conduct of our lives and that we should instead trust to our instincts and sentiments – is best understood not as an ethical theory but as a piece of advice about how to conduct our individual lives. Philosophers and theorists ought not to be blamed for failing to conform their conduct to their philosophical theories. The wiser course of action is to let our sentiments and instincts guide our conduct. Fundamentally, Peirce's sentimental conservatism is a piece of advice about how *individual persons* should conduct their lives. When Peirce was writing, Millian and Kantian theories of morality were in their ascendency, and Henry Sidgwick's highly theoretical approach to ethics framed discussions of the subject matter. What Peirce could not have foreseen when he was writing is the recent emergence of practical ethical theories – most notably, the principlism of Tom L. Beauchamp and James Childress and the new casuistry of Albert R. Jonsen and Stephen Toulmin – that do not appeal to highly theoretical, abstract moral principles. What I aim to do here is extend the application of Peirce's theory to the field of practical ethics. How should we *corporately* reach decisions about how to conduct our lives? If, for instance, a commission is charged with outlining policies for biomedical research or for the use of technology in government surveillance programs, how might that commission proceed in its deliberations, given Peirce's views? And why should the conclusions of those deliberations hold any weight? Why should we regard them as trustworthy? Peirce's views can be developed to carve out a distinctive position with respect to these questions, a position that incorporates the key insights of both principlism and casuistry.

Highly Theoretical Approaches to Practical Ethics

One way of broaching issues in practical ethics – a way that is no longer in vogue – is to take a highly theoretical approach. On this approach, we begin by taking a theoretical stance and then see what follows from it practically. This manner of broaching issues in practical ethics may be either heroic or skeptical. On the heroic approach, one endorses some abstract ethical principle – say rule utilitarianism or Kantian deontology – and then applies the principle directly to the issue at hand. On the skeptical approach, one might deny that there are any moral principles or rules at all or one might deny that there are any moral truths.

The Heroic Approach

Consider the heroic approach wherein we take some abstract, philosophical, moral principle and apply it to a concrete moral issue or dilemma. One might, for instance, embrace Rawlsian contractualism and then attempt to apply this principle to a concrete case. Suppose we are wondering whether we should implement policies restricting the sorts of data the government may glean from personal computers and web searches. We might pause, wonder whether free, equal, and rational agents behind a veil of ignorance would agree to some rule that enacts such restrictions, and set our policies accordingly. Now it takes little reflection to see how absurd this is in a novel, concrete situation, especially when one is pressed for time. When it comes to vitally important matters, as Peirce calls them, we cannot possibly follow this method through. Nonetheless, we might think that this is how practical ethics *should* be done even if we will not always be able to avail ourselves of its insights. It would be ridiculous to claim we first need to work out the intricacies of philosophical ethics to make decisions. Policies, whether ideal or not, need to be implemented and, sometimes, implemented quickly. This does not preclude, though, working out the intricacies of an ethical theory and applying it directly to our lives when we can.

Yet as many others have noted, a significant problem the heroic approach faces is determining which ethical theory is true. If we are making corporate policy decisions on the basis of a theory, we had better make them on the basis of the correct theory. For different theories may well yield different pieces of advice – if they are capable of delivering specific counsel in a concrete situation at all – and it might prove disastrous to trust ourselves to bad counselors.

That is one reason to be doubtful of heroic practical ethics, and Peirce provides two other reasons. The second reason is that even if we were to pare down the number of acceptable ethical theories to one or two, we should still regard those theories as being on probation for the short term. Perhaps only one or two theories have survived our critical scrutiny, but it is yet another step to assert that the theory is true and a trustworthy guide to the conduct of our lives. There may be some criticism of the surviving theory we have yet to recognize, or there may be some other ethical theory of which we have yet to conceive but that is true.

This might seem like a doubtful claim for a pragmatist to make, especially for Peirce who states that truth is "the opinion which is fated to be ultimately agreed to by all who investigate" (W 3:273, 1878) and that "if we can find out the right method of thinking and can follow it out, – the right method of transforming signs, – then truth can be nothing more nor less than the last result to which the following out of this method would ultimately carry us" (EP 2:380, 1906). But two points are in order here. The first is that these considerations do not preclude some belief from being true even if *we* have not reached ultimate agreement. Peirce's later statement is that truth is what would be believed, not what is or will be believed. The second point is that by identifying those beliefs that survive critical scrutiny as true, Peirce does not mean that those beliefs that survive *our* critical scrutiny are true. For Peirce makes inquiry rest on three logical sentiments: "hope in the unlimited continuance of intellectual activity," "interest in an indefinite community," and "the possibility of this interest being made supreme" (W 3:285, 1878). Truth is the predestinate opinion, but only on the conditions that intellectual activity never ceases, that it embraces not merely human inquiry but inquiry by whatever form rational life might take, and that inquiry is conducted rigorously and not limited to our local or trivial concerns. These two points together get to the heart of why Peirce endorses sentimental conservatism. While some one of our moral theories may well be true, the limited scope of human reason and experience means that we ought not to regard them as trustworthy at least in the short term, and in the long term we should proceed cautiously. What we can regard as trustworthy guides to conduct in the here and now, on Peirce's view, are our instincts and our instinct-based sentiments, for evolutionary processes have honed these. I shall say more about this later.

The third reason to be doubtful of heroic approaches to practical ethics is that those who endorse such approaches trust to their instincts and sentiments anyway. On the one hand, it is surely true that diverse, plausible ethical theories will give the same advice in a variety of normal cases. Otherwise, we would not even find the ethical theory attractive in the first place. There is a reason few philosophers endorse ethical egoism, the theory that we ought to act so as to promote our own interests exclusively and over the long run. That reason, I opine, is not because they have some knockdown, drag-out theoretical argument against it. It is because the theory gives advice about how we should conduct our lives that runs directly contrary to what we commonly believe and excites in us intense sentiments of disapproval. We simply cannot countenance a moral theory that would permit murder, rape, or torture under any circumstances, however far-fetched the circumstances under which they may be to one's own benefit may be. A Peircean would say that this is a knockdown, drag-out *practical* argument against employing the principle of ethical egoism in our everyday decision making. It runs contrary to our instincts and sentiments to promote our own interests exclusively. As we saw in the previous chapter, Peirce rejects psychological hedonism; in Chapter 2, we saw that Peirce believes we have both suicultural and civicultural instincts. Yet we must tread carefully here. For Peirce would deny that this is a conclusive argument against the *theory* of ethical egoism. Ethical egoism may well be true; the question of its truth must be left to our theoretical researches. Yet whether it be true or not, we should not treat it as a sound principle for the conduct of our lives.

To return to our line of thought, diverse, plausible ethical theories will deliver the same counsel about a myriad of cases, but, on the other hand, they will also deliver different counsel in a handful of cases. Consider, for instance, the standard case we teach in introductory philosophy courses: whether we have a right or duty to lie to save the life of another person. Whereas Kant concludes we do not, Mill presumably believes that we do in the right circumstances. Now most of us, I suppose, believe that Mill has the right side of this disagreement. Presumably for this reason, those attracted to Kant's deontological ethics have sought to show that lying under certain conditions is in fact permissible on Kant's view, as for instance Christine Korsgaard (1986) famously does. Similarly in the area of practical ethics, in a particularly astute comment, Jonsen writes,

Authors who begin their works with erudite expositions of teleology and deontology hardly mention them again when they plunge into a case. Indeed, Beauchamp, who espouses rule utilitarianism, and Childress, who favors deontological theory, admit that "for both of us the most satisfactory theory is only slightly preferable" and that the distinction between the theories "can be and has been overestimated." They are almost always in agreement about the resolution of cases. (1990, 34)

Whereas Beauchamp and Childress – authors of *Principles of Biomedical Ethics* – endorse different normative ethical theories, in their practical ethics they defend a view known as principlism, about which I shall say more later. For the moment, notice that in particular cases, it is not the ethical theory that is doing the real work – they "hardly mention them again" – but something else, something such as a shared set of practical principles.

Now setting aside whether Korsgaard and others are right in their theorizing and setting aside the empirical and (possibly) personal questions of what motivates any given philosopher to reconcile a philosophical theory with her intuitions about what is right or wrong, the Peircean point is that we do not even need to engage in such theorizing in the conduct of our lives. The mere fact that we do attempt such reconciling projects testifies to the fact that we think our instincts and sentiments are sufficient guides for the conduct of our lives. Otherwise, we would feel no compunction to bring our moral theories into accord with our pre-theoretical moral attitudes. Whether we ought to or not, we do trust to our moral instincts and sentiments, and we let that trust inform our ethical thinking. On Peirce's view, it is those instincts and sentiments that are doing the real work in resolving particular cases. Reason, as he says, is the fly on the wheel.

Another question here is whether we ought to let that trust of our instincts and sentiments inform our ethical theorizing. The Peircean worry about heeding those instincts and sentiments in our theorizing (and not merely in our practical decision making) is that doing so might involve sham reasoning, where our conclusions are made in advance of our investigations and our reasonings are formed to those conclusions. As we saw in Chapter 1, Peirce maintains that "it is far better to let philosophy follow perfectly untrammeled a scientific method, *predetermined* in advance of knowing to what it will lead" (RLT 114, 1898). The worry here is not that our sentiments and instincts are wrong. To the contrary, Peirce would maintain that, from a practical, non-theoretical point of view, they have evolved to track the real moral features of the universe, presuming the universe has such real moral features. I argued for this in Chapters 2 and 4, and I shall take it up again in this chapter. For now, the more significant worries are that our instincts and sentiments are not infallible in the theoretical domain, on the one hand, and that they can lead us to err in our scientific investigations, on the other. They may lead us to err because we may be blind to some evidence or misjudge the weight of other evidence. To be certain and as Peirce consistently maintains from his earliest writings to his last, we must enter into a course of inquiry with all our prejudices: "We cannot begin with complete doubt. We must begin with all the prejudices which we actually have when we enter upon the study of philosophy" (W 2:212, 1868). The relevant difference between this claim and the worry about sham reasoning that Peirce records in "Philosophy and the Conduct of Life" is how those prejudices inform our theorizing. They are surely the starting points of our inquiries. What we must not take them for are the end points of inquiry, too.

Importantly, Peirce is not denying that our sentiments and instincts and our ethical theories need to be consistent. Much to the contrary, his very commitments imply that in the long run, they must be. For on his view, our sentiments and instincts will evolve to accord with the real moral order of the universe. Moreover, our inquiries, provided they are pushed far enough, will eventually discover what the real moral order of the universe is. His claims are rather that for now we ought not block the road of theoretical inquiry into ethics just because some theory is inconsistent with our sentiments and instincts and that we ought not allow whichever moral theory we do endorse to directly and suddenly influence how we conduct our lives.

The Skeptical Approach

We might be doubtful of heroic applied ethics – that is, attempts to take an abstract ethical principle and derive from it counsel about what to do in particular cases – for the three reasons just recorded. But there are also highly theoretical ways to be skeptical about such attempts. One way is to deny that there are abstract moral principles at all. This is not to deny that there are no moral facts of the matter; it is only to deny that the moral facts are determined or made what they are by general moral principles. Jonathan Dancy (2004), most notably, develops and defends such a view in his work on moral particularism. A second way is to deny that there are moral truths at all. We may opt for some variety of error theory about moral judgments, for instance. In that case, while moral judgments do purport to state the facts, they are nevertheless all false just because there are no moral facts. Richard Joyce (2006) has given forceful expression to this position.

The Peircean response here is to remain theoretically neutral when it comes to the conduct of our lives. We need not be theoretically neutral from a scientific point of view. Quite possibly, Dancy, Joyce, or the several defenders of moral skepticism may be correct. But, again, it can hardly be justifiably asserted that there is a consensus on these matters, that investigation into them has reached even tentative conclusions, much less probable ones. Consequently, we ought not to allow the views of Dancy or of Joyce – let alone Kant or Mill – to precipitately inform how we conduct our lives.

I would be remiss not to note, though, that when it comes to our actual theorizing independent of the conduct of our lives, Peirce would also be skeptical of these skeptical approaches to ethics. In particular, his later distinctive view of pragmatism – what he calls "pragmaticism," where the suffix "–icisim" is introduced to denote a more specific version of a doctrine – emphasizes the importance of our instinctive beliefs in our theorizing. He writes that his pragmaticism is a variety of positivism, taken in a broad sense, and is marked by "its retention of a purified philosophy" as well as "its full acceptance of the main body of our instinctive beliefs" (EP 2:339, 1905). That is, on Peirce's conception of pragmatism, philosophy is to be a theoretical science severed from the conduct of our lives, at least until it reaches conclusions on which we are willing to risk our lives. And yet, in its theoretical activities, it accepts the mass of our instinctive beliefs, such as the beliefs that there is some reality independent of our minds, that we can know that reality, and even that there are other minds. Now one of those instinctive beliefs, I would think, is that that there are in fact moral principles we are obliged to follow (whether at all times and under all conditions I leave aside). Consequently, the pragmatist as a theoretician is obliged to accept this instinctive belief at least until she has strong reasons to reject it.

Of course, the belief may well be false, as might the other three instinctive beliefs just recorded, but that is not Peirce's point. All of our theorizing begins with prejudices and the firmest of those prejudices, on Peirce's view, are our instinctive beliefs. Accordingly, we ought to regard the belief that there are moral principles as the much more plausible hypothesis even in the face of the brilliant argumentation of Dancy, Joyce, and others. But, again, that is not to claim that we ought to allow our own hypotheses regarding those moral principles to directly influence the conduct of our lives. Neither is it to deny that developing these theories is a worthwhile intellectual endeavor; we ought not to block the road of inquiry.

To sum up, as I argued in Chapter 2, it is entirely consistent with the Peircean position to maintain that if philosophers animated with the "true scientific Eros" should reach the conclusions of their ethical investigations and find that some moral theory – be it Rawlsian contractualism, rule utilitarianism, or some theory yet to be articulated – is true, then we ought to allow that theory to inform our everyday conduct by a "slow process of percolation" and to guide our policy making. The problem, Peirce maintains and I believe the numerous and still hotly contested issues in ethics show, is that philosophers have not reached the conclusions of their investigations. Moreover, the conclusion of those investigations is surely far off in the indefinite future. Furthermore, skepticism about moral principles, such as we find defended in Dancy's moral particularism, and skepticism about morality *tout court*, such as we find in the error theory of Richard Joyce, remain viable philosophical positions. Accordingly, it may well turn out that there are no moral principles to inform our conduct. Perhaps what we now regard as moral principles are merely heuristics abstracted from the conduct of our lives and wrongly imported into the domain of theory. Peirce's view, unlike heroic practical ethics, can countenance this possibility. A Peircean practical ethics need not take a theoretical stand on whether there are in fact general moral principles and much less on what those principles might be. When it comes to the conduct of our lives, we can remain neutral on these questions even if we are not neutral on them in the theoretical domain. As Peirce states, "in my logic there is a great gulf between the methods proper to practical and to theoretical question[s]" (SS 19).

Minimally Theoretical Approaches to Practical Ethics

As noted, highly theoretical approaches to practical ethics are no longer in vogue. In their place, a variety of minimally theoretical approaches have been proposed. These theories are, of course, theoretically articulated. But they are minimally theoretical in the sense that their methods for resolving particular cases do not make an appeal to abstract moral principles or theories from which are derived concrete counsels. Two minimally theoretical approaches have gained considerable traction, the new casuistry – for which Jonsen and Toulmin, especially, advocate, and principlism – developed and defended, most notably, by Beauchamp and Childress. My aim in the remainder of this chapter is to show that a Peircean view of practical ethics can accommodate both casuistry and principlism while setting them on firmer footing. In the next sections, I briefly canvas the methods and commitments of casuistry and principlism. Then, I bring Peirce's insights to bear on them.

Casuistry

Peirce, I argued in Chapter 2, maintains that the science of ethics is useless. He does not deny that we should study ethics scientifically, and he believes that we should develop and defend ethical theories. When he claims that the science of ethics is useless, he is claiming that we ought not to conduct our lives according to our preferred ethical theory – at least not until that ethical theory has been proven by careful and honest investigation. The ponderous tomes of philosophers of ethics have their place; it just so happens that their place is not in the conduct of our lives.

Nevertheless, Peirce does see a value in books of casuistry for the conduct of our lives, and Cornelis de Waal (2012, 97) has also noted that a Peircean approach to ethics and casuistry is amenable. Peirce does not seem to have in mind the high casuistry of the late Middle Ages and Renaissance, though. His example of a book on casuistry is Amelia Alderson Opie's *Illustrations of Lying* (R 435:30), which Peirce describes as both entertaining and diverting. Notably, she begins that book by stating that she "pretend[s] not to lay before my readers any new knowledge; my only aim is to bring to their recollection knowledge which they already possess, but do not constantly recall and act upon" (1825, ix). That is, she is not "prying into the philosophical basis of morality" (R 435:30), as Peirce says, but bringing to mind what we already know about morality. Again, as Peirce states, "we all know what morality is" (R 435:30). Excavating the philosophical foundations of morality will not change what we already know even if it may shed new light on it.

Notably, an endorsement of casuistic approaches to practical ethical decision making is one point on which William James and Peirce agree. In "The Moral Philosopher and the Moral Life" from *The Will to Believe*, James notes that the casuistic question is "what is the *measure* of the various goods and ills which men recognize, so that the philosopher may settle the true order of human obligations" (WWJ 6:142). However, he denies that this can be ascertained by deduction from some abstract moral principle. Instead, it must be discerned in the actual "experiments" that we make in the conduct of our lives: "So far as the casuistic question goes, ethical science is just like physical science, and instead of being deducible all at once from abstract principles, must simply bide its time, and be ready to revise its conclusions from day to day" (WWJ 6:157). Peirce would distinguish between the methodologies proper to physical science and casuistry, if physical science be understood as pure theoretical (rather than applied) science. Nonetheless and as we saw earlier, he would endorse James's claim that ethical principles for the conduct of life should not be deduced from abstract principles. What we should do instead is trust to our collective instincts and sentiments and to the counsel of wise persons, revising our policies and commitments as future experience demands.

Jonsen and Toulmin (1988) have given new life to casuistry in their *The Abuse of Casuistry*. Casuistry, they argue, had fallen by the wayside following Pascal's attacks on it, in *Provencial Letters*, for its laxity. For instance, some casuists of the 1500s defended the outrageous view that a nobleman may meet a slap to the face with lethal force. Moreover, the emergence of highly theoretical approaches to ethics, most obviously the deontological ethics of Kant and the utilitarianism of Bentham and Mill, contributed to the decline of philosophical interest in casuistry. Nonetheless, the method of casuistry provides a framework for moral deliberation when the correct moral theory is doubtful, as it surely is today. In fact, what brought Jonsen and Toulmin to an interest in casuistry was their participation in the National Commission for the Protection of Human Subjects of Biomedical and Behavioral Research. While serving on this commission, they realized that when it came to concrete moral decisions and policies, persons of vastly different religious and ethnic backgrounds and with highly divergent moral points of view could nevertheless come to consensus about what should be done in particular cases. Controversy tended to erupt not with respect to what the correct decision was but the reasons – the principles, the theories – that explained why the decision was correct or that justified the decision. They write,

> Members of the commission were largely in agreement about their specific practical recommendations; they agreed what it was they agreed about; but the one thing they could not agree on was *why* they agreed about it.
>
> ... The *locus of certitude* in the commissioners' discussions did not lie in an agreed set of intrinsically convincing *general* rules or principles, as they shared no commitment to any such body of agreed principles. Rather, it lay in a shared perception of what was *specifically* at stake in particular kinds of human situations. (1988, 18)

The members of the commission could perceive – they had a sense of or an insight into – what should be done. Excavating the foundations of morality is what led to disagreement.

The method of casuistry is particularist in the sense that it begins with specific, detailed moral cases with respect to which the correct decision is clear. Suppose, for example, that I have an acquaintance (not friend) of modest means who will give me a sizable sum of money if I make a false promise to repay it and suppose, moreover, that I do not need the money but will spend it on personal luxuries. Is it morally permissible to make the false promise? The obvious answer is *no*. We can then extend our considerations to other cases. Imagine a similar scenario but my plan is to donate the money to a charity. Is it then morally permissible to make a false promise? Again, presumably the answer is *no*. What if the acquaintance is not of modest means but quite wealthy though miserly? Here again, I take it the answer is *no*. What if I will use the money obtained by a false promise made to my wealthy but miserly acquaintance to pay for a life-saving surgery for his own child and I cannot afford to pay for the surgery myself and have no other means of raising the money needed for the surgery? Here it is much less clear that the answer is *no*. Making the false promise may well be licit.

Importantly, casuistry is not inconsistent with the view that there are *practical* moral principles that we may use to help guide our decisions in these particular cases. Neither is it inconsistent with the theoretical view that there are in fact highly abstract moral principles. To the first point, Jonsen and Toulmin note that one of the leading casuists of the high era – Juan Azor – "established an important feature of casuistical methodology: the general principle is first exhibited in an obvious case and only then in other cases in which circumstances make its application increasingly less clear" (1988, 155). The principles that Azor employed were the Ten Commandments. As the argument of Chapter 2 suggests, Peirce would surely endorse using those principles that reflect our instincts and sentiments, giving the greatest weight to those principles that reflect our instincts and urging us to be cautious with regard to those sentiments that are based on mere prejudices. Regardless of these details, the key point is that casuistry is consistent with the recognition that practical moral principles can guide our decision making, principles such as *we should not lie* or *we should not kill*. However, the casuists also recognize that in specific circumstances, there might be exceptions to these principles. To the second point mentioned earlier about casuistry being consistent with the theoretical view that highly abstract moral principles exist, it is natural to ask what is the status of these practical principles. Here, Jonsen and Toulmin are in disagreement. In Toulmin's view, these principles are merely heuristics that mark how cases were decided in the past and that serve as guidelines for future decisions. Jonsen, on the other hand, is a moral realist. Toulmin adopts a skeptical theoretical stance with respect to the status of principles whereas Jonsen does not. Nonetheless – and this is Peirce's view, too – what matters in resolving particular cases is not our theoretical stance regarding the status of such practical moral principles. That is a question we can put on hold until our theoretical researches reach their conclusion. What matters is the mutual recognition and application of those principles to the particular cases. As Jonsen and Toulmin write,

Casuistry had never been intended as a substitute for ethical theory or moral theology. It was not, in itself, a doctrine about what is the best life for man, what virtues characterize the good person, or what ideals humans should strive for. It did not even offer a general or fully elaborated doctrine about what sorts of acts are right, or about how principles and rules are to be justified. It was a simple, practical exercise directed at attempting a satisfactory resolution of particular moral problems. (1988, 242)

Paul Cudney (2014, 209) provides a summary of how casuistry proceeds. Casuists begin with paradigms that are used to establish initial presumptions and are conclusive for those cases. Next, casuists move to particular cases. They first consider which paradigm the particular cases are most like. If the particular case is unambiguously like a paradigm, then the case is decided in the same manner as the paradigm case. Problems arise only when either the particular case does not unambiguously fit any of the paradigms or when two or more paradigms apply to the particular case in conflicting ways. In these cases, we must recur to the details to try to resolve the ambiguity and defer to the wise person who is able to discern what to do in these cases. Then, through our social practices and the refinement of our moral sensibilities, we are able to progressively clarify exceptions to the paradigm cases.

Principlism and Its Rapprochement with Casuistry

Jonsen and Toulmin turned to casuistry as a particularist response to putatively "deductivist" tendencies in the principlism of Beauchamp and Childress. The early editions of their *Principles of Biomedical Ethics* suggest that the principles that comprise the core of principlism are somehow deduced or derived from more fundamental moral principles found in deontological ethics. This suggestion appears most clearly in the second edition of their book, where they write, "our approach to moral reasoning by deliberation and justification can be diagrammed in the form of hierarchical tiers or levels" (1983, 4). Beauchamp and Childress then provide a tiered chart where we move up from particular judgments and actions to rules, then principles, and finally ethical theories. Rules and principles are distinguished in that principles are more general and less restricted in scope: *Do not lie* is a rule that is subsumed under the principle of respect for persons. Taken in reverse order, then, we might think that the principles are somehow deduced or derived from ethical theories, the rules from principles, and the particular judgments from the rules.

In the third edition, however, Beauchamp and Childress back away from this earlier suggestion. Instead, they write, "moral justification is appropriate *whenever there is a need to defend one's moral convictions*" (1989, 6, emphasis added). One need only move up this hierarchy when there is such a need. When there is no such need, one might be satisfied to stay at the level of particular judgments. For example, we can all concede that Smith murdering Jones for personal profit is immoral, and we feel no special need to justify this judgment at all. Or one might be satisfied to stay at the level of principles. For example, we might all recognize that the principle of nonmaleficence – that we ought to do no harm to one another – entails that doctors ought not to perform invasive and unnecessary tests, and we can come to this recognition without needing to justify the principle of nonmaleficence itself provided we agree to the principle.

Moreover, Beauchamp and Childress begin to shift away from identifying ethical theories as the *source* of our practical ethical principles. As mentioned, Beauchamp and Childress hold differing moral theories themselves but note that they "find that some (not all) forms of rule utilitarianism and rule deontology lead to virtually identical principles and rules and recommended actions" (1989, 44). Peirce would maintain that this is just evidence we do not even need to engage in such theorizing in the conduct of our lives. In later editions of their book, Beauchamp and Childress identify the source of practical ethical principles to be the common morality and not primarily abstract ethical principles.

Morality "refers to norms about right and wrong human conduct that are so widely shared that they form a stable social compact" (2013, 2–3), and the common morality is "the set of universal norms shared by all persons committed to morality" (3).[1] Morality is not exhausted by the common morality – some people might endorse principles or practices not found among the principles of the common morality and the practices it permits – but at the core of morality is nevertheless a shared set of norms "applicable to all persons in all places, and we rightly judge all human conduct by its standards" (3). On their view, "all persons committed to morality accept the standards found in what we are calling the common morality" (5). Though there are surely people who do not endorse the common morality – sociopaths, for example – they are people who are not committed to morality in the first place. Moreover, the common morality includes both standards of action – that is, rules or principles – and standards of character, such as

---

[1] Bernard Gert (2004) also proposes a theory of the common morality. My focus here shall be on Beauchamp and Childress, since their theory is more amenable to a Peircean point of view.

the virtues. The standards of action are not absolute but prima facie binding, for they may come into conflict.

Beauchamp and Childress focus on those principles of the common morality that are directly relevant to biomedical ethics, but they acknowledge that there may well be other principles. They do not presume to give an account of the whole of the common morality. However, their conception of the common morality has come under attack, especially on the grounds that there may not be such a thing as the common morality that is universally shared. But from a Peircean perspective, we can rest content with a weaker claim. As explained in Chapter 2, humans have evolved a number of instincts to guide the conduct of their lives, just as all animals have. Those instincts are universally – or nearly so – shared across the human race. Moreover, we have various sentiments, some of which have their basis in instinct, to help guide the conduct of our lives. On the basis of these instincts and sentiments, we can identify a series of moral principles or rules to guide our conduct. For instance, we have strong feelings of disapproval when we consider actions that inflict harm on others for no reason. We also have feelings of warmth and approval when we consider actions that promote the well-being of others. From the mere fact that we have these sentiments and that they are (nearly) universally shared, we can assert that the principles of nonmaleficence and of benevolence are prima facie morally binding. This may appear to involve an attempt to derive an "ought" from an "is," but I shall argue that it is not.

The manner in which Beauchamp and Childress have refined their views has led some to hope there might be a rapprochement between the casuistry and principlism. In an essay from 1995, Jonsen remarks that casuistry and principlism are complementary in that "principles, such as respect, beneficence, veracity, and so forth, are invoked necessarily and spontaneously in any serious moral discourse: indeed, it would be difficult to distinguish moral discourse from any other sort of talk without such reference" (1995, 246). Both theories involve the use, the scaffolding, of principles to give structure to moral decision making. However, Jonsen does maintain that casuistry and principlism are differing scholarly practices: "A person can choose to do the work of the casuist or the work of the moral philosopher ... The moral philosopher may be the architect of the moral 'memory palace' but the casuist is its interior decorator. The palace, constructed of theory and principles, is empty without the interior design, finishing, and furniture of circumstance" (247, 248). Jonsen's point is that princip-lists are concerned with the "psychological and metaphysical . . . origins and meanings of principles and their relationship to theory" (247). As we have just seen, however, Beauchamp and Childress have turned away from a reliance on ethical theory to justify particular moral judgments and instead begun to emphasize common morality as the foundation for moral justification. Moreover, Beauchamp and Childress recognize the complementarity of these two methods when they write, "both are helpful as long as we have a solid knowledge base that allows us to use them. However, to obtain that knowledge, the casuistical method must be supplemented by norms of moral relevance that incorporate prior judgments of right and wrong conduct" (2013, 403). This is just Jonsen's point: The principlist gives us the structure; the casuist gives us the finishing touches.

A second apparent point of difference is that Beauchamp and Childress recognize only four principles – autonomy, nonmaleficence, benevolence, and justice. Casuists, in contrast, admit a great diversity of principles, including popular adages and aphorisms. But this apparent difference is misleading, for as noted Beauchamp and Childress also recognize that principles can be further specified into rules, including rules along casuis-tical lines, such as *don't lie*. Moreover, Beauchamp and Childress concede that they are identifying only a part of the common morality.

A third apparent point of difference is the procedure they follow. Casuists begin with paradigm cases and then turn to consider how close other cases are to that paradigm. Principlists, in contrast, consider which principles apply to a given case and then attempt to determine what weight should be given to which principle in the case. Yet Mark Kuczewski maintains that if we distinguish between finding an answer to a particular moral dilemma and justifying the answer, we find that,

Casuistry and principlism are identical theories if they both hold that answers are found by examining cases, circumstances, maxims, mid-level principles and other common sense considerations. Nothing prevents the casuist or principlist from adding an explanatory story, i.e., a justification, regarding why this solution is "for the best" or achieves the appropriate balance of mid-level principles. (1998, 520)

As I shall argue in more detail, casuists and principlists alike must employ practical wisdom in finding an answer to any particular moral dilemma.

They both must make judgments as to which principles or rules are relevant to the given case and consider how close the particular case is to those that have already been decided. Yet each method is neutral when it comes to climbing the ladder of theoretical justification. One might appeal to utilitarian, deontological, or contractualist views or one might deny that there is any sense to providing a higher justification at all. These further theoretical justificatory moves, though, are independent of what casuists and principlists must do to find a solution to a given case.

Recently, Paul Cudney has argued that claims that casuistry and principlism are methodologically distinct stem from three confusions. The first is the belief that casuistry rejects the use of mid-level principles; what it rather critiques is high-level moral theory for practical decision making. The second is that principlism is purely deductivist, and the third is that casuistry is purely inductivist. Rather, Cudney argues, on the "two relevant methodological questions [of] how should one go about confronting issues in bioethics? and how should one go about explaining these decisions to others? . . . Casuists and principlists mostly agree" (2014, 222). Where Cudney believes casuistry and principlism diverge is with respect to their views on the justification of ethical judgments and the semantic content of moral principles. Whereas principlists appeal to common morality to account for the justification of ethical judgments, casuists appeal to the practically wise person. Whereas casuists maintain that for moral principles to have content, one must understand the cases of which they are "summaries," the principlist can maintain that principles can have meaningful content without a grasp of the cases to which they refer.

However, it is not clear that much sense can be made of Cudney's attempt to distinguish principlism and casuistry on metaethical grounds. With respect to the justificatory claim, he writes,

> If I were confronted with a group of people who did subscribe to some system for guiding and justifying their behavior, but that system did not issue in judgments corresponding sufficiently to correct judgments about paradigmatic cases, what they had developed would not make sense as a system of moral justification at all. Moreover – and this is the difference from principlism – this would still be the case even if these people claimed to support the same basic set of general principles to which I subscribe. (224)

But how much sense can be made of two groups of persons endorsing the same principles but not making the same judgments with respect to paradigm cases? Suppose, for instance, a group of people should endorse a principle of nonmaleficence but think that it is permissible to abuse children. I should think they are deeply confused about the meaning of the term "nonmaleficence," do not regard children as members of the moral community, or think that the principle of nonmaleficence in some cases (viz. those in which they abuse their children) is outweighed by some other good. But then it turns out that we do not endorse the same moral principle (we are equivocating on "nonmaleficence"), or we do not share the same moral outlook (in which case one of us may not participate in the common morality), or we need to carefully examine, based on cases, whether the abuse really is outweighed by some other good. In each of these cases, though, it would turn out that principlism and casuistry are not distinct. With respect to the semantic content of ethical judgments, Cudney writes the casuist but not the principlist is committed to the view

that moral principles derive their content from the cases of which they are summaries means that if someone were committed to a set of moral principles, but had no grasp of what cases count as the types of right- or wrong-doing the principle is meant to pick out, then what that person had in mind would not count as a set of moral principles at all. (226)

Yet again it is not clear what sense can be made of the denial of this view or that the principlist should deny it. One thinks of Kant's famous statement that concepts without intuitions are empty and intuitions without concepts are blind. What sense can be made of grasping a moral principle without also a grasp of cases to which it may apply?

Nevertheless, Cudney does put his finger on one important difference between principlism and casuistry: that the former makes moral justification in practical matters rest on the common morality, whereas the latter makes it rest on what the wise person would do. In the next section, I aim to show that there is a third, Peircean way to ground moral justifications that can accommodate the insights of both the common morality of Beauchamp and Childress and the casuists' appeal to the practically wise person.

Justification in Peircean Practical Ethics

Thus far I have been arguing that Peirceans should eschew highly theoretical approaches to practical ethics. Instead, Peirce endorses a casuistic approach to practical ethics. I have argued that this approach is minimally theoretical in that it requires theoretical commitments only to the claims that we have a certain insight into – an instinct for – morality such that we can "see" what is morally required in paradigm cases; that we can abstract moral principles, rules, or maxims from these paradigm cases; that we can extend the applicability of these rules to non-paradigmatic cases; and that the wise person in particular is able to "see" how the principles apply to especially complex moral dilemmas. Moreover, I have argued that casuistry's main competitor, the principlism of Beauchamp and Childress, is also minimally theoretical in that its theoretical commitments are to the common morality and its principles and to our ability to grasp how those principles are specified into rules that are relevant to particular cases. Furthermore, as noted, some scholars have maintained that casuistry and principlism are complementary theories. Their main difference lies in the sorts of appeals that are made in moral justifications. Whereas the casuist appeals to the judgments of the wise person, the principlist appeals to the common morality. My aim here is to show that Peirce offers us a *via media* between these two views that incorporates their core insights.

Let us begin by considering casuistry, since that is the theory with which Peirce most clearly identifies. In *Ethics and the Limits of Philosophy*, Bernard Williams writes, "the repertory of substantive ethical concepts differs between cultures, changes over time, and is open to criticism. If casuistry, applied to a given local set of concepts, is to be the central process of ethical thought, it needs more explanation. It has to claim that there are preferred ethical categories that are not purely local" (1985/1993, 96). Williams especially doubts that an account of human nature will "adequately determine one kind of ethical life as against others" (52). I take it that three aspects of casuistry need explanation. The first is to explain how it is possible that diverse people are able to reach consensus at all. If ethical concepts change and are culturally conditioned, then how is consensus possible? What explains the fact that we sometimes do reach consensus on ethical issues – such as on the moral impermissibility of murder – and what merits our hope that we will reach consensus on other issues? Second, casuist judges need to explain how their judgments can hold any weight when they are mutable and possibly distorted by their cultural prejudices. Third and closely related to the second issue, casuists need to explain why we *corporately* should regard the methodology as trustworthy. Notice that this is different from particular judgments of casuists holding any weight; the issue here is why we should think that the method of casuistry yields trustworthy insights into the sorts of policies we should employ in the conduct of our corporate lives. Notice, also, that this third call for explanation is different from the question of why I should trust to my sentiments and instincts. To be sure and as we shall see momentarily, Peirce thinks that an explanation for the trustworthiness of the casuistic method will appeal to our sentiments and instincts, but why those sentiments and instincts are corporately trustworthy or may be regarded as trustworthy is a question different from why *I* should trust them. As argued in Chapter 2, *I* should trust them because I have nothing better to rely on. As we shall see, the Peircean argument for the trustworthiness of casuistry is analogous, but it is also different in important respects.

If we can provide an explanation for the third of these, then we will be in a position to explain the first two. To embark on such an explanation, we will do well to begin with Peirce's critique of psychologism. Broadly speaking, psychologism is the thesis that logic is somehow importantly informed by or rests on psychology. As Christopher Hookway explains (2012, 89–91), those who endorse psychologism might be committed to one of several claims. Peirce is primarily concerned with attacking those who think that the normativity of logic somehow rests on the psychological description of mental operations. As Hookway writes, "Peirce's main criticisms of [psychologistic theses] depend upon the distinction between the descriptive character of psychological laws and the normative character of logical laws" (90). On Peirce's conception, logic is a normative science that studies how one ought to think insofar as one is capable of exerting self-control over her thinking; it is not to be limited to formal logic.

As psychologism is not widely endorsed and minimally requires engaging in the doubtful enterprise of deriving an ought from an is, Peirce's own criticisms of psychologism need not detain us here (see Stjernfelt 2014, ch. 2, and Hookway 2012, ch. 5, for detailed discussions). What is of importance in the present context is that while Peirce rejects psychologism, he would not deny that our actual reasoning practices are trustworthy. Hookway indicates this when he writes,

Suppose that I am justified in believing that someone is an extremely successful poker player. When I learn that they make use of a particular strategy of reasoning in the course of their play, then, we might suppose,

I have good, albeit defeasible, reason for thinking that the kinds of reasoning they employ are indeed good ones. I would not have an explanation of what their goodness consists in. But I do have strong inductive evidence that the inferences they use can be trusted. (2012, 95–96)

The poker player's success gives us grounds to believe that the rational procedures are trustworthy. Notice that we can extend this beyond the narrow considerations of poker players and their success. Most persons, while not trained logicians, are nevertheless successful reasoners. To be sure, they are very far from infallible. Yet they reason well enough – they have sufficiently well-developed habits of reasoning, a *logica utens* – that they need not rely on a *logica docens*, an elaborated doctrine of how one ought to reason. And this is indeed Peirce's view. As noted in previous chapters, Peirce believes that our instinct of just reasoning has undergone geometrical growth since the time of Homer and for most of us a *logica utens* is all we need. We can concede that our habits of reasoning are trustworthy without maintaining that they provide an account of the normativity of logic.

However, we must make one important qualification to this extended line of thought. In the poker player case, it is quite easy to recognize that the poker player has succeeded. We can directly infer from the fact that the poker player regularly wins that the rational procedures the poker player utilizes are trustworthy. We could, moreover, confirm the soundness of the player's methodology mathematically if she told it to us. But in the case of reasoning, that we have succeeded is less obvious. Such reasoning – since in this context we are discussing psychologism – issues in belief. On Peirce's view, what we aim at is settled belief (see W 3:248, 1877). Moreover, the true belief will be a settled or fixed belief; it will stand up to future experience. Clearly, we may well have some settled, true beliefs. The difference as compared with the poker player example, though, is that it is much harder to *recognize* that one has a true, settled belief. Of course, we may recognize the belief to be settled for now and, on this basis, judge that the belief is likely to be true. But, as Peirce writes, "if man were immortal he could be perfectly sure of seeing the day when everything in which he had trusted should betray his trust, and, in short, of coming eventually to hopeless misery. He would break down, at last, as every great fortune, as every dynasty, as every civilization does. In place of this, we have death" (W 3:283, 1878). "Perfectly sure" is doubtless an overstatement of the point Peirce wishes to make, which is simply that for any given belief that we take to be settled, it is quite possible that belief is not true and so will be overturned by future experience. The recognition of this possibility is at the heart of Peirce's fallibilism.

Yet for Peirce the right lesson to draw from this possibility is not despair at ever having a true belief but a cheerful hope that in fact we may be able to divine the truth. That is, *if* there is an "affinity of the human soul to the soul of the universe" (EP 2:152, 1903) – if we have evolved an instinct of just reasoning – *then* our reasoning procedures are trustworthy. Peirce thinks that we can affirm there is such an affinity because "there is a reason, an interpretation, a logic, in the course of scientific advance" (EP 2:444, 1908), but his appeal to scientific *advance* obviously begs the question. Perhaps – outrageous though the suggestion may be – the current state of science is nothing but a protracted error. What he ought to have said is simply that we have nothing better than the rational procedures we (*not* I) currently have on hand to use. To be certain, we can develop and refine those procedures. We might elaborate a *logica docens*, or our reasoning instinct can be improved simply through study and practice, much as college students have their *logica utens* improved even if they never take a course in logic. The key point, though, is that either we have evolved the instinct for just reasoning or we have not. If we have not, we can do nothing about it. Even an attempt to develop a *theory* of reasoning will depend on our instinct for reasoning. If we have evolved an instinct of just reasoning, then we can trust our reasonings. Let us hope, then, that we have evolved that instinct for just reasoning and trust to it. After all, as Peirce writes, "despair is insanity. True, there may be facts that will never get explained; but that any given fact is of the number, is what experience can never give us reason to think; far less can it show that any fact is of its own nature unintelligible. We must therefore be guided by the rule of hope" (W 6:206, 1887–88).

Peirce rejects psychologism: The normativity of logic does not rest on how we in fact reason. Nevertheless, how we in fact reason is trust-worthy supposing that our minds are attuned to the natural order, and, anyway, we have nothing better to go on. What I propose here is that Peirce would employ an analogous argument with respect to our prac-tical reasoning about ethical matters. That is, what we ought to do – the norms of action – are not to be explained by our psychology, culture, or evolutionary history. The naturalistic fallacy really is a fallacy.

The mistake is to think that this must drive us to a highly theoretical approach to practical ethics, which may be either heroic or skeptical. The alternative approach is to claim that if we have evolved to be attuned to the real moral features of the universe, if we have evolved an instinct of morality, then our *logica utens* about practical matters is trustworthy. That is, our instinctive capacity for navigating the various pushes and pulls of desire, instinct, sentiment, and reason is trustworthy. As explained in Chapter 2, this is what Cornelis de Waal calls our *ethica docens*. Alternatively, if we have not evolved such an instinct, then there is nothing we can do about it anyway. Certainly, we might theorize about ethics, but the conclusions of those researches are indefinitely far in the future. Even if we did reach the conclusion of those researches, we should have to wonder why we should care about them if we have no instinct of morality in the first place. As Peirce says of Kant's categorical imperative, "Why *should* we pay any more attention to it than we would to the barking of a cur" (EP 2:202, 1903)? Let us instead hope that we have evolved an instinct of morality and trust to it.

Notice, moreover, that just as we can improve and refine our instinct of just reasoning by elaborating a *logica docens* or by study and practice, we can also improve and refine our instinct of morality by elaborating a *logica docens* for practical matters or by study and the practice of making judgments about ethical matters. Now a *logica docens* for ethical matters would require us to adopt a highly theoretical approach to practical ethics, and I have already argued on Peircean grounds against the direct application of such theories to the conduct of our lives and to policy making. Instead, we will have to refine our instinct of morality through study and practice. It is precisely this that casuistry does, and it is precisely for this reason that the casuist must appeal to the wise person's discernment with respect to non-paradigmatic cases. The paradigmatic cases are not particularly interesting because we all recognize what should be done in the case at hand. Nevertheless, it is by gaining a clear comprehension of the paradigmatic cases and those that are closely allied to them that we can begin to refine our insights into the non-paradigmatic cases. Just as a scientist who has labored for years on a particular issue has her instincts for the right answers refined through her study without herself being a logician or a philosopher of science, so also we can have our instincts for the right answers on practical matters refined through the study of and reflection on particular cases.

Furthermore, the principlist will have to make this same appeal to the wise person's discernment. To be sure, the common morality will be a trustworthy guide to conduct just because we, as a social organism, have (hopefully) evolved an instinct of morality. But our instincts can sometimes lead us astray: "Such animals as dogs and ants are sometimes betrayed by their instincts" (EP 2:467, 1913), Peirce writes, and we are no different from dogs and ants in this respect. What we will need for the difficult cases are people whose instincts of morality have been developed and refined through studious reflection. Beauchamp and Childress gesture to this point when they write that "balancing is the process of finding reasons to support beliefs about which moral norms should prevail" (2013, 20) and "we are proposing a model of moral judgment that focuses on how balancing and judgment occur through practical astuteness, discriminating intelligence, and sympathetic responsiveness that are not reducible to the specification of norms" (22). While they acknowledge rational constraints on moral judgment and balancing – such as that no other morally preferable option be available – they still must cede ground to the casuist in recognizing the weight of those judgments made by the astute, discriminating, sympathetic – in a word, wise – person.

It is here that there is a rapprochement between casuistry and principlism on the question of justification. If practical ethicists are not to appeal to highly theoretical – likely heroic – principles for moral justification, then the best grounds they can appeal to for paradigmatic cases are the principles of the common morality, and the best grounds they can appeal to for non-paradigmatic cases are the judgments of wise persons. A casuistry that does not take seriously the common morality will be prone to laxism. It may indeed result in the opinion that a nobleman may respond to a slap with lethal force. A principlism that does not take seriously the judgments of wise persons will not reach satisfactory settlements of complex moral cases, for it is not always easy to tell which principles have the greatest weight. Casuistry and principlism are complementary not merely with respect to their methodologies but also with respect to justification in practical matters. The casuist employs principles when she classifies paradigmatic cases. The principlist makes use of cases to give determinate content to the principles themselves. Yet both must make an appeal to our shared common moral sensibilities, and both must make an appeal to authority of the wise persons in justifying their moral conclusions. To be sure, these are not theoretical justifications of those decisions on the basis of principles. But they are *pragmaticistic* justifications that appeal to the body of our instinctive beliefs.

We are now in a position to turn to the other two issues that stand in need of explanation. The first issue noted earlier is what explains the fact that we sometimes do reach consensus on ethical issues and what merits our hope that we will reach consensus on other issues. What merits our hope is simply that we have nothing else to put our hope in. Moreover, by now it ought to be clear that the Peircean explanation for consensus about ethical issues is simply that we have evolved an instinct of morality. There is, of course, an important question about the scope of such consensus. Williams appears to think that what is required is that an appeal to human nature settle in favor of one sort of ethical life to others. But this demand is too strong. All that is required is that an appeal to human nature yields a core set of principles related to paradigm cases. The core set of principles may be few and the applicable scope of that core set of principles might be quite small. This is open for further debate and certainly calls for more detailed research into the common morality. Moreover, accretions to that core set of principles might be many or a few, and those accretions may change how the core set of principles is weighted in specific circumstances. But this does not rule out that there is such a core set of principles on the basis of which ethical deliberation may proceed. Furthermore, by considering which principles are instinctual and which are mere prejudices – in Chapter 2, I gave some marks by which they may be distinguished, such as the intensity of our sentiments relative to their breadth – we can discern which are mere accretions to that core and which are not. For these reasons, Bernard Gert (2004) is surely right to start his account of the common morality with a description of it, and the first order of practical ethical business ought to be an examination of the accuracy of his and similar accounts, a task outside of the purview of this book on Peirce.

The second issue in need of explanation is why the casuist's judgments hold any weight when they are mutable and possibly distorted by their cultural prejudices. On the one hand, as already noted, the casuist must cede ground to the judgments implied by the common morality. Any judgment inconsistent with that is doubtful. To be sure, the common morality is fallible and mutable – who knows what sentiments and instincts we might evolve over the next 1,000 years? – but it is also the best we have. On the other hand, what gives the judgments of casuists weight is that they have refined their instinct of morality – supposing we have any such instinct – through study and reflection. As Jonsen and Toulmin note,

> We have to reconcile ourselves to the fact that the conditions of human life are always changing and that from time to time new historical circumstances are liable to put us in situations of moral embarrassment where we can no longer continue relying on the "common sense" and "common morality" that have served us more or less well hitherto, and are forced to reconsider the goals of moral life and reflection at a deeper level. (1988, 322)

The wise person is the person who is best able to see this just because her instincts have been honed through study and reflection. That is what gives her judgments weight: They are the judgments of expertise. And this is why we appoint experts to commissions and not just anyone. To sure, they may be wrong; their judgments may not stand up to future experience. We may need to form new commissions and revise the decisions of previous ones. But that does not entail that we may presently ignore them when they do not suit us. For collectively, we still must make policy decisions and in making those decisions we will want to defer to the judgments of the wisest among us, to the judgments of those who have honed their instincts of morality.

Conclusion

Peirce would eschew highly theoretical approaches to practical ethics. Instead, he endorses casuistry. His practical ethics, insofar as he has one, hangs its hat on the hope that we corporately have evolved an instinct of morality. If we have evolved such an instinct, then it is trustworthy. If we have not, then there is nothing we can do about it anyway. Presuming we do have such instincts, our moral instincts are sufficient guides to policy making, though we can develop and refine them through study and practice. When we confront moral dilemmas, we will have to rely on the counsel of wise persons who have done precisely that. They, moreover, may conclude that we should implement policies contrary to our instincts, for it is "the essence of conservatism to refuse to push any practical principle to its extreme limits, – including the principle of conservatism itself" (RLT 111).

Bibliography

Abbreviated References

CP: Peirce, Charles. 1931–58. *Collected Papers*. 8 vols. Ed. Charles Hartshorne, Paul Weiss, and Arthur Burks. Cambridge, MA: Belknap Press of Harvard University Press.

CWJ: James, William. 2000. *The Correspondence of William James*. Vol. 8. 1895–June 1899. Ed. Ignas K. Skrupskelis and Elizabeth M. Berkeley. Charlottesville: University Press of Virginia.

EP: Peirce, Charles. 1992 and 1998. *The Essential Peirce*. 2 vols. Ed. Nathan Houser and Christian Kloesel and The Peirce Edition Project. Bloomington: Indiana University Press.

HP: Peirce, Charles. 1985. *Historical Perspectives on Peirce's Logic of Science*. Ed. Carolyn Eisele. Berlin: De Gruyter Mouton

NEM: Peirce, Charles. 1979. *New Elements of Mathematics*. 4 vols. Ed. Carolyn Eisele. Atlantic Highlands, NJ: Humanities Press.

PPM: Peirce, Charles. 1997. *Pragmatism as a Principle and Method of Right Thinking*. Ed. Patricia Ann Turrisi. Albany: State University of New York Press.

R: Peirce, Charles. *The Charles S. Peirce Manuscripts*. Cambridge, MA: Houghton Library at Harvard University. Citations are by manuscript number (as assigned in Robin 1967 and 1971) and, where available, page number.

RLT: Peirce, Charles. 1992. *Reasoning and the Logic of Things: The Cambridge Conferences Lectures of 1898*. Cambridge, MA: Harvard University Press.

SS: Peirce, Charles and Lady Victoria Welby. 1977. *Semiotic and Significs*. Ed. Charles S. Hardwick. Bloomington: Indiana University Press.

W: Peirce, Charles Sanders. 1982–Present. *The Writings of Charles S. Peirce: A Chronological Edition*. Ed. The Peirce Edition Project. 8 vols. Bloomington: Indiana University Press.

WWJ: James, William. 1975–1998. *The Works of William James*. Ed. Frederick H. Burkhardt, Fredson Bowers, and Ignas K. Skrupskelis. Cambridge, MA: Harvard University Press.

Other References

Alston, William. 1991. "The Inductive Problem of Evil and the Human Cognitive Condition." In *Philosophical Perspectives*. Vol. 5. Atascadero: Ridgeview Publishing, 29–67.

Anderson, Douglas. 2004. "Peirce's Common Sense Marriage of Religion and Science." In *The Cambridge Companion to Peirce*. Ed. Cheryl Misak. Cambridge: Cambridge University Press, 175–193.

1995. *Strands of System*. West Lafayette: Purdue University Press.

1990. "Three Appeals in Peirce's Neglected Argument." *Transactions of the Charles S. Peirce Society*. 26:3, 349–362.

Atkin, Albert. 2016. *Peirce*. New York: Routledge.

Atkins, Peter. 1994. *Creation Revisited*. New York: Penguin.

Atkins, Richard Kenneth. Forthcoming. "Peirce on Truth as the Predestinate Opinion." *European Journal of Philosophy*.

2014. "The Inferences That Never Were: Peirce, Perception, and Bernstein's The Pragmatic Turn." In *Richard J. Bernstein and the Pragmatist Turn in Contemporary Philosophy*. New York: Palgrave Macmillan, 55–67.

2006. "Restructuring the Sciences: Peirce's Categories and His Classification of the Sciences." *Transactions of the Charles S. Peirce Society*. 42:4, 483–500.

Ayim, Maryann. 1982. *Peirce's View of the Roles of Reason and Instinct in Scientific Inquiry*. Meerut, India: Anu Prakashan.

Baldwin, James Mark. 1902. *Development and Evolution*. New York: The Macmillan Company.

1894. *Handbook of Psychology*. Vol. 2. New York: Henry Holt and Company.

Beauchamp, Tom and James Childress. 2013. *Principles of Biomedical Ethics*. 7th ed. Oxford: Oxford University Press.

1989. *Principles of Biomedical Ethics*. 3rd ed. Oxford: Oxford University Press.

1983. *Principles of Biomedical Ethics*. 2nd ed. Oxford: Oxford University Press.

Bedell, Gary. 1980. "Has Peirce Refuted Egoism?" *Transactions of the Charles S. Peirce Society*. 16:3, 255–275.

Beeson, Robert J. 2008. *Peirce on the passions: The role of instinct, emotion, and sentiment in inquiry and action.* Ph.D. dissertation. University of South Florida.

Bergman, Mats. 2010. "Serving Two Masters: Peirce on Pure Science, Useless Things, and Practical Applications." In *Ideas in Action: Proceedings of the* Applying Peirce *Conference.* Eds. M Bergman, A.V. Pietarinen, and H. Rydenfelt. Nordic Studies in Pragmatism 1. Helsinki: Nordic Pragmatism Network, 17–37.

Black, Joshua. 2013. "Peirce on Habit, Practice, and Theory." M.A. Thesis. University of Waikato. http://researchcommons.waikato.ac.nz/bit stream/handle/10289/7847/thesis.pdf?sequence=3&isAllowed=y.

Bloom, Paul. 2010. "The Moral Life of Babies." In *New York Times Magazine.* www.nytimes.com/2010/05/09/magazine/09babies-t.html? pagewanted=all&_r=0.

Boyd, Kenneth. 2012. "Levi's Challenge and Peirce's Theory/Practice Distinction." *Transactions of the Charles S. Peirce Society.* 48:2, 51–70.

Brent, Joseph. 1998. *Charles S. Peirce: A Life.* Bloomington: Indiana University Press.

Broad, C. D. 1950. "Egoism as a Theory of Human Motives." *The Hibbert Journal.* 48, 105–114.

Campos, Daniel. 2014. "Peirce's Prejudices against Hispanics and the Ethical Scope of His Philosophy." *The Pluralist.* 9:2, 42–64.

2011. "On the Distinction between Peirce's Abduction and Lipton's Inference to the Best Explanation." *Synthese.* 180: 419–442.

Clanton, J. Caleb. 2014. "The Structure of C. S. Peirce's Neglected Argument for the Reality of God: A Critical Assessment." *Transactions of the Charles S. Peirce Society.* 50:2, 175–200.

Colapietro, Vincent. 2007. "C. S. Peirce's Rhetorical Turn." *Transactions of the Charles S. Peirce Society.* 43:1, 16–52.

2006. "Practice, Agency, & Solidarity: An Orthogonal Reading of Classical Pragmatism." *International Journal for Dialogical Science.* 1:1, 23–31.

1998. "Transforming a Philosophy into a Science: A Debilitating Chimera or a Realizable Desideratum?" *American Catholic Philosophical Quarterly.* 72:2, 245–278.

1989. *Peirce's Approach to the Self: A Semiotic Perspective on Human Subjectivity.* Buffalo: State University of New York Press.

Cudney, Paul. 2014. "What Really Separates Casuistry from Principlism in Biomedical Ethics." *Theoretical Medicine and Bioethics.* 35, 205–229.

Dancy, Jonathan. 2004. *Ethics without Principles.* Oxford: Clarendon Press.

Darwin, Charles. 1870. *The Origin of Species.* New York: D. Appleton and Company.

Davidson, Donald. 1986/2001. "A Coherence Theory of Truth and Knowledge." In *Subjective, Intersubjective, Objective.* Oxford: Oxford University Press.

Davis, William H. 1972. *Peirce's Epistemology.* Dordrecht: Springer.

Dawkins, Richard. 2006. *The God Delusion.* New York: Houghton Mifflin.

de Waal, Cornelis. 2012. "Who's Afraid of Charles Sanders Peirce?: Knocking Some Critical Common Sense into Moral Philosophy." In *The Normative Thought of Charles S. Peirce.* Eds. Cornelis de Waal and Krzysztof Piotr Skowroński. New York: Fordham University Press, 83–100.

Frankfurt, Harry. 1971. "Freedom of the Will and the Concept of a Person." *Journal of Philosophy.* 68, 5–20.

Forster, Paul. 2011. *Peirce and the Threat of Nominalism.* Cambridge: Cambridge University Press.

Gavin, William J. 1980. "Peirce and the 'Will to Believe.'" *The Monist.* 63:3, 342–350.

Gert, Bernard. 2004. *The Common Morality.* New York: Oxford University Press.

Girel, Mathias. 2011. "Peirce's Early Re-Readings of His Illustrations: The Case of the 1885 Royce Review." *Cognitio.* 12:1, 75–88.

Hausman, Carl R. 1993. *Charles S. Peirce's Evolutionary Philosophy.* Cambridge: Cambridge University Press.

Hawkins, Stephen B. 2007. "Desire and Natural Classification: Peirce and Aristotle on Final Cause." *Transactions of the Charles S. Peirce Society.* 43:3, 521–541.

Helvétius, Claude Adrien. 1777. *Treatise on Man, His Intellectual Faculties, and His Education.* Trans. W. Hooper. London: Law and Robinson.

Hobbes, Thomas. 1660/1994. *Leviathan.* Ed. Edwin Curley. Indianapolis: Hackett.

Holmes, Larry. 1966. "Peirce on Self-Control." *Transactions of the Charles S. Peirce Society.* 2:2, 113–130.

Hookway, Christopher. 2012. *The Pragmatic Maxim.* Oxford: Oxford University Press.

2000. *Truth, Rationality, and Pragmatism.* Oxford: Clarendon Press.

Hornsby, Jennifer. 1997. "Truth: The Identity Theory." *Proceedings of the Aristotelian Society.* 97, 1–24.

Howat, Andrew. 2014. "Peirce on Grounding the Laws of Logic." *Transactions of the Charles S. Peirce Society.* 50:4, 480–500.

Hull, Kathleen. 2005. "The Inner Chambers of His Mind: Peirce's 'Neglected Argument' for God as Related to Mathematical Experience." *Transactions of the Charles S. Peirce Society.* 41:3, 483–513.

Hutcheson, Francis. 1756. *Essay on the Nature and Conduct of the Passions and Affections with Illustration on the Moral Sense.* 4th ed. London: Innys and Co.

　1753. *An Inquiry Concerning the Original of Our Ideas of Virtue and Moral Good.* 5th ed. London: Ware and Knapton.

Isaiah. 1973. In *The New Oxford Annotated Bible.* Ed. Herbert May and Bruce Metzger. New York: Oxford University Press.

James Sr., Henry. 1863. *Substance and Shadow.* Boston: Ticknor and Fields.

Jonsen, Albert R. 1995. "Casuistry: An Alternative or Complement to Principles?" *Kennedy Institute of Ethics Journal.* 5:3, 237–251.

　1990. "Practice versus Theory." *Hastings Center Report.* 20, 32–34.

Jonsen, Albert R. and Stephen Toulmin. 1988. *The Abuse of Casuistry.* Berkeley: University of California Press.

Jouffroy, Théodore. 1851. *Introduction to Ethics, Including a Critical Survey of Moral Systems.* Trans. William H. Channing. Boston: James Munroe and Co.

Joyce, Richard. 2006. *The Evolution of Morality.* Cambridge, MA: MIT Press.

Kant, Immanuel. 2000. *Critique of the Power of Judgment.* Ed. Paul Guyer. Trans. Paul Guyer and Eric Matthews. Cambridge: Cambridge University Press.

Kasser, Jeff. 1999. "Peirce's Supposed Psychologism." *Transactions of the Charles S. Peirce Society.* 35:3, 501–526.

Kent, Beverley. 1987. *Charles S. Peirce: Logic and the Classification of the Sciences.* Montreal: McGill-Queen's University Press.

　1976. "Peirce's Esthetics: A New Look." *Transactions of the Charles S. Peirce Society.* 12:3, 263–283.

Ketner, Kenneth Laine and Hilary Putnam. 1992. "Consequences of Mathematics." In *Reasoning and the Logic of Things.* Cambridge, MA: Harvard University Press.

Khachab, Chihab El. 2013. "The Logical Goodness of Abduction." *Transactions of the Charles S. Peirce Society.* 49:2, 157–177.

Korsgaard, Christine. 1986. "The Right to Lie: Kant on Dealing with Evil." *Philosophy and Public Affairs.* 15:4, 325–349.

Kuczewski, Mark. 1998. "Casuistry and Principles: The Convergence of Method in Biomedical Ethics." *Theoretical Medicine and Bioethics.* 19, 509–524.

Lane, Robert. 2009. "Persons, Signs, Animals: A Peircean Account of Personhood." *Transactions of the Charles S. Peirce Society.* 45:1, 1–26.

　2007. "From Set Theory to Pragmaticism: Peirce's Modal Shift." *Journal of the History of Philosophy.* 45:4, 551–576.

　1999. "Peirce's Triadic Logic Revisted." *Transactions of the Charles S. Peirce Society.* 35:2, 284–311.

Lefebvre, Martin. 2007. "Peirce's Esthetics: A Taste for Signs in Art." *Transactions of the Charles S. Peirce Society.* Bloomington, 43:2, 319–344.

Liszka, James. 2014. "Peirce's Idea of Ethics as a Normative Science." *Transactions of the Charles S. Peirce Society.* 50:4, 459–479.

2012. "Charles S. Peirce on Ethics." *The Normative Thought of Charles S. Peirce.* Eds. Cornelis de Waal and Krzysztof Piotr Skowroński. New York: Fordham University Press.

Lucy, John A. 1997. "The Linguistics of 'Color.'" In *Color Categories in Thought and Language.* Eds. C. L. Hardin and Maffi Luisa. New York: Cambridge University Press, 320–346.

Lutz, Catherine. 1988. *Unnatural Emotions: Everyday Sentiments on a Micronesian Atoll and Their Challenge to Western Theory.* Chicago: University of Chicago Press.

Mackie, J. L. 1955. "Evil and Omnipotence." *Mind.* 64:254, 200–212.

Mandeville, Bernard. 1723/1997. *The Fable of the Bees and Other Writings.* Ed. E. J. Hundert. Indianapolis: Hackett.

Massecar, Aaron. 2013. "The Fitness of an Ideal: A Peircean Ethics." *Contemporary Pragmatism.* 10:2, 97–119.

Mayorga, Rosa Maria. 2012. "Peirce's Moral 'Realicism.'" In *The Normative Thought of Charles S. Peirce.* Eds. Cornelis de Waal and Krzysztof Piotr Skowroński. New York: Fordham University Press, 101–124.

McKaughan, Daniel. 2008. "From Ugly Duckling to Swan: C. S. Peirce, Abduction, and the Pursuit of Scientific Theories." *Transactions of the Charles S. Peirce Society.* 44:3, 446–468.

Migotti, Mark. 2005. "The Key to Peirce's View of the Role of Belief in Scientific Inquiry." *Cognitio.* 6:1, 44–55.

2004. "Critical Notice: Christopher Hookway, *Truth, Rationality and Pragmatism.*" *Canadian Journal of Philosophy.* 34:2, 287–310.

Misak, Cheryl. 2011. "American Pragmatism and Indispensability Arguments." *Transactions of the Charles S. Peirce Society.* 47:3, 261–273.

2004. "C. S. Peirce on Vital Matters." In *The Cambridge Companion to Peirce.* Ed. Cheryl Misak. Cambridge: Cambridge University Press, 150–174.

2000. *Truth, Politics, Morality: Pragmatism and Deliberation.* London: Routledge.

Niño, Douglas. 2009. "Peircean Pragmatism and Inference to the Best Explanation." www.academia.edu/2046722/Peircean_Pragmatism_and_Inference_to_the_Best_Explanation_first_draft.

Noble, N. A. Brian. 1989. "Peirce's Definitions of Continuity and the Concept of Possibility." *Transactions of the Charles S. Peirce Society.* 25:2, 149–174.

Opie, Amelia Alderson. 1825. *Illustrations of Lying.* 2 vols. London: Longman, Hurst, Kees, Orme, Brown, and Green.

Orange, Donna. 1980. *The Development of Peirce's Theism.* Ph.D. dissertation. Fordham University.

Paavola, Sami. 2005. "Peircean Abduction: Instinct or Inference?" *Semiotica.* 153:1/4, 131–154.

Pape, Helmut. 2012. "Self-Control, Values, and Moral Development: Peirce on the Value-driven Dynamics of Human Morality." *The Normative Thought of Charles S. Peirce.* Eds. Cornelis de Waal and Krzysztof Piotr Skowroński. New York: Fordham University Press.

Parker, Kelly A. 1998. *The Continuity of Peirce's Thought.* Nashville: Vanderbilt.

Petry, Edward S. 1992. "The Origin and Development of Peirce's Concept of Self-Control." *Transactions of the Charles S. Peirce Society.* 43:3, 667–690.

Plantinga, Alvin. 2000. *Warranted Christian Belief.* New York: Oxford.

Potter, Vincent G. 1967. *Charles S. Peirce on Norms and Ideals.* Worcester: University of Massachusetts.

Raposa, Michael. 1989. *Peirce's Philosophy of Religion.* Bloomington: Indiana University Press.

Reynolds, Andrew. 2002. *Peirce's Scientific Metaphysics: The Philosophy of Chance, Law, and Evolution.* Nashville: Vanderbilt University Press.

Richards, Robert J. 1987. *Darwin and the Emergence of Evolutionary Theories of Mind and Behavior.* Chicago: The University of Chicago Press.

Robin, Richard. 1967. *Annotated Catalogue of the Papers of Charles S. Peirce.* Amherst: The University of Massachusetts Press.

1971. "The Peirce Papers: A Supplementary Catalogue." *Transactions of the Charles S. Peirce Society.* 7:1, 37–57.

Rohaytn, Dennis. 1982. "Resurrecting Peirce's "Neglected Argument" for God's Reality." *Transactions of the Charles S. Peirce Society.* 18:1, 66–74.

Rowe, William. 1979. "The Problem of Evil and Some Varieties of Atheism." *American Philosophical Quarterly.* 16:4, 335–341.

Savan, David. 1981. "Peirce's Semiotic Theory of Emotion." In *Proceedings of the Charles S. Peirce Bicentennial international Congress.* Ed. Kenneth Laine Ketner, et al. 319–333.

Shapiro, Gary. 1973. "Habit and Meaning in Peirce's Pragmatism." *Transactions of the Charles S. Peirce Society.* 9:1, 24–40.

Short, T. L. 2007. *Peirce's Theory of Signs.* New York: Cambridge University Press.

Sidgwick, Henry. 1884. *The Methods of Ethics.* London: Macmillan and Co.

Smith, C. M. 1972. "The Esthetics of Charles S. Peirce." *The Journal of Aesthetics and Art Criticism*. 31:1, 21–29.

Smith, John E. 1983. "The Tension between Direct Experience and Argument in Religion." *Religious Studies*. 17, 487–497.

Sober, Elliott. 1992. "Hedonism and Butler's Stone." *Ethics*. 103:1, 97–103.

1989. "What Is Psychological Egoism?" *Behaviorism*. 17:2, 89–102.

Spencer, Herbert. 1852. "A Theory of Population." *The Westminster Review*. Vol. 57/8. New York: Leonard, Scott, and Co.

Stjernfelt, Frederick. 2014. *Natural Propositions*. Boston: Docent Press.

Talisse, Robert B. 2007. *A Pragmatist Philosophy of Democracy*. New York: Routledge.

Thomas Aquinas. 1964. *Summa Theologiae*. Vol. 2. Trans. Timothy McDermott. Cambridge: Cambridge University Press.

Thompson, M. H. 1953. *The Pragmatic Philosophy of C. S. Peirce*. Chicago: The University of Chicago Press.

Tillich, Paul. 1951. *Systematic Theology*. Vol. 1. Chicago: The University of Chicago Press.

Trammell, Richard L. 1973. "Charles Sanders Peirce and Henry James the Elder." *Transactions of the Charles S. Peirce Society*. 9:4, 202–220.

1972. "Religion, Instinct, and Reason in the Thought of C. S. Peirce." *Transactions of the Charles S. Peirce Society*. 8:1, 3–25.

Trout, Lara. 2010. *The Politics of Survival: Peirce, Affectivity, and Social Criticism*. New York: Fordham University Press.

Turrisi, Patricia Ann. 1986. *Charles S. Peirce's Evolutionary Metaphysics: The Growth of Reasonableness in Nature, Mind and Science*. Ph.D. dissertation, Pennsylvania State University.

Welchman, Jennifer. 2006. "William James's 'The Will to Believe' and the Ethics of Self-Experimentation." *Transactions of the Charles S. Peirce Society*. 42: 2, 229–241.

Westrbrook, Robert B. 2005. *Democratic Hope: Pragmatism and the Politics of Truth*. Ithaca: Cornell University Press.

Williams, Bernard. 1985/1993. *Ethics and the Limits of Philosophy*. London: Routledge.

Index

9 781316 613856